REBECCA DAVIES is Senior Lecturer in the Department of International Relations at Plymouth University where she teaches African politics. She holds a DPhil from the University of Stellenbosch in South Africa where she remains a visiting fellow at the Centre for Comparative and International Politics. She has taught at universities in Australia, South Africa and New Zealand.

INTERNATIONAL LIBRARY OF AFRICAN STUDIES

1. *Military in the Making of Modern South Africa* – Annette Seegers
978 1 85043 689 8

2. *The Diplomacy of Liberation: The Foreign Relations of the ANC Since 1960* – Scott Thomas
978 1 85043 993 6

3. *A History of East Africa, 1592–1902*
R. W. Beachey
978 1 85043 994 3

4. *The Nigerian Military and the State*
Jimmy Peters
978 1 85043 874 8

5. *Adjusting Society: The World Bank, the IMF and Ghana*
Lynne Brydon & Karen Legge
978 1 86064 000 1

6. *The Horn of Africa: Politics and International Relations*
Peter Woodward
978 1 85043 741 3

7. *State of Emergency: Nyasaland 1959*
Colin Baker
978 1 86064 068 1

8. *From Colonization to Democracy: A New Historical Geography of South Africa* – Alan Lester
978 1 86064 091 9

10. *South Africa in Transition: The Misunderstood Miracle*
Adrian Guelke
978 1 86064 343 9

11. *Security and the State in Southern Africa* – Agostinho Zacarias
978 1 86064 328 6

12. *Coming to Terms: Zimbabwe in the International Arena* – Richard Schwartz
978 1 86064 647 8

13. *Britain, Kenya and the Cold War: Imperial Defence, Colonial Security and Decolonisation* – David Percox
978 1 85043 460 3

14. *Apartheid South Africa and African States: From Pariah to Middle Power, 1961–1994* – Roger Pfister
978 1 85043 625 6

15. *A History of the Left in South Africa: Writings of Baruch Hirson*
Baruch Hirson
978 1 85043 454 2

16. *An African Trading Empire: The Story of Susman Brothers & Wulfsohn, 1901–2005*
Hugh Macmillan
978 1 85043 853 3

17. *The Place of Tears: The Novel and Politics in Modern Zimbabwe*
Ranka Primorac
978 1 84511 120 5

18. *Mineworkers in Zambia: Labour and Political Change in Post-Colonial Africa*
Miles Larmer
978 1 84511 299 8

19. *Reconstructing the Nation in Africa: The Politics of Nationalism in Ghana*
Michael Amoah
978 1 84511 259 2

20. *Revolt and Protest: Student Politics and Activism in Sub-Saharan Africa*
Leo Zeilig
978 1 84511 476 3

21. *The Other Way Around* – Frank Verdon
978 1 86064 030 8

22. *The Politics of Neoliberal Democracy in Africa: State and Civil Society in Nigeria*
Usman A. Tar
978 1 84511 656 9

23. *Afrikaners in the New South Africa: Identity Politics in a Globalised Economy*
Rebecca Davies
978 1 84511 785 6

24. *The Politics of Water in Africa: The European Union's Role in Development Aid Partnership* – Chris Rowan
978 1 84511 685 9

AFRIKANERS IN THE NEW SOUTH AFRICA

Identity Politics in a Globalised Economy

REBECCA DAVIES

TAURIS ACADEMIC STUDIES
an imprint of
I.B.Tauris Publishers
LONDON • NEW YORK

Published in 2009 by Tauris Academic Studies, an imprint of I.B.Tauris & Co Ltd
6 Salem Road, London W2 4BU
175 Fifth Avenue, New York NY 10010
www.ibtauris.com

In the United States of America and in Canada distributed by
St Martins Press, 175 Fifth Avenue, New York, NY 10010

Copyright © 2009 Rebecca Davies

The right of Rebecca Davies to be identified as author of this work has been asserted by the author in accordance with the Copyright, Designs and Patent Act 1988.

All rights reserved. Except for brief quotations in a review, this book, or any part thereof, may not be reproduced, stored in or introduced into a retrieval system, or transmitted, in any form or by any means, electronic, mechanical, photocopying, recording or otherwise, without the prior written permission of the publisher.

International Library of African Studies 23

ISBN: 978 1 84511 785 6

A full CIP record for this book is available from the British Library
A full CIP record for this book is available from the Library of Congress

Printed and bound in India by Thomson Press
from camera-ready copy edited and supplied by the author

CONTENTS

Acknowledgements   vii

1. **Rebuilding the Future or Revisiting the Past?**   1
   Introduction   1
   A political economy of post-apartheid Afrikaner identity   4
   Theorising identity in a global era   9

2. **The Afrikaner Nationalist Project**   18
   Appropriating the past: The development of an Afrikaner identity   19
   Moving towards consensus   25
   A volk in retreat?   31
       The nationalist project unravels   37
       A class apart: The maturation of Afrikaner capital   39

3. **The Nature of Consensus in the 'New' South Africa**   44
   Consolidating dominance? The shape of the new hegemonic order   45
   Neo-liberal orthodoxy and the capital transition   51
       Connecting with the global consensus   56
       Compromise on the domestic front   59
   An African Renaissance?   63

4. **Contemporary Manifestations of Afrikaner Identity in an Era of Increasing Globalisation**   71
   Rethinking the cultural: The future of the Afrikaner past   72
       The politics of transformation   74
       The new discourse of minority rights   76
       The culture industry   81
   The rise of a globalised capital consensus   92

5. **The 'Logic of the Local' in Contemporary Afrikaner Identity Politics**   99
   The local tradition in Afrikaner nationalist politics   100
   An alternative Afrikanerdom?   105
       Recreating the cultural: New visions of Afrikaans   117
       Reorienting the local: Politics at the provincial level   123

6. **Renewing the Consensus in a Post-Apartheid Era?**   130

Notes   139
Bibliography   177
Index   193

ACKNOWLEDGEMENTS

A great many people deserve my thanks for their help and support during the course of this project. Among those scholars and colleagues to whom I owe considerable gratitude are Janis van der Westhuizen, Karen Smith, Scarlett Cornelissen, Ken Good, Richard Gibb, Simon Payne, Jamie Gaskarth, Patrick Holden, Karl Cordell, Alex Cunliffe, Ian Murphy, Noah Bassil, Kath Sturman, Natalie Klein, Rosemary Oetojo, Andrew Mack, Hennie Kotze and Philip Nel. During the early days of my research and throughout the entire development of this book, Ian Taylor has been an invaluable source of support and direction.

Across Africa, friends and colleagues have taught me far more about Afrikaners in the new South Africa than I might have learned from any book. A number of Afrikaans speaking scholars, writers, businessmen and activists all gave up considerable time to offer valuable thoughts and insights for which I am very grateful. Some are named in the course of this book, others are not. I would also like to thank Deirdre Holcroft, Vladimir Guerrero, JoAnne Taylor, Kiki Tremeer, Paul Cronje, Carinus Lemmer, Rachel Darlami, Sally Drewe, Gaspard Serrat and Mark Cornell who supported me more than they could realise. In France, Guillaume Sers, Mark Woodhatch, Alexandre Odier, Jean-Pierre Zelcer, Catherine Cournot, and Nigel and Dawn King ensured that the final stages of this project were possible.

This book has benefited from the guidance of Elizabeth Munns and Rasna Dhillon at I.B.Tauris who have been unfailingly supportive. I would also like to thank the anonymous reviewers at the *Review of African Political Economy* for their challenging feedback and advice.

It is hard to describe the debt I owe to Beyers who inspired me with the possibilities of the idea for this study and so much else. I hope that I have done his vision some justice: he has been sitting on my shoulders throughout. This book is dedicated to him and to Mollie. Finally, my greatest debt is to my family. I could not have begun or completed this project without them.

1

REBUILDING THE FUTURE OR REVISITING THE PAST?

Introduction

The first democratic elections in South Africa during 1994 marked the formalisation of a power shift away from the minority Afrikaner grouping. Today, a profound dislocation is apparent in post-apartheid Afrikaner identifications. Despite the fact that Afrikaner nationalism has lost its centrality to South African politics, it remains an important political issue due to the economic and cultural importance of Afrikaans speakers. Nonetheless, the measure of contemporary group cohesion and the evolution of a once coherent collective identity, bound together by the strength and versatility of the social coalitions of Afrikanerdom,[1] are largely unremarked upon in the scholarship.[2] At the same time, it is widely acknowledged that certain Afrikaans constituent parts, most notably an increasingly globalised middle class and capital or business elites, are flourishing in the new South Africa.[3] Typically adapting by seeking economic independence, their success is borne out by the position of Afrikaner capital, which now ranks second only to declining English capital on the Johannesburg Stock Exchange (JSE).[4] Since the negotiated settlement of the 1990s the ANC government under both Presidents Mandela and Mbeki has not wavered from its commitment to dialogue with particular elements of this disparate community in graphic recognition of their significance.[5]

It would appear then that Afrikaner identity politics remains important in post-apartheid South Africa, even whilst it varies substantially. Most striking has been the manner in which this has had to adapt to the loss of political power at the same time as a substantial rise in economic influence.

This chapter is based on my article: 'Rebuilding the Future or Revisiting the Past? Post-apartheid Afrikaner identity politics in a globalised era' Review of African Political Economy 2007; 112(34): 357–74.

This incidence of identity adjustment is not unique. Quebec, Catalonia and Scotland all provide examples of nationalist movements that have made considerable adjustments to contemporary conditions.[6] But what is unprecedented is the simultaneous collapse of a political economic system dedicated to a racial means of achieving material advantage and political leverage. From a historical standpoint, the position of the Afrikaner community within South Africa and on the global stage has undergone major transformation. Determining the extent of this change requires a consideration not merely of the subjective definition of the phenomenon — the self-understanding Afrikaans speakers have of their identity — but likewise its objective aspect. That is, the characteristics of culture, descent and language (that form the obvious structural bases for ethnic differentiation), as well as the material context of society, economics, politics and history in which it functions.[7]

With the end of minority rule, many analyses painted a bleak future for Afrikanerdom subjugated beneath a state dominated by the ANC government and broadly aligned against Afrikaner interests. Some scholars predicted the tendency of important groups and sectors to simply 'opt out' of the state,[8] whilst a resurgence of rightwing militancy and the Boeremag's thwarted bombing campaign raised the spectre of a race war.[9] None of these situations has materialised. The once sound link between an Afrikaner nationalist identity, regime and state which characterised the years of apartheid government, and that sustained a delicate balance of ethnic, racial and class forces, has been irretrievably broken. Notwithstanding the recent and marked increase in white poverty levels,[10] it is evident that this newly disempowered minority still commands a vast material and cultural capital accrued under the previous dispensation.[11] Whilst certain of these constituent parts have been increasingly marginalised in the new order, others have become important players in the new South Africa and upon the world stage, embracing elements of the wider politico-economic order. It is suggested that a select number have been able to refigure the character of the government's hegemonic project itself due to their position within the leading historic bloc.

There is evidence to suggest that those groupings within the ruling party fold enjoy far greater influence than those outside it.[12] From its inception as a resistance movement to its contemporary populist manifestation, the ANC has relied on a wide range of alliance partners and constituencies to achieve three successive electoral victories. Indeed, it is a trend that is likely only to strengthen with the acknowledgement that the ANC government today is:

> 'leaning towards construction of a procapitalist, interventionist state prepared to use its power, influence and divestment of assets to create

a black bourgeoisie, expand the black middle class, and to generally produce a seismic transfer of wealth from white to black over a ten to twenty year period.'[13]

Given the centuries-old white economic and political hegemony, the importance of these capital elites within the new order, as well as their connections and business ideology,[14] cannot be overstated. Regular meetings with business leaders within forums including President Mbeki's Big Business Working Group attest to the enduring relationship between government and capital.[15] In this atmosphere business has declared itself 'broadly satisfied' with the government's fiscal and monetary policies, as well as its macro-economic policy and micro-economic programmes.[16] It is a position of considerable strength which has only intensified during Mbeki's presidency with its strong focus upon the transformation of the economy.[17]

The paradigm shift in political economic context within a post-apartheid South Africa – where the national political and economic landscape demonstrates compelling continuities with the old, and the present government is 'heavily conditioned' by the foundations of the negotiated transition[18] – received comparatively little attention until recently and remains the subject of considerable debate.[19] Moreover, the parameters of this new hegemonic order, exhaustively detailed with regard to ANC constituencies and tripartite alliance partners,[20] remain comparatively unexplored vis-à-vis current manifestations of Afrikaner identity politics. In order to understand the simultaneous paradigm shift in the political economic context of identifications among Afrikaans speakers in South Africa, it is argued that it is necessary to understand both the subjective *and* objective experiences of the Afrikaner against the prevailing structure of power relations. For whilst a pervasive sense of 'being Afrikaner' exists, characteristically expressed in terms of cultural attributes and less frequently descent, the significance attached to this self-understanding varies considerably.

At the onset of majority rule, the new bases of Afrikaner identity politics were judged to be fragile at best.[21] Since then empirical observation appears to suggest a simultaneous decline and acceleration in ethnic affiliations. The range and even lack of identification among Afrikaans speakers is considerable. A large section of the coloured community, black Afrikaans speakers and *verloopte* (walked away) Afrikaners remain firmly outside of or even reject any formal grouping. Much of the dialogue during this period has concerned the possibility and desirability of divorcing Afrikanerness from Afrikaner nationalism. Thus, Nash can claim that the 'new politics of Afrikaans' is concerned with defending Afrikaans language and culture without regard to 'ethnic background'[22] whilst *Die Burger's* former editor Arrie Roussouw announced that the newspaper would no longer refer to Afrikaans speakers as Afrikaners but more inclusively as 'Afrikaanses'.[23]

At the same time, however, a resurgence of group-based politics has placed the legitimacy of minority cultural rights at the top of the agenda.[24] A very small number of Afrikaners are encamped in the Northern Cape demanding a territorial homeland, many are no longer choosing to associate on a traditional group basis, whilst others go abroad either on a temporary or permanent basis in search of better prospects.[25] Others have gone the route of attempting to preserve a more formal minority grouping, working within the ambit of the 1996 Constitution, various United Nations conventions and a globalised liberalism.[26] In that sense, the electoral collapse and then dissolution of the New National Party, historically the political home of Afrikanerdom, during April 2004, was largely symbolic given that its traditional support base had long since ebbed away. It is suggested that coherence within each of these movements has been influenced both by the success of key Afrikaans constituent parts within the ANC's hegemonic project and on the global stage, as well as significant tensions at the local level. To all intents and purposes then, contemporary Afrikanerdom is experiencing a period of unprecedented change within its rank and file.

This book attempts to provide a new basis for understanding Afrikaner identity in a post-apartheid era. It argues that a wide array of factors informs these identifications, so that conceptions of identity politics based on reductionist frameworks inherent in both structuralist or agency-orientated approaches do not properly capture the multilevel dynamics of identity adjustment in an era of globalisation. Instead, it assesses the analytical tools of global political economy and a neo-Gramscian analysis as a means of breaking down the barriers between the global, national and local levels, as well as between the interconnected structural and subjective dimensions of the phenomenon. This approach forms part of a larger effort to provide a richer, more critical framework for understanding identity politics under conditions of increasing globalisation.

A political economy of post-apartheid Afrikaner identity

Using this framework, the principal aim of this book is to demonstrate that transformation within the globalised political economy has served to constrict or empower different Afrikaner constituencies by analysing their responses to these wider structural changes on a national and sub-national or local level. It is contended that the global character of the current world order has had a major effect on the political economy of post-apartheid Afrikaner identifications as a globalised neo-liberal consensus has taken hold on the domestic front. Here, globalisation is considered as the ongoing transformation of power on a global scale which involves:

> 'the relations – class, economic, social, gender, financial and political – that are generated by the impulses associated with the globe-wide diffusion of capital's power in our current epoch.'[27]

Identity is both a structural and subjective condition determined by historical forces and the prevailing structure of power relations. That is, a balance must be struck between the agency (or subjectivity) of the phenomenon and the structural backdrop against which it is realised. What this means is there must be a balance between these interconnected structural and subjective dimensions so that a proper comprehension of post-apartheid Afrikaner identity politics may be realised. By so doing, it is possible to locate these identifications within a historical and global context.

Despite increasing recognition of the importance of these structural factors, there has not been any substantive attempt to address the complexities of these identifications, and the methodology and history that link identity to context, in the scholarship.[28] These flaws have been worsened by mainstream (territorial or state-based) accounts of identity in a global era where diasporic pluralism, cultures of hybridity and transnational solidarities take precedence. Tooze argues that the imperative must be the identification and assessment of the social forces that 'orthodox analysis' does not recognise.[29] Yet these forces have been largely overlooked in past analyses which privilege 'the relationship of Afrikaner culture to the state and to state power' as the 'pivotal issues' in Afrikaner group politics.[30] More recently, Giliomee has elaborated on the survival of the Afrikaners as a group without problematising the notion of survival.[31] This same ahistoricism is apparent in earlier accounts of Afrikaner history in South African historiography where it is contended that Afrikaners' points of reference entered a virtuous circle, propagating ideas of community and a collective identity that were perpetuated by their very rise to power.[32] Du Toit shattered this Calvinist paradigm which he argued served as the root of modern Afrikaner nationalism and apartheid ideology.[33] Even where globalisation is raised, it is viewed in the context of cultural homogenization,[34] and without any thorough regard to a globalised political economy perspective that privileges a wide spectrum of social forces.

Historically, the study of Afrikaner identity has been broadly dominated by the primordial and constructionist perspectives accentuating either cultural resilience or a materialist realpolitik whereby social identities are realised as the products of human agency or choice.[35] Yet neither of the leading analyses of the development of the Afrikaner nationalist project fit straightforwardly within these respective camps. Thus, Giliomee admits that ethnic identification 'sought to attain political and cultural goals and meet diverse psychological needs',[36] whilst recognising that 'the construction of an Afrikaner political ethnicity must be sought in broad economic and social processes and not merely in the realm of cultural innovations.'[37] Placing more stress on the constructionist dimension, O'Meara's broadly Marxist perspective pays testimony to the fragmented nature of the class forces who, mobilised by the concept of *volk*, entered into what was to be a fragile nationalist class alliance that effectively subsidised mass economic empowerment by using the savings of the majority to facilitate the elevation of Afrikaner capital.[38]

Important questions as to the depth and power of ethnic identifications – external categorisation and self-understanding, objective commonality and subjective groupness[39] – the complex process by which class alignments subvert and even supersede ethnic ideologies, as well as the advent of new ethnic groups and identifications or scarcity thereof, have all too frequently been missing from the scholarship. Instead, a more historicist account joins with both agency and structure and implies that change or transformation occurs within the 'limits of the possible'. These limits:

> 'are not fixed and immutable but exist within the dialectics of a given social structure (comprising the inter-subjective aspect of ideas, ideologies and theories, social institutions, and a prevailing socio-economic system and set of power relations).'[40]

Both the constructivist and primordialist perspectives, to varying degrees, fail to acknowledge the changing salience and significance of ethnic identifications within such a context. In this study it is suggested that wider structural shifts should be related to changes in identification among Afrikaans speakers by analysing connections between social forces in South Africa and the globalised economy. The Gramscian framework introduced below makes it possible to analyse the openings for particular Afrikaans constituencies in real historical conditions, and across a number of levels of analysis, by addressing the level of hegemony (the nature of a post-apartheid consensus emerging from the connections between local and global structures of social forces) as an empirical question.

By developing a theoretically informed and historically specific treatment of power, this study examines how contemporary manifestations of Afrikaner identity justify or challenge existing power relations. Although South Africa remains a society characterised to a notable degree by group politics, it is contended that whilst Afrikaans speakers exhibit a wide range of identifications not all are connected to an ethnic, language or even racial heritage. Nonetheless, with the demise of apartheid and the decline of Afrikaner nationalism, the issue of who or what comprises an Afrikaner is as relevant as it has ever been. One enduring legacy of apartheid has been the resonance of the race issue. The existence of non-white or 'brown Afrikaners' remains controversial and the three-fold definition of the term Afrikaner introduced below acknowledges the importance of race. The historical relationship between the coloured and white Afrikaans speaking communities has been beset by contradictions, ranging from inclusion to discrimination and racial classification, to partial political and economic integration. Today the position of the four million-strong Afrikaans speaking coloureds within any wider Afrikaner community remains one of considerable ambiguity,[41] with contemporary tensions extending to land claims amongst other issues. Determining the depth and power of these identifications is possible only by acknowledging the dynamic and historical balance between structure and agency. Returning to the agent-structure debate effectively fixes the logic of power as essential to questions of identity. The definitions of ethnicity and ethnic identity proposed here therefore build upon a broadly structuralist interpretation that is linked to an equal attention towards the role of purposeful subjects. Thus ethnicity is best viewed as a continuum, varying widely in terms of salience, intensity and meaning.[42]

This study contends that there are significant inconsistencies among Afrikaans speakers in South Africa today which are part of a distinct historical genesis and contemporary structural change. Whilst it focuses upon the development of post-apartheid identifications, distinctions can thus be drawn between the different but historically linked stages of Afrikaner nationalism, namely: group consciousness, the consciousness of being a *volk*, and national consciousness.[43] Indeed, the term 'Afrikaners' for whites was first used early in the eighteenth century alongside other terminology; it was not until the mid-twentieth century that the term was set aside only for white Afrikaans speakers.[44] The uneven and fractured class, racial and ethnic awareness which characterises this grouping has fluctuated considerably since 1652, most coherent during the years of Nationalist government when an organisational axis of the state and the National Party offered this minority 'systematic access to the ear, agency and largesse of the state'.[45] With the onset of the accumulation crisis during 1974 and the unprecedented success of the socio-economic transformation of the grouping,[46] the very same tensions returned to afflict this conditional unity. The process of managed reform which followed only laid these divisions bare as it sought to 'rearrange the relationship between the state, race and class interests which lie at the core of Afrikaner nationalism'.[47]

Despite the presence of a pervasive sense of Afrikanerness or 'being Afrikaans' then, the meanings and significance attached to this subjective groupness or self-understanding are now so varied that it is moot whether an Afrikaner grouping exists in any formal sense. Given this diversity, and the historical controversy that surrounds the act of classification itself, employing one definition of the term Afrikaner is problematic. This book introduces three different definitions in order to acknowledge the complexity of the experiences of Afrikaner identity.[48] In the first instance, the ascriptive category of Afrikaner will denote everyone who has Afrikaans as their mother tongue. Secondly, an auxiliary ascriptive definition will comprise all whites that boast Afrikaans as their mother tongue. Finally, a more circumscribed experience of identity will be covered by a self-definition that describes an Afrikaner as someone who identifies himself/herself as belonging to a distinct group, defined in terms of (a) an identification with cultural homogeneity converging on the Afrikaans language, and (b) in terms of a self-consciousness at being a political minority in South Africa. Whilst the empirical section of this study will focus primarily upon an Afrikaans speaking white elite and middle class, this categorisation is intended to allow a broadening of the term in order to inform a wider research agenda in the context of global restructuring.

It is clear then that the concept of identity needs to be carefully re-examined and framed within a new global context. Problematically, little agreement has been reached on the relationship between identity and globalisation. Traditional orthodoxies are being unevenly disrupted by a new politics so that Cerny alludes to the subnational, transnational and supranational cleavages, tribalism and other revived or *invented* identities that flourish in the wake of the uneven erosion of national identities, national economies and national state policy capacity apparent in the contemporary global era.[49] Much of the literature is not fully cognisant of the paradox between 'homogenising global flows and continued cultural heterogeneity',[50] which give expression to ethnic fundamentalisms as well as new diasporic or transnational identities. Yet closer examination demonstrates that 'locality has survived alongside globality'.[51] Robertson defines this concern with spatial and temporal issues as 'glocalisation' where globalisation represents the compression of the world as a whole, and involves the linking of localities, whilst alluding to the 'invention' of 'locality' as well as its imagination.[52] Thus Hall suggests that social identities now fluctuate along a spectrum between tradition and translation, whereby those which adapt are capable of substantive reconfiguration, revision and even renewal.[53] Together these trends suggest a paradigm shift in the political economic context of identity politics.

It is intended that the framework introduced below will advance a new research agenda to explore identity politics within a global context. Whilst contemporary globalisation does provide a fundamental reconfiguration of political space, 'globalisation is not really global.'[54] It is necessary to examine the key structures within which this politics is practised as well as the politics of different agents therein. The nuances of these 'transformed social semantics' can be felt throughout every aspect of society, informing the (re)constitution and/or creation of identities.[55] Whilst this new global equation does provide openings and opportunities, these are fundamentally uneven so that the implications of such profound structural change for the economic, territorial and cultural resources that give meaning to a distinct identity politics should not be underplayed. Globalisation is considered here as one of the foremost explanations for the structural realignment and possible reconfiguration of Afrikaner identity.

Theorising identity in a global era

The concept of power is clearly fundamental to an analysis of identity under conditions of globalisation. Recent scholarship has confirmed that a 'historical-structural' analysis of the transition (including the strength of the meta-discourse of neoliberal global capitalism) is a *sine qua non* of any understanding of post-apartheid South Africa. Taylor and Vale are emphatic that:

> 'the realisation by the minority elite that a continuation of their privileged position within society rested on a renegotiated political understanding was derivative of, if not dependent upon, the thrust of what was increasingly called "globalisation."'[56]

Although a global political economy analysis highlights only certain aspects of the transition, it is contended that it draws attention to a sphere that has been largely overlooked in the study of identity politics. And this is nowhere more apparent than vis-à-vis prominent constituent parts such as capital elites, a globalised middle class and cultural intelligentsia who have participated to very different extents in the neo-liberal revolution, and in measures to protect their material position and manufacture a new cultural commentary. For it is this transformation which provides the backdrop to the structural shifts in South Africa that have impacted upon the process of identity adjustment and the reconfiguration of Afrikaner identifications.

At the same time, the local or sub-national level of analysis must take equal precedence in representing the variety in the observable behaviour of Afrikaans speakers. These non-elite actors also respond to the same global and hegemonic forces which have shaped the transition, as their identifications are in turn shaped by local circumstances. The 'local orientation' of the 'new nationalist movement' has been remarked upon,[57] and the concerns of this politics have indeed taken a more markedly provincial turn in recent years.[58] This slant should also be reconciled with other levels of analysis to show how identification with Afrikaans is similarly affected by the global and national logics of the neo-liberal hegemonic consensus and the ANC's hegemonic project respectively. The so-called local logics of geographic location, generation and provincial politics help to account for this variety. More specifically, this analytical frame allows a focus on the manner in which certain Afrikaans speakers have disconnected entirely from any notion of a formal grouping, but remain connected to a pervasive if subjective understanding of Afrikanerness. Indeed, each of these constituent parts is grounded within the more sophisticated categorisation of Afrikaners raised above.

It is a central contention of this study that an assessment of these structural factors and social forces is best represented within a Gramscian analysis. The strength of the dynamic historical analytic framework that Antonio Gramsci promotes lies in its richer formulation of these phenomena, and their deeper connection to particular historical junctures.[59] It operates on different (local, national, regional and global) levels of analysis simultaneously, assigning each equal analytical weight. It offers a non-reductionist and non-essentialist means of examining the negotiated and contextual properties of social identities. His reading goes far beyond a simple economism to include political, ethnical and ideological components within an autonomous political dynamic. With the introduction of the crucial concept of hegemony he in effect loosens the notion of power – hegemony represents one form of power – from a tie to historically specific social classes and, in one fell swoop, gives it a broad applicability to *all* relations of domination and subordination.[60] His dialectic comprehension of history offers a simultaneous attention to both structures and agents so that identity is exposed as a structural and contested condition, punctuated by systemic transactions and moulded by agents. Moreover, Gramsci's analysis of hegemony:

> 'necessarily draws our attention to regional, religious, ethnic and national – as well as class – lines of cleavage and connection [which] are the subject of a common analytic frame.'[61]

Overall, certain of these concepts and this new 'sociology of power' are exceptionally relevant to an understanding of how consent – measured in all the cultural, ideological, political and economic spheres of the prevailing global hegemonic project – is currently being reproduced in post-apartheid South Africa, and thus how wider structures of power impact upon the transformation of social identities.

Despite the 'continued vitality' of Gramsci's legacy in international relations and political theory,[62] there is a substantial lacuna within the neo-Gramscian perspectives which has emerged in global political economy in regard to culture and identity politics. Yet, a Gramscian approach is a novel starting point for a rethinking of some of the most fundamental and potentially divisive issues in the recent scholarship concerned with these identifications. To begin with, it supports an awareness of power relations that is necessary in the study of ethnicities and related social phenomena. Further, it concentrates on both the global nature of these phenomena and their local variances and influences by placing them within a global context that is sensitive to historicity and path-dependence. As Hall reasons, the point is not to apply Gramscian theory 'literally or mechanically but to use his insights to unravel the changing complexities [that] historical transformation has brought about'.[63] This study attempts to answer how consensus has been empowered both by linkages with a variety of domestic partners, and connections with the transnational hegemonic order. It is contended that connecting the domestic and global hegemonic orders explains the structural shifts underway in South African society, and thereafter the changing composition of identifications among Afrikaans speakers in South Africa today. Moreover, this process of adjustment is framed within the more complex three-fold categorisation introduced above.

At the centre of this configuration rests the Gramscian concept of historic bloc. It prescribes a complex conception of how different social forces can be joined so as to create a set of alliances and promote common interests or a new historic order. As Rupert suggests:

> 'For Gramsci, an historic bloc is more than a simple alliance of classes or class fractions. It encompasses political, cultural, and economic

aspects of a particular social formation, uniting these in historically specific ways to form a complex, politically contestable and dynamic ensemble of social relations. An historic bloc articulates a world view, grounded in historically specific socio-political conditions and production relations, which lends substance and ideological coherence to its social power.'[64]

To succeed, the bloc must devise a worldview that appeals to different communities and to reasonably claim that the interests of the bloc emulate those of the wider society it professes to represent. Thus, in post-apartheid South Africa it is argued that the formation of a historic bloc is underway that, whilst preferring the interests of capital, also favours other constituent parts including the middle classes, the African petite bourgeoisie and, to a lesser degree, the organised working classes.[65] In recent years, growing disillusionment in the tripartite alliance over imbalances in the partnership with the private sector has led to a 'GEAR shift' whereby:

'The principles of macroeconomic stability remain. But because such stability has essentially been attained, there is more space for massive social and economic interventions by the government. In that sense, we are in a post-stabilisation phase, a post-GEAR period.'[66]

Nonetheless, a precarious but workable equilibrium remains whereby these divergent interests are joined within a broad development strategy, and are broadly aligned with a transnational historic bloc of social forces fashioned by the ideological dominance of neo-liberalism.

Only by acknowledging both the ideological composition of the ANC's hegemonic project then, as well as the dynamics whereby a consensus is manufactured around this ideology, can the nature of contemporary Afrikaans identifications be properly demonstrated. Likewise, only by linking this notion to a transnational historic bloc that demarcates a particular, neo-liberal developmental paradigm can any analysis of the nature of relations between the government and various Afrikaans speaking constituent parts be attempted.[67] The comprehensive social revolution initially prescribed by the ANC liberation movement and later government has irretrievably faltered. Indeed, the task of building a new order distinguishable from and inimical to the former dispensation has been uneven. It has been suggested that contemporary globalisation discourse has projected certain elements of 'common sense' onto the transformation process and transition in post-apartheid South Africa.[68] The so-called 'ideology' of globalisation is constituted within a neo-liberal historic bloc where the ideological, institutional and material elements of neo-liberalism have attained hegemonic status amongst a transnational elite, among which a number of ANC and other domestic elites include themselves. For the time being neoliberal economic ideas remain hegemonic ideologically and in terms of policy.[69] This is despite changes to industrial policy and the widely mooted emergence of a new developmental path,[70] as well as a vicious leadership succession which is assuming an ideological edge on important policy issues.[71]

The 'new' South Africa is not so much the fêted break with the past as the outcome of a sequence of compromises and consensus building. Instead, Marais contends that this transition should:

'be understood less as a miraculous historical rupture than as the (as yet inconclusive) outcome of a convergence of far-reaching attempts to resolve an ensemble of political, ideological and economic contradictions that had accumulated steadily since the 1970s.'[72]

In the economic sphere in particular, little is distinguishable from the later years of the former dispensation. It would appear then that the antecedents of Afrikaner nationalism and its communal ethos have changed as the liberalisation of the domestic economy has kept pace with global developments. Thus, the 1970s saw the beginnings of change as, for Afrikaner capital elites, the 'virtues of economic growth and participation in the international economy began to conflict with the virtues of nationalist identity'.[73] The upshot of this 'broad coincidence of business and government over economic policy' was that, with the National Party employing neo-liberal economic policies by the late 1980s, the government and 'its allies in capital worked hard to circumscribe efforts by the ANC to forge a different economic path', embarking on the transition with 'considerable confidence'.[74] Indeed, today, despite striking ambiguities at the heart of government thinking on globalisation and macro-economic policies, there is likewise a dominant 'ideological posture' in the inner sanctum of ANC government which is reflected among Afrikaans speaking capital elites. Bond argues that the ideological variant that has won out, at least for the time being, is a 'techno-economic' perspective on globalisation which stresses that there is no alternative to capitalism in the present global context.[75] The government's stance on this issue, echoing the neo-liberal line on market liberalisation and deregulation even whilst overtly pushing a redistributive agenda, has seen macro-economic policy making become ever more circumscribed within the narrow confines of ministerial and business circles.

Nowhere has this been more evident than the paradigm shift between the Keynesian focus of the Reconstruction and Development Programme (RDP) of 1994, and the market-orientated Growth, Employment and Redistribution (GEAR) strategy which was adopted in 1996. This radical change of direction was born of the clout of both domestic – including Afrikaans capital elites – and international capital, forces within the ANC's leadership, and the global balance of social forces as opposed to the concerns of its tripartite alliance partners.[76] Indeed, Mbeki and his allies promoted GEAR with persistent assertions that South Africa 'had no choice but to play by the rules of the globalised economy'.[77] While it is widely acknowledged that an 'elite compromise' permeated the entire settlement resulting in significant shifts in the ANC's economic policy during the pre- and post-1994 election period,[78] this spirit of compromise has only strengthened during Mbeki's presidency. Over time he has consolidated considerable power in the presidency where his 'technocratic style of policy-making' and reforms have tended to come from above:

> 'Mbeki is not one for the big hall meeting. He excels at formulating policy in small, bilateral groups, and resolves conflict by talking to the parties concerned individually and securing separate agreements. Official policy is increasingly the product of bilateral meetings.'[79]

Indeed, the lack of deliberation outside these narrow circles which characterised the presentation of GEAR has continued with the government still motivated by the belief that it must send 'strong signals to the international financial community about its determination to pursue a "responsible" fiscal stance'.[80]

It is now more than a decade since the ANC government assumed power. As the political axis of the settlement, it remains sandwiched between several conflicting prerogatives; indulging capital forces has done little to placate its marginalised constituencies, whilst the Africanist turn of nation-building initiatives has not assuaged increasingly vociferous minority group demands. Indeed, the historical development of the ANC and its hegemonic project has ensured that existent ideological discrepancies on the level of ideas and material forces have become ever more pronounced with the advent of government and the demands of transformation. Today there are many signs of genuine cracks in this settlement as crises at the local level suggest that the ruling ANC is now facing a 'growing credibility crisis',[81] and allegations of corruption within leadership circles have accumulated.[82] Recent years have proved that there are substantial qualifications to the loyalty of the hegemon's junior if more progressive alliance partners, the South African Communist Party (SACP) and Congress of South African Trade Unions (COSATU).[83] Later chapters will elaborate further on these rifts; it is now apparent that the tripartite alliance is troubled and the divisions worsening.[84] Although the neo-liberal agenda continues to dominate the economic policy agenda, it is clear that capital elites retain concerns about the government's ambitions for socioeconomic transformation, most prominently Black Economic Empowerment (BEE) legislation. And that these are concerns that the government takes seriously.[85]

Hegemony then supplies a methodology for the study of change. As a consequence, it is possible to monitor the openings for groups in real historical conditions – the possibilities for action, innovation and manoeuvre – with the level of hegemony to be addressed as an empirical question. These spaces are constituted not only by ideas but also material and institutional factors, stretching across the sub-national, national, regional and global spectra to provide opportunities for a reconfiguration of Afrikaner identity. It has become apparent that only certain Afrikaans speaking constituent parts have taken advantage of these openings. Because of this it is suggested what is emerging is a plurality of subjective meanings of Afrikanerness which are derived from structural conditions, and which intersect most prominently with identities such as race and class, as well as others including generation and gender.

This study examines the dynamics of identity adjustment more closely by illuminating how key groups behave in real historical conditions. Empirical evidence is presented demonstrating the manner in which capital elites have bolstered their position by endorsing the neo-liberal macroeconomic policies of the ANC government whilst paying lip service to the associated agenda of social transformation and its opportunities. The engagement of elements of an increasingly globalised middle class with the global division of labour and power is also evaluated. Thereafter, on the level of ideas, the emergence and nature of a cultural politics involved in the defence of the Afrikaans language and culture forms the focus of discussion. Finally, by examining how the responses of non-elite actors differ under local circumstances, the development of local forms of community, identification and disengagement is considered.

Evaluating these dynamics requires a deeper, structural understanding of how compliance in all the symbolic, institutional and material bases of the ANC's hegemonic project and interconnected ideology of globalisation is being manufactured. Exactly how this agenda has come to be so widely accepted and an exploration of the global and domestic constraints upon the shape and depth of the ANC's hegemonic project is unravelled in the next chapters. Both the nature of the transition and the ongoing if uneven consolidation of liberal democracy 'increasingly resembles a corporatist pact between state, labour and business, which implies that the [ANC government] has to play to two audiences at the same time, with different sets of expectations'.[86] Thus the national consensus rests, at least in the economic realm, upon familiar territory. As a consequence, this work will attempt to resolve whether the development of a neo-liberal consensus in domestic circles has eroded the ethnic slant of communal solidarity and sentiments once espoused by a synergy of the National Party government, state and Afrikaner nationalist elites. More simply, in fostering a domestic variant of the transnational ideological hegemony, have these class coalitions shattered the terms of the ethnic bargain? The value of a Gramscian frame here lies in its attention to difference and historical context. Within this frame, the complexity of the economic, social, cultural and political formation of any population – and among both popular and elite actors – can be assessed.

In this setting the choices for Afrikanerdom are legion and an evaluation of the divisions *and* connections within this diverse grouping is long overdue. Certainly, history suggests that these same social coalitions were more or less constantly reformed over time so as to enhance Afrikaner material and cultural interests in chorus. More philosophical and intellectual disputes concerned with perceptions of marginalisation, entitlement and belonging, together with pragmatic quarrels regarding institutional and symbolic power, have become increasingly prominent.[87] A concentration upon the status of the Afrikaans language and associated contention of cultural space has bestowed an agenda beset by contradictions. On the one hand, an influential number among the intelligentsia are wholly committed to a narrow, linguistic and local focus that retains some ethnic undertones in spite of protestations to the contrary. At the same time, this is countered by another, patently more progressive, framework. What is impossible to ignore is that both share an uncritical understanding of the current milieu. Neither grouping properly acknowledges the highly salient fact that any community today represents a minority that still retains a sizeable material *and* cultural inheritance, an aspect of apartheid's historical legacy that has been reinforced by contemporary global restructuring.

Although South Africa remains a society characterised to a notable degree by group politics, this book asserts that Afrikaans speakers exhibit a wide range of identifications, not all of which are connected to an Afrikaans ethnic or language heritage. Indeed, Chapter two examines the historical development of an Afrikaner identity and nationalist project. It does not suggest that ethnicity as a form of identification among the Afrikaans populace is disappearing but rather that the attributes which previously assumed great significance are being eroded as other, different distinctions are seizing centre stage. In his study of ethnic identity among white Americans, Alba suggests such a trend pre-empts the on-going formation of a new ethnic group based on ancestry from anywhere on the European continent.[88] Set against the shape of the post-apartheid order explored in Chapter three, it is too early to say whether a similar transformation is proceeding among Afrikaans speakers. Nonetheless, providing a broad overview of the dynamics of identity adjustment, Chapters four and five demonstrate that a metamorphosis of sorts is occurring. Regarded in this way, it is contended that post-apartheid identifications suggest a loosely bound grouping apparently in the process of both retrenching and rebuilding under a new regime ambivalent towards the fortunes of this population as a whole, and within an increasingly hospitable global context in which important constituent components of Afrikanerdom are now functioning.

2

THE AFRIKANER NATIONALIST PROJECT

A distinctive Afrikaner social identity was deliberately cultivated by the regime, state and other organisations that permeated both the public and private spheres during the apartheid era. The task of building what became the Afrikaner nationalist project and Afrikanerdom itself fell to this heterogeneous range of actors who increasingly cemented the nationalist ethos with distinctive ethnic overtones. Yet beneath the surface of this ostensibly monolithic community was a grouping beset by regional variations, increasing class stratification and other, compelling divisions that no deft manipulation could entirely conceal. With electoral victory during May 1948 a somewhat nebulous nationalist movement reached a new stage of maturity. Exactly how a diverse coterie of nationalists with fundamentally disparate concerns and agendas managed to transform and sustain the meaning of *volk* within the auspices of a popular nationalist project will thus occupy a large part of this chapter.

Whilst this book focuses upon the development of post-apartheid identity politics, a number of observations are held to be consistent throughout the development, reproduction and adjustment of Afrikaner identifications. The dynamics of identity adjustment are conceived as historically rooted so that a clear distinction can be drawn between the earlier stages of identity formation, and during the apartheid era when a pronounced grouping became readily apparent. Any one definition of an Afrikaner during the formative years covered in this chapter is problematic. For that reason, an Afrikaner will be defined both ascriptively – whites who have Afrikaans as their mother tongue – and in terms of a self-definition which comprises a process of group identification. In line with these assumptions, a distinction will be drawn between the different but historically linked stages of nationalism manifested at various stages of Afrikaner political thought, namely: group consciousness, the consciousness of being a *volk*, and national consciousness.[1] Essentially, this chapter aims to demonstrate the importance of both historical context and the changing balance of social forces in any proper analysis of this nationalist project.

Appropriating the past:
The development of an Afrikaner identity

For a long period, any understanding of Afrikaner nationalism was shrouded in myth so that its development was established as nothing less than inherently nationalistic: the behaviours of a fully-fledged and conscious grouping. In this sense, Afrikaners' points of reference entered a virtuous circle, propagating ideas of community and a collective identity that were perpetuated by their very rise to power.[2] Thus the realities of the past were effectively distorted and embellished as the dislocations wrought by the racial-capitalist path of modernisation became increasingly evident.[3] Yet neither of the contending approaches to the development of Afrikaner identity comes fully to terms with the reality of identity as a historical process that assumes shape within the context of a particular political, economic and social system. Leaning towards a primordialist approach, Giliomee admits that ethnic identification:

> 'sought to attain political and cultural goals and meet diverse psychological needs. It was more than a struggle for material rewards, but the outcome of the Afrikaners' struggle in the economic field would be decisive in determining whether they would see themselves primarily as an ethnic group or as a class.'[4]

During the 1930s, therefore, Afrikaner cultural and business elites constructed a scheme with both materialist and ethnic appeal to raise an ethnic mobilisation capable of improving and securing the economic position of an Afrikaner grouping. In order to do so, a programme of political and ideological engineering stirred up nationalist sentiments to fix conceptions of group interests, whilst simultaneously acquiring material rewards for this same grouping. Although Afrikaner capital and the middle class stood to benefit the most, at the heart of this movement lay the conviction that only a combination of ethnic mobilisation and *volkskapitalisme* could improve the lot of the economically and politically marginalised Afrikaner.[5] Giliomee's analysis is appreciative of the material sensibilities of Afrikaner nationalism, accepting the constructed nature of the movement and consequently its readiness for transformation.

In both his iconoclastic earlier work *Volkskapitalisme* and later *Forty Lost Years*, O'Meara's broadly Marxist perspective analyses Afrikaner nationalism by introducing the imperatives of political economy and mode of production. In his analysis, the central protagonists were the economic entrepreneurs contained largely within the ranks of the *Broederbond*. These entrepreneurs systematically won over large sections of nascent Afrikaner business and workers to the nationalist project using not so much the complexities of Christian nationalism, as much as concrete, everyday issues within a network of overlapping social, economic and cultural organisations.[6] In this picture, the Afrikaner Economic Movement, begun with the *Economic Volkskongres* and the *Reddingsdaad* (Rescue Action) of 1939, is perhaps the most important piece of the nationalist puzzle, responsible for the platform which led to the later election victory during 1948.

O'Meara's account is sensible of the fractious elements within this class alliance – organised around Transvaal, Cape and Orange Free State (OFS) farmers, specific categories of white labour, the Afrikaner petty bourgeoisie and the emerging capitalists of the *reddingsdaad* movement[7] – each of which had their own, often divergent interests that were pulled together by a form of racial protectionism which offered welfare, subsidies and job reservation. His concentration upon the relations between particular class forces and the capitalist economy ultimately affords the ideology of Afrikaner capital central stage within the nationalist ideology.[8] And his resonant and nuanced account of capital, classes and the state itself is a useful depiction of the early politics of the Afrikaner nationalist project.

Nonetheless, the approach is not without flaws. In the main, critics have emphasised the materialist or class reductionism that hinders many Marxist approaches and, more specifically, the economic determinism inherent in O'Meara's answer to the motive of support for Afrikaner nationalism. For example, Posel directs attention to the contested and non-hegemonic version of apartheid expounded by Afrikaner capital within the nationalist alliance.[9] Giliomee refers to the wheat farmers in the Cape who he alleges could not have supported Malan over Hertzog within this class scenario given the fact that there was no particular economic policy to reward such a move.[10] However, O'Meara's account retains considerable power due to the cogent and organic record it provides of the constructed and contextual nature of Afrikaner identity. What is most useful about his analysis is the manner in which it can be utilised to address the early tensions and splits, as well as the unravelling of the Afrikaner nationalist alliance during the post-apartheid years. Indeed, this account is fully cognisant of the power relations inherent in the formation and thereafter reproduction of Afrikaner identities.

It is beyond the scope of this book to provide more than a concise overview of this formative period. By briefly reintroducing the complexities of these years during the remainder of this section, it will adhere to Butler's four-fold periodisation of South African history prior to 1990: South Africa before minerals (pre-1870); the age of mineral revolutions and unification (1870–1910); the age of established segregation and early apartheid (1910–60); and, the age of high apartheid (1960–90).[11] Indeed, the notion of an ethnic awareness was first given substance in nationalist ideology prior to 1870. Giliomee suggests that by this stage a distinct grouping had emerged, all of whom spoke Dutch, had a common religion and managed a certain racial endogamy.[12] In short, the somewhat diluted ingredients of what would later become Afrikanerdom could be discerned.

Racial hierarchies were present from the beginnings of the colony. These represented not so much an ideology as an inherent ethnocentrism that, during the Dutch period, was transformed into a hierarchy of legal status groups that established the basis for a racial order which survived even through the upheavals of the 1820s and 1830s.[13] There was also concern and resentment over British control's being extended over the Cape Colony begun in 1795, and made permanent during 1805. Imperial hegemony was increasingly felt in many quarters with the prohibition of the slave trade during 1807 and, more significantly, a battery of legislation from 1833 onwards that served to weaken the colonialists' authority over their native workers. The situation in the colony was complicated further by the incomplete incorporation of the settlement into the British Empire during the 1850s, stepping up what was perceived by many Dutch settlers to be hostile interference.

Although imperial intervention expanded significantly during this pre-minerals stage, relations between the British and Dutch settlers, as well as those between the Dutch and native inhabitants, were governed largely by a form of pragmatism. Indeed:

'Precapitalist and capitalist modes of production existed side by side, as did state forms of varying size with their own ruling groups and systems of exploitation.'[14]

Prior to the closing of the frontier, Guelke contends that the trekboers were far from being subsistence farmers, instead nurturing trade and other economic relations with the Cape in order to market their produce and buy supplies. He distinguishes between two distinct frontier communities: the first 'orthodox' or trekboer communities dedicated to maintaining an exclusivist 'European' way of life; and, the second, 'pluralist' community that involved the blending of cultures and peoples within an informal social framework.[15] Indeed, Butler suggests that the Great Trek, later to become the seminal event of this period and the focus of many claims for Afrikaner political self-determination, was no more than a series of episodic migrations of around 12 000 migrants who left the Cape between 1836 and 1840.[16] For the most part, the different colonies and semi-autonomous republics subsisted, if uneasily at times, side by side. Following Du Toit, it is proposed that this interval comprised the prenationalist phase of Afrikaner history,[17] a stage prior to the subsequent refinement of a genuine group consciousness.

Between 1870 to 1910, however, what had been no more than a wavering sense of solidarity evolved into a group awareness even whilst the boundaries of this group remained a matter of dispute. With the discovery of diamonds and gold in 1867 and 1886 respectively, the advent of modern capitalism in South Africa ushered in an era leading to the establishment of the contemporary South African state which was characterised by tumultuous, deep-seated change. Butler outlines four processes that indelibly marked the country during this period and thereafter, namely: the Anglo-Boer War, unification, economic development and quasi-proletarianisation.[18] As the piecemeal capitalist transformation of early settlement was entirely superseded so a new politics took hold in each of the three regional Afrikaner groupings. Urbanisation and migration proceeded at an unprecedented rate accompanied by a bona fide policy of segregation that catered to the vociferous demands of the increasingly omnipotent mining industry: the modern South Africa was being born.

In these few short years, the comparative stability of social relations in the preceding decades had disappeared entirely. Development progressed at vastly different rates through different sectors and regions, effectively contributing to the fractured class and ethnic awareness upon which an Afrikaner nationalist identity would be founded. Any group consciousness was thus slow to develop. Whilst the Jameson Raid of 1895–96 irrevocably harmed the integration promised during the late nineteenth century, it provided the term 'Afrikaner' with anti-British and anti-imperialistic undertones.[19] Elsewhere uneven economic development aggravated regional and class differentiation among Afrikaans-speakers, injuring hopes of unity. Conversely, this same process shaped perceptions among Dutch-Afrikaner professionals that a significant section of their group was faced with economic and cultural degeneration.[20] Thus, in 1875 the *Genootskap van Regte Afrikaners* (Fellowship of True Afrikaners) was established in Paarl to champion the cause of the Afrikaans language and thus build a culturally based means of ethnic recognition. It was the first of an increasingly number of such associations that were to follow.

It was, however, the outbreak of war that broke the bitter stalemate and heralded a vital progression in Afrikaner nationalist history. Schutte captures the importance of this event:

> 'The old themes of purification through suffering reappear. The British were seen to be sent as a scourge. Their colonial expansionist tendencies were understood to be part of a larger plan that fitted the Afrikaner ethnic eschatology. God had a purpose with the humiliation of his people, namely to purify and sanctify them more than ever before. God's standards were set very high for His elect. The materialism and selfishness of the mineral- and money-grabbing British were contrasted with the righteous suffering of the Afrikaners, who were the designated holders of the land. Among all this suffering and humiliation the Afrikaners believed in the divine promise of justice through the restitution of their land.'[21]

Defeat demanded a high price of the Boer forces, inflicting a policy of Anglicisation as well as laying the foundations of Milner's race-based, modern South African state. As whites, and thus the principal beneficiaries of the new political structure, the Afrikaners were forced to accept the permanent position of the victorious British enemy in this state. Thus, a period that had begun with the pragmatic coexistence of the region's diverse populations had ended with nascent racial hierarchies securely in place; republicanism, language policy and white poverty inscribed firmly upon the nationalist agenda; and, a previously resentful if fragmented grouping having conceived a tangible and separate culture.

The ensuing three decades were perhaps the most critical in the formation of the Afrikaner nationalist project. At the time of electoral victory in 1948, the nationalist alliance could celebrate the unexpected success of a programme of cultural and economic engineering that had borne fruit with the maturity of Afrikaner nationalism as a cross-class and nationally supported enterprise. No small achievement, this process of unification had been hard won from the plethora of divisions that had periodically managed to derail progress towards unity. Indeed, the successes of this period can be broadly located within the material and social dislocations evident during the inter-war years.

Cohabitation in the aftermath of defeat reconciled little around the Afrikaner-English split. Although political power was essentially shared, and a succession of supportive governments lent financial backing to Afrikaans speakers with subsidies and job reservation schemes, even middle class Afrikaners failed to compete equally with English speakers or to capture all-important civil service positions. The Depression of the early 1930s and late Afrikaner urbanisation took their toll so that even with the deepening of segregation, the blue collar and other manual workers and struggling farmers who comprised nearly two-thirds of the Afrikaner grouping by 1948 required state support to maintain some sort of parity within the dominant white grouping.[22] Even the second industrial revolution wrought by the gold and export boom of the mid-1930s failed to make real inroads, unable to wholly erase the militancy apparent as mining capital and white workers clashed over the inequalities of this form of racial capitalism.

Circumstances did not improve with the advent of World War Two, despite the fact that it excised the lingering aftermath of the Depression and substantially enlarged the country's industrial base and production. Instead, the relaxation of segregation and concomitant influx of blacks to the cities ostensibly served further to threaten the position of the largely Afrikaans speaking unskilled and semi-skilled workers. Accompanied by the revitalisation of the African National Congress (ANC) into a mass populist movement with far more conspicuous and militant democratic demands,[23] these immense social changes effectively collapsed the final pillars of the then 'Native Policy', shattering the ruling 'South Africanist' consensus and its definition of the interests and project of white South Africa.[24]

If the poor white problem had been established as a genuine concern by the 1932 Carnegie Commission – which had concluded that, out of approximately 300 000 poor whites, the majority were Afrikaans speakers – by the end of the war it had become a compelling political issue. Deliberately accorded a platform during the centenary celebrations of the Great Trek in 1938,[25] capitalism, traditionally viewed as the domain of the imperial power, was imbued with a distinctly anti-Afrikaner character. Accompanied by the Fusion Pact of 1934 between Hertzog's NP and Smuts' South Africa Party which formed the United Party, an act seen by many Afrikaners as a betrayal, the politicisation of the Afrikaner culture began in earnest.

Since its inception in 1918, the Afrikaner *Broederbond* had been at the centre of this process. Utilising a network of overlapping cultural and economic organisations, the

> 'belief-system which characterised the traditional Afrikaner was propagated both in theory and practice during this period, so that

Afrikaners could identify themselves on all levels with Afrikaner cultural values,'[26]

and a unitary Afrikaner nationalism. Forceful strategies of cultural assertion centring upon the Afrikaans language, recognised as an official language with parity beside English in 1925,[27] were formulated by the middle class and urban-orientated elite who made up the majority of *Bond* members. Gradually a reworking of Afrikaner nationalist ideology along Christian-nationalist lines was fixed. It represented a genuine break from earlier manifestations and, translated into a concern with tangible issues, was far better equipped to tackle the traumatic social transition and economic inequalities that had so profoundly affected the Afrikaner grouping.[28] Most importantly, this new political ideology overturned the anti-capitalism evident in the ranks of Afrikanerdom as it set Afrikaner capital to work for the Afrikaner. Allied with the NP, the *Broederbond* had effectively ensured the survival, for a time at least, of a distinctive Afrikaner grouping.

Moving towards consensus

The legacy of the formative decades between 1910 and 1948, and endeavours to build consensus among a disjointed and divided grouping, were later to cast a long shadow over the nationalist alliance. In the years immediately following the electoral breakthrough it was difficult to disguise the less than fortuitous rise to power. Only latterly did the election year become the watershed it has remained to this day. Butler contends that:

> 'Three factors in combination – the electoral win of the National Party, the later importance that the term apartheid adopted and the moral repugnancy and seeming triviality of early NP legislation – made 1948 a year of seemingly unprecedented importance.'[29]

Indeed, NP policy at the time was little more than a 'pragmatic continuation' and 'reactive' intensification of the existing government policy of segregation: a series of '*ad hoc* attempts' to resolve enduring issues.[30] That said, the influential alliance between the NP and *Broederbond* would effectively shore up support for the nationalist project which was emerging, legitimated by the simple expediency of electoral victory. Elsewhere within the nationalist edifice, and even more markedly within the ranks of these two pivotal organisations, divisions and conflict festered which had significant bearing upon the nationalist project itself. The recommendations of the

Sauer Report of 1947 – allegedly the precursor to full-blown apartheid – itself only:

> 'manifested an unresolved conflict between disparate sets of policy proposals, rather than a single, consistent plan. The newly elected Nationalist government therefore lacked a compelling, unambiguous, and uncontested blueprint from which state policies could simply be read off, step by step. Instead, after 1948 the contest between the opposing factions within the Nationalist alliance was transposed into the state itself.'[31]

In the meantime, however, little attempt was made to rectify these contradictions.

The negotiated character of the nationalist project can be surmised from the necessity of subduing these contradictions within an expanding hegemonic project. Consensus became the name of the game so that first and foremost the hegemonic project served to draw the disparate constituent forces of Afrikanerdom together. In order to do so the Christian-national ideology associated with the 1930s and 1940s was to be made more pertinent to existing political realities. In short, 'vigorous' political and ideological engineering had to provide:

> 'a legitimating philosophical basis for the draconian structures of white political power that was group-based, historically grounded, and modern.'[32]

This ideology was to be elaborated in the shape of policies to protect and advance the Afrikaans language alongside the encroachment of the state into the economic realm to overturn both real and perceived sources of disadvantage and grievance within the wider Afrikaner population. If the *volkseenheid* (unity of the volk) and its survival were to be secured, the character of this ideology was crucial. Indeed, a prominent characteristic of the apartheid era was the:

> 'almost desperate attempts made by successive NP heads of state to crystallise a new ideology which would legitimise (or mystify) the continuation of white supremacy and the structures of racial exploitation.'[33]

Unity and legitimacy were to prove problems that never entirely went away.

These political manoeuvrings bore considerable fruit in the shape of a nationalist alliance of Afrikaner farmers, labour, the petty bourgeoisie and embryonic Afrikaner financial and commercial capital, first conceived in the decades before electoral victory.[34] The challenge for the regime thereafter was to retain some measure of stability and consistency within this vital alliance even as its social base altered conspicuously. During the 1970s the white middle classes and capital were at its core. By the mid-1980s it was constituted by:

> 'a multi-racial co-opted elite, consisting of the upper echelon of the National Party; large sections of the Afrikaner and English-speaking business communities (with close patronage relations with government); key securocrats in the State Security Council; and co-opted African, coloured and Asian leaders.'[35]

Even whilst the alliance was broadened, the centre could only hold whilst the common ideology held firm and its adherents could appreciate a tangible return. The lowest common denominator was initially white authority and the integrity of the white race. Apartheid ideology nurtured 'incompatible conceptions' from the start, essentially over the basic issue of the relationship between political segregation and the economic integration of Africans in white (urban) areas.[36] Most tellingly, the fundamentally irreconcilable needs of different factions of capital could not be overcome:

> 'It was precisely because the Afrikaner nationalist alliance comprised an alliance of class groupings that consensus was *not* reached over the meaning of apartheid.'[37]

And these divergent interpretations of apartheid were to plague the nationalist establishment throughout the apartheid era.

Worsening tensions within the nationalist project were initially papered over, encouraged by the highly successful and rapid socio-economic transformation of the status of the majority of Afrikaners. If the fundamental political issue was survival, then consensus was to be achieved through a balance of class, racial and ethnic forces within Afrikanerdom itself, and the success of the nationalist project. With growing confidence, the social coalition that had sustained the rise to power was continually refashioned so as to advance Afrikaner material and cultural interests simultaneously. Uniformity of a sort was secured about an organisational axis comprising the state and NP, with the nationalist project itself constructed on two main pillars, namely: racial domination that affirmed the power of whites to determine the political meanings of self-determination and citizenship; and, the Afrikaner group's 'systematic access to the ear, agency and largesse of the state'.[38] Both were born of 'deprivation and necessity', and both were intended to elevate the Afrikaner minority over a protracted period. The former was as a corrective to marginalisation and an intervention to legitimate racial difference and integrity in everyday life. The latter was to supply the necessary 'cohesiveness', bought of 'a pervasive confidence among Afrikaners that the state would recognise and promote their particular interests'.[39] Race and an activist state thereby supplied the foundations of a readily adaptable nationalist ethos and project.

Perhaps the most definitive feature of this project of social engineering was the *volksbeweging* (national movement) of organised Afrikaner nationalism, charged with creating consensus and cementing unity across the broad stretch of Afrikaner and later white society. This mechanism:

> 'was composed of a gamut of political, cultural, economic, religious, labour and educational organisations. Sharing many of the same leaders, this interlocking organisational network generated a broad consensus and common notion of the particularity of Afrikaner identity and Afrikaner culture. Whatever their often ferocious internecine conflicts, all Afrikaner nationalist groups came to share the view that the real purpose of the South African state was to advance Afrikaner interests and realise Afrikaner destiny (*volkseie*). This conception of the state as the vehicle for Afrikaner advance meant that once the NP arrived in office, each of the constituent elements of the volksbeweging had a legitimate claim on the new administration. The social forces and organisations comprising the Afrikaner nationalist social movement each demanded a unique access to the NP government. Each played a role in the definition of the government agenda. Each expected its own conception of 'its particular interests to be defended in the NP Cabinet and guaranteed by the NP government as an essential element of the interest of the volk as a whole.'[40]

Entrusted with both the practical justifications of apartheid and promoting Afrikaner interests, this increasingly unwieldy mix of organisations sank its tentacles into every aspect of Afrikaner existence. Yet the consequences of this 'bureaucratisation' were manifold, introducing integrated leadership at the apex of Afrikaner organisations; organisational independence into everyday routines; collective goals for Afrikaner organisations and a unity of purpose into corporate Afrikaner action; and, finally, presenting the ordinary Afrikaner with his or her own 'establishment'.[41] In order to achieve this solidarity, all manner of organisations were accommodated even whilst each zealously guarded its own allegiances. Despite such diversity, this organisational union was nonetheless to furnish a bona fide measure of consensus throughout Afrikaner civil society for a considerable and critical period.

Any popular and enduring nationalist project requires more than a simple organisational ethos. In addition, it demands an ideological axis which must bear the brunt of changing historical context and modifications to features of the project itself. The regime's very own 'ideological coup d'état' apartheid – literally separateness – was to perform this ideological duty with considerable success. Indeed, the initial vagueness of the doctrine worked to the nationalist alliance's considerable advantage. Not only did it eloquently express the belief of inundation (*oorstroming*) of the cities by the black population that it was widely believed would endanger the majority of Afrikaners and their various interests, but it also thereby condensed into a 'symbolic whole' all the divergent interests within the auspices of the nationalist alliance.[42] Apartheid provided the ideological glue for and justification of a nationalist order that merged elements of race, ethnicity and class within a remarkably cohesive system.

For the duration of Afrikanerdom's nationalist project, apartheid retained considerable appeal to all elements of this broad social coalition. In the early years of rule the implementation of this ideology was staggered and at times even leisurely. The period 1948–60, so-called 'low apartheid', represented an extension of extant segregationary practices. It did, however, witness the elaboration of a three-fold programme that essentially supplied the foundations of the later season of 'high' or 'grand plan apartheid'. This centred upon new discriminatory laws, enlarged bureaucratic and parastatal sectors, and a range of welfare programmes. The first element focused on African labour regulation, principally influx control and the pass law system, which preserved strict control over the movement and use of this labour, fortified by a battery of petty but nevertheless damaging apartheid legislation. By the close of the 1950s, racial segregation had been effectively guaranteed. These same policies of exclusion and privilege were carried over into the state itself where departments and employment were progressively politicised and expanded to benefit the Afrikaner grouping. Providing a welfare state for this constituency in the shape of increased employment opportunities, white job reservation and a sprawling bureaucracy became an indelible fixture of the apartheid regime.

By the early 1960s, however, separate development or 'formal equality' between ethnic groups became ascendant. For the first time there was a 'genuine departure' from the decades-old segregationist policies and an emphasis instead on a 'retribalisation' of the African political sphere. Despite compelling continuities, and facilitated by:

> 'important political realignments within Afrikanerdom, [this] second phase of apartheid inaugurated a series of new premises, objectives, and ideological tenets, in an attempt to remedy the perceived failures of existing urban policies.'[43]

Not only did the rise of overt statism guide this distinct policy shift, so too did revolutionary elements – the abandoning of white supremacy for self-government; the self determination doctrine and associated policy of industrial decentralisation; and, the inauguration of mass forced removals and the deliberate creation of tribalism in the African population[44] – evidenced in a sea change in apartheid ideology.

What this brief summary of these critical decades has demonstrated is an unmistakable tendency to shift both the direction and gear of the nationalist project in order to maintain cohesion. Price maintains that:

> 'as the historical context facing the ruling group changed over time, the mix of consummatory and instrumental significance attached by the governing elite to the apartheid project could be and was modified . . . [so that] apartheid's instrumental purpose incorporated a number of components whose relative salience for policymakers shifted as the historical context changed and the governing elite's perception of key challenges and threats was consequently refashioned.'[45]

If apartheid served as the ideological premise of unification, there was no illusion that apartheid meant anything otherwise than *'different things to different groups of Afrikaners'*.[46] No less a scion of the establishment than Piet Cillié would proclaim apartheid as a 'pragmatic and tortuous' process of consolidation.[47] The real issue lay, however, not so much with the nationalist project per se but with the ideology that accompanied it. Even whilst separate the two were chronologically and conceptually joined so that apartheid represented a social and political programme advanced by an already modern and modernising Afrikaner elite.[48] Indeed, fractures within the alliance were to converge initially upon economic development to a greater degree than the ideological system apartheid itself elaborated.

These internal differences mattered less during the earlier decades of pragmatic 'low' apartheid. Right until the structural crisis of the mid-1970s the NP was able to steer the nationalist alliance within:

> 'a broader programme which intensified the rate of exploitation and profit in South Africa and which ensured that the benefits were dispersed intensively within the white community.'[49]

Earlier and contentious conceptions of apartheid were coupled with differing opinions of economic development that were, for the most part, buried by the 'successful match' between the prevailing accumulation strategy and the project of Verwoerdian apartheid.[50] Later dissension claimed a heavier cost of the populist coalition because, at its core, it reflected deep-rooted tensions over the true nature of the *volk* and exactly which interests within the alliance should be privileged. As *volkskapitalisme* proceeded apace, the stratification of Afrikaner interests visible in an antecedent fractured group awareness rapidly deepened. Indeed, disturbing and divisive tendencies threatened to undo the hard-won cohesion of the nationalist alliance.

A volk in retreat?

With the onset of the accumulation crisis during 1974, the honeymoon was over and with it the ideological hegemony that characterised the wider Afrikaner community during the 1960s. The nationalist alliance began to flounder and lost a momentum it was never to recover. Reaping the benefits of apartheid – the much fêted achievement of the republic during May 1961 and the unprecedented socio-economic transformation of the Afrikaner minority into a largely urbanised middle class – left Afrikanerdom in uncharted territory. The very different task now confronting the NP required the provision of:

> 'political cohesion to a changing class alliance in a period of apparent prosperity for all its elements – when the early demands of its original constituents had been largely met. The conditions which had first given rise to the nationalist alliance no longer existed, and its burning sense of political and economic mission was dissipated precisely by the NP government's achievements.'[51]

With the economic crisis paralleled by a similar predicament in the political sphere, Botha's infamous injunction to 'adapt or die' set the tone for a prolonged attempt by the nationalist establishment to rejuvenate an ailing nationalist project via a broadening and deracialisation of its support base and concerns.

Unsurprisingly this was less easily achieved in practice. The depth of the economic emergency was unprecedented. The postwar accumulation strategy had comprised a form of racially-based capitalism lodged in historically specific foundations, namely: an industrialisation strategy based on import-substitution and an ongoing dependency on cheap African labour.[52] A number of structural weaknesses and other obstacles troubled this exploitative partnership between racial domination and capitalism. In essence, boom and bust alike had been engineered by the same perverse racial qualifications on economic growth. Apartheid had engendered 'racial restrictions on the Fordist link between mass production and mass consumption'[53] so that economic capacity was overwhelmingly geared to the small white domestic market. This unhealthy liaison manifested itself in many quarters of the economy, not least the persistent skills shortage, foreign exchange constraints, poor domestic markets and high productivity costs.[54]

Not only was this deep-rooted malaise compounded by the variant of capitalism promoted through the period of *volkskapitalisme* and apartheid, but likewise by the peculiar character of South Africa's industrialisation which centred almost completely upon the export of gold and other minerals. The strength of the mining sector within the economy was premised on the inflow of investment capital and a distinctive regime of labour relations. Moreover, these demands impacted on the very nature of state-capital relations ensuring that South African mining corporations have been 'entities as much political as economic'.[55] In this equation, and given the political clout still exhibited by these mineral conglomerates that has only begun to taper off in recent decades – as late as 1987 Anglo American accounted for 60 per cent of the JSE's market capitalisation – the wants of mining capital were increasingly favoured by the apartheid state over and above the subsidy and protectionist demands of agricultural and other industrial capital. First apparent in this economic realm, the structural crisis was pre-empted by the oil emergency of 1973. In reality it derived from the simple fact that racial Fordism and its associated handicaps were not capable of substantive adjustment. These internal pressures were further accentuated by external pressures from the 'developing international crisis' of Fordism.[56] At this particular juncture, the dynamics of apartheid capitalism could no longer conceal labour instability and the profound alienation of the African majority.

Outside the nationalist establishment and beyond the scope of this book, political resistance was being resurrected following the post-1960 period of repression and relative quiescence. The racial perversions and structural impediments of the economy only compounded the domestic crisis which soon became a fully-fledged recession, casting into doubt the very foundations of the country's economic order. The implications were potentially severe given the uneven assimilation of different capital factions and classes within the NP's nationalist project. Indeed, O'Meara portrays 'mutually reinforcing' crises that afflicted the regime: a crisis of accumulation, of domestic and regional hegemony, and of international relations. Together these precipitated a wholesale rejection of the old order by key constituent parts and from within the body of white politics, inaugurating both a 'crisis of representation within the power bloc', a well as 'a crisis of political organisation and political culture within the hitherto relatively cohesive Afrikaner nationalist movement'.[57] The time of even a conditional unity was emphatically over.

Resolving these tensions would require a renewal of the consensus that underpinned the basis of apartheid rule. However, instead of confronting the issue, capital and the state treated the crisis merely as a socio-economic problem.[58] Reinvention or renewal of the nationalist project was neglected as, left more or less intact, it lurched from one legitimacy crisis to the next. What was needed was a new system of legitimation beyond the discredited orthodoxy of separate development. But, as the new concord would show, efforts at reform served only to expose the immorality of the methods with which the state had subdued the non-white populace, and the highly questionable foundations upon which the entire nationalist edifice rested.

Begun in 1977 and lasting roughly until 1989, the process of modernising apartheid or managed reform was tentative at best. Laid out in various White Papers the so-called 'total national strategy' was born of the threat of 'total onslaught' and promised:

> 'a comprehensive plan to utilise all the means available to the state according to an integrated pattern in order to achieve the national aims within the framework of specific policies.'[59]

It signalled a critical shift in the relationship between the state and NP which had been a long time coming. Indeed, celebrated as the 'custodian of the Afrikaner's group interests and cultural aspirations',[60] the NP had from necessity started life as a 'highly mobilised mass political party':

> 'Its populist origins and traditions, its tight structure of branch committees, local organisers, regional structures and provincial and federal congresses, all worked to generate lively and sharply contested

internal politics. Until the 1980s, the NP leadership generally remained in touch with, and responsive to, its large and active membership, which itself enjoyed some policy input.'[61]

However, sharp deviations from this style of government were initiated with the inauguration of Vorster in 1966. Lacking a provisional or institutional power base, he rapidly propelled the government to the centre of what had previously been party-based struggles. In so doing, he transformed the NP from 'the political embodiment of a *volksbeweging* in the service of the volk, into a party of pluralist power centres held together by patronage and insider access'.[62] It was a trend that reached a high point during the administrations of Botha and De Klerk as a heavily centralised state replaced the populist machinations of the party, and critical constituent parts such as capital elites were brought closer within the fold.

These incremental but definitive power shifts underlined a similar transformation in the legitimatory ideology of the nationalist project. Henceforth, the racial idealism of separate development was jettisoned for the dynamics of survival. Whilst white supremacy remained critical, it was to be deftly hidden by the premise of the Total Strategy. Alongside a more obtrusive regional policy and blinding obsession with security:

> 'Overt official racism gave way to a discourse of economic growth and the wonders of supply-side economics. Blacks would be given access to the system and its benefits . . . Now the old Verwoerdian maxim of 'better poor and white than rich and mixed' was replaced by a vision of 'power-sharing' and rapid economic growth by private initiative freed of the interventionist shackles of the past. Economic growth would guarantee living standards and make it possible to raise those of blacks.'[63]

The Total Strategy represented a cynical and expedient attempt to create a new national basis of consent, as well as an increasingly 'aberrant mix of repression and reforms' aimed at restructuring the social and economic basis for capital accumulation.[64] The problem was, with the NP effectively alienated from its social base, the regime was unprepared to deal with the unravelling social cohesion of Afrikanerdom itself. Farmers in particular bore the brunt of reform efforts aimed at economic liberalisation. Elsewhere, a burgeoning and autonomous African labour movement was causing concern to the Afrikaner working class. In short, certain political alliances of Afrikanerdom were 'critically at odds with reform'.[65]

At the crux of this new strategy, the reform package sought to realise a new system of domination without completely dismantling the old and:

> 'followed a classic pattern of cautious liberalisation, which aimed neither to relinquish any significant trappings of power nor to abandon the political alliances that lay at the base of Afrikaner nationalism. Nevertheless, it did propose *to rearrange the relationship between the state, race and class interests which lay at the core of Afrikaner nationalism.*'[66]

This expansion of the *volk* or nation had been initiated by Verwoerd's insistence on white or racial unity, and was continued during the reign of Vorster, who was concerned to relocate the greater white establishment within the political confines of the NP. These profound ideological transformations were given extra impetus after the mid-1970s, and as the NP espoused a more 'defensive nationalism'[67] seeking allies beyond the racial partition. Hardly a new direction then, it was swiftly cemented by the overall thrust of the reform agenda that followed three dominant motifs: firstly, a stronger commitment to the market abetted by a depoliticisation of the social order so that the market, and not the state, became the focus of social conflict; secondly, the principle of exclusive white access to the state was abandoned; and, finally, power was progressively centralised within the state or, more accurately, the National Security Council.[68] All in all, it was a last ditch venture to preserve white control on the basis of an expanded consensus and in vastly altered socio-economic conditions.

Each stage of reform was characterised by an inherent logic dedicated to a realigned nationalist project and emphasised three goals: the re-establishment of domestic security, the attainment of international legitimacy, and the return to a trajectory of rapid economic growth.[69] The first phase centred upon the somewhat piecemeal reform of discriminatory labour and urbanisation policies. The Total Strategy dictated a renegotiation of these relations with various population groups in order that a non-white middle class be included within the prevailing nationalist regime. Thus, capital's demands for more skilled labour to fill the crippling shortages were accommodated at the same time as the cooperation of particular elements of the black populace was sought. With the end of influx control and limited attempts at democratisation in the shape of the Tricameral Parliament and 1984 Constitution, concerted efforts to build and co-opt a black, urbanised elite heralded an end to the aspirations of apartheid. By the final years of reform apartheid, the high stakes game of enlarging consent across racial boundaries was at an end. Democratisation was halted and security once again took precedence. However, the abortive reform process continued, sheltered within a security-orientated framework, in order to 'combine reforms and repression in ways that could alter the balance of forces'.[70]

Playing this reformist tune, the apartheid regime sought to head off the rising tide of discontent both from within its own ranks and among other constituent parts. The instrument of this process of legitimation was to be a popular nationalist project and the reform initiative contained therein. If large tracts of the previous ideological consensus were unceremoniously dumped, it was because the most profound aspects of the reform package were concerned chiefly with sustaining a successful accumulation strategy. Resolution of the national question came a poor second, proceeding along familiar racial lines by promising to satisfy certain (class) interests. Without conforming to a concrete ideological outlook, the regime was to stretch itself far too thinly trying to cover these bases as well as the priorities of big business. In a indictment of the years of reform, O'Meara suggests that:

> 'Through the Total Strategy the apartheid regime effectively conceded the moral, ideological and cultural initiative. It sought to replace its abandoned ideology with a technocratic modernising discourse. This would work only should it be able to live up to its own ideological claims and deliver social stability and general prosperity while it slowly did away with the petty inequities of the past. By clinging to its modernised version of neo-apartheid, the Botha government held on to a policy which its own expressed ideology now clearly labelled as illegitimate. Here was the central contradiction of all its reformist pretensions – because it refused to abandon the central elements of Grand Apartheid theory, it could not legitimate its own reforms. Because its analysis failed to grasp that the central problem was the theory and practice of apartheid itself, its solutions were doomed to failure.'[71]

For all the hand-wringing and ideological conflict that had consumed Afrikanerdom's response to the economic crisis, it was patently obvious that changes to the white elite – a modification of the power basis from race to class – without any significant and corresponding redistribution of this power were merely cosmetic gestures to preserve white privilege. Reform of the nationalist project from above had proved to be an abject failure.

The nationalist project unravels

The internal discord that precipitated some of this reform process materialised most prominently during the late 1960s and early 1980s, in the form of the bitter battles between *verkrampte* (conservative) and *verligte* (enlightened) factions within the regime. A history of the nationalist alliance demonstrates a record of friction between disparate constituents. Indeed, the much vaunted monolithic character of Afrikanerdom was little but a fiction held together by a potent mix of respect for both ideological dogma and material interests. For a long period political domination and the apartheid dividend cloaked any dissent. But, by the close of the 1960s, real differences were apparent in the policy arena between the line supported by Afrikaner business and that backed by the NP's populist base.

There remains considerable debate over the character of these quarrels. Giliomee contends that until 1982 the NP was a 'purely ethnic party',[72] so that the splits reflected 'symbolic and status issues [more] than economic conflicts'.[73] In contrast, O'Meara's account points to the divergent class interests – particularly within different capital camps – which matured within the nationalist alliance of 1948. Growing pains emerged between these more established interests and 'those who sought to adapt the ideology and policies of Afrikaner nationalism to the changing social composition of the volk'.[74] The latter represents a more substantive explanation, privileging material concerns over ethnic interests alongside an acknowledgement of the salience of these latter sentiments.

The repercussions of these so-called *broedertwis* (divisions between brothers) within both the party and government were to become ever more pronounced as the coalition matured. Untried alliances hardened as the stakes were raised in a deteriorating political and economic climate. At the heart of this struggle for ascendancy between *verligte* and *verkrampte* elements lay the pivotal issues of the very character of the *volk* itself: the 'proper' composition of the nationalist alliance, and the best means of ensuring its survival. The problem was:

> 'the achievement of both the political and economic aims of Afrikaner nationalism meant the disappearance of a single symbolic target against which all classes of Afrikaners could be mobilised with the promise of the good life once these demons were replaced by an authentic Afrikaner government. Given the increased economic and social stratification of Afrikaans speaking whites, by the mid-1960s it was very difficult to identify the common, collective interest of this highly differentiated Afrikaner volk. The only feasible way of doing

so was to claim that the interests were those of this or that social class – or, in a more radical *verligte* way, those of the broader white nation.'[75]

Earlier divisions had been less pronounced and certainly less bitter. With the achievement of the republic this intra-group conflict assumed more of an internecine character. Indeed, political power had ensured there was far more to fight over and far higher political costs to the discord.

The inauspicious beginnings of this hostility occurred with the departure of Verwoerd, and centred upon Vorster's support for a white nation and broader South African nationalism to the detriment of an exclusively ethnic Afrikaner representation. Lesser issues including the easing of apartheid in the sporting arena and lowering the colour bar in certain areas only added to the acrimony. But the crux of the debate revolved about the changing composition of the volk and the social transformation taking place within the ranks of Afrikanerdom. Giliomee concurs that it had become clear that 'large numbers of Afrikaner workers, farmers and civil servants in the lower-income groups had become disaffected.'[76] From now on, the class tensions which had progressively pervaded the nationalist bond now beset the NP itself. Those Afrikaners who had profited least from redistribution policies sided with Albert Hertzog and his *Herstigte* (Reconstituted) National Party (HNP), as economic favouritism lost the NP its crown as the 'sole authentic representative of the *volk*'. This split signalled the beginning of the end for the nationalist alliance and popular nationalist project inaugurated during 1948.

As a precursor to the final, irredeemable political split of 1982, these earlier clashes had demonstrated a NP far from immune to the disparate material concerns and changing political culture of its wider electorate. The final nail in the coffin of any genuine *volk* unity appeared within the arena of NP nationalism. The NP had been drifting gradually towards a class-based political programme. It had progressively abandoned a bias toward identity politics and appeals to ethnic sentiments in a 'major realignment'[77] of white politics as its new constituent parts became business and the white urban middle class. The familiar strains between the beneficiaries of the embourgeoisement of the Afrikaner nationalist pact surfaced to endanger and ultimately destroy the populist collaboration that had dominated since 1948. This time, there was to be no renewal of the hard-won *volkseenheid* (unity of the *volk*). Instead, the NP split of March 1982 – Andries Treurnicht's *verkramptes* left to form the Conservative Party (CP) – for ever:

'destroyed Afrikaner political unity, [representing] the culminating moment of the process begun after shattering in the 1960s of the myth of the classless *volk* united by a common ethnic project.'[78]

Political pragmatism had won out over symbolic politics.

This second set of *broedertwis* rent Afrikanerdom and the ideological cohesion of its nationalist project to its very core. All the organisations of Afrikaner nationalism were involved, from the grass roots through to the seemingly inviolate Dutch Reformed Churches and *Broederbond*. These later schisms represented a more mature version of past conflicts. The NP was caught on the one hand between those white groupings that depended on the generosity of the state and, on the other, those with more flexible political needs capable of operating beyond the orbit of the state.[79] In many respects the old *volksbeweging* political style had become surplus to the requirements of the latter, and the increasingly prominent capital elites and professional middle classes. By the time of Botha, the *verligte* reformists and their appreciation of the necessity of realigning the nationalist project had triumphed: the reforms that characterised his administration were the result. Winning consensus had been no small victory but preserving it within the nexus of party, government and state, and across an ever-expanding Afrikaner grouping had proved beyond the limits of the possible for the existing nationalist project.

A class apart: The maturation of Afrikaner capital

Within the popular project of Afrikaner nationalism, a distinctive accumulation strategy premised upon racial Fordism was pivotal. Alongside it a number of key strategic alliances comprised what became a scheme for the material upliftment of Afrikanerdom as a whole. This economic project or *reddingsdaad* was an exceptional achievement mirroring similar developments in the ideological and institutional realms. But, whereas prior to the economic movement the wider Afrikaner populace had exhibited a notable lack of class stratification, the very success of the scheme increasingly came to weaken this homogeneity. For the first time during the 1960s, a progressively deeper separation between the economic, ideological and cultural bases of the nationalist project forced a number of confrontations between capital and other constituent parts within the nationalist alliance. For the remainder of this section, the changing nature of the NP's constituency represented within this capital class will be examined.

After barely two decades of nationalist rule these differences had become too pronounced to ignore. Economic favouritism assisted albeit very differently all the Afrikaner constituent parts within the NP's social base. Within the occupational structure of the economy, a triad of breakthroughs transpired: firstly, Afrikaners moved rapidly into the higher income sectors of the economy alongside their English speaking counterparts; secondly, the proportion of Afrikaner males in lower occupational categories fell drastically; and, thirdly and most significantly, the closing gap between the English and Afrikaans speaking populations underlined the growing stratification of the latter group.[80] Moving up the class ladder, the majority of Afrikaners settled into white collar positions – by 1977 this had reached 65.2 per cent of the community after a low of 29 per cent during 1946[81] – predominantly in the professional, administrative and skilled employment arenas. Most marked were the massive rise of an urbanised managerial middle class and the growth of an extensive base of Afrikaner entrepreneurs. These shifts pushed up the Afrikaner grouping's share in the private sector of the economy, and were paralleled by a similar and substantial increase in per capita income that approached parity with the English speaking grouping by 1976.

Availed of these remarkable economic developments, a confident and relatively independent strata of Afrikaner capitalists began to emerge on the national stage. Whereas previously the economic interests of the NP's electorate had been overwhelmingly agricultural and linked with the petty bourgeoisie, socio-economic transformation gave a prominent voice to a growing coterie of Afrikaner capitalists within the commercial and financial sectors, and the demands of *geldmag* (finance power). Most significant was the loosening of the economic dependence between these figures and the Afrikaner farmers and workers as 'their interests became less tied to the economic well-being of these social forces'.[82] As this earlier solidarity faded, and the realities of a class alliance welded together with an ethnic glue made themselves ever more clearly felt, so the ambitions of these capital elites became more overt. The maturation of Afrikaner capital was echoed by an increasing intra-group interpretation of themselves as 'a politically based class with vested interests'.[83] Many among this 'emergent and entrepreneurial' elite began to side with their white class counterparts 'across the ethnic divide' as much as with their fellow Afrikaners further down the ladder.[84] They demanded the liberalisation of the state-controlled areas of the economy and aligned themselves squarely with free-market tendencies very much against the nationalist tradition.

With these developments the order that had characterised Afrikaner nationalism thus far began to give. Stability was shaken in all the ideological, material and institutional arenas of the hegemonic project as, with the ascent of the Botha administration, large-scale Afrikaner capital fixed itself as the principal element in Afrikaner nationalism.[85] This seminal shift reflected a process of acclimatisation and negotiation initiated by the Vorster era's levelling of the restrictions between Afrikaner and English business cooperation which was strengthened by the recessional tendencies towards conglomeration in capital that mitigated in part the 'linguistic and political tensions' between the two capital camps.[86]

Following close behind the structural crisis, the real changes in the capital-state equation arrived during the years of the Botha administration. Botha was especially keen to paint his government as the partner of capital. Yet the political cost of opening the door to capital as an equal partner in the reform project left Botha increasingly exposed to the requirements of a grouping that had little allegiance beyond the profit margin. What began as a satisfactory association for both parties, solidified during a round of conferences where Botha urged business to cooperate in the economic development of the region, soon soured. Initially the regime had played its part, loosening the restrictions on labour and urbanisation policies and proceeding with a liberalisation of the economy. However, the after-shocks of the organic crisis were still being felt, and the government's piecemeal and circuitous reforms were soon to prove a case of too little too late.

Botha's reforms essentially gave free rein to the vagaries of capital which meant that capital elites were able to engage with the state on a far more equal footing. It was, in many respects, a complete change of tack:

> 'Capital traditionally engaged the South African state through discreet channels, mostly through engagements performed by business organisations grouped according to sector and even language. Its input into political and social policy tended, therefore, to be hide-bound and parochial. Concentrated pressure and coherent macro-reform proposals did not materialise. Instead capitalist organisations generally preferred to slipstream behind state policies, intervening when specific interests were at stake. The result was a *political distance* between state and capital, despite the state's attempts during the 1980s to rationalise the political input of capital by organising consultative conferences and channels.'[87]

However, the old rifts had not been entirely overcome and cooperation between Afrikaner and non-Afrikaner capital should not be overemphasised. The height of this expedient collaboration between different business cliques lay ahead in the post-1990 negotiations process. For the time being, capital recognised that the NP government and its rapidly changing economic agenda was the best option it had, and it was sticking to this economic straw man.

Although the nadir of this relationship was most probably Botha's infamous Rubicon speech of August 1985[88] – the 'Manifesto for a new South Africa' that was anything but – that witnessed the most critical business opposition to date and initiated the rush to Lusaka, in reality the coherence of capital had long been lacking. Corrupted by 'linguistic and organisational divisions' a divided capitalist class was more or less crippled in the political realm. And these rifts were compounded by further divisions:

> 'overlaying but also cutting across the historical divide between English and Afrikaner capital, between a more internationally oriented bourgeoisie and one which [was] more domestically oriented.'[89]

Due in no small part to this incoherence, capital's short-lived renaissance in the political sphere left it with no real option, even had it so wished, of anything but a grinding down of apartheid orthodoxies. Lacking the support of a programme of political reform acceptable to the black population or a credible political vehicle,[90] an agonised debate over reconstituting the accumulation strategy was about as far as the business community was prepared or able to go.

There were of course a number of moot exceptions. During 1977, Andreas Wassenaar, the then chairman of SANLAM, launched a stinging if highly expedient assault on the government's economic policy.[91] During January 1985, the AHI and Chamber of Mines amongst other organisations outlined their limited opposition to some fundamental tenets of apartheid in a memorandum presented to a visiting overseas delegation. And Anton Rupert was pivotal in founding the South Africa Foundation during the early 1960s to bolster the country's faltering image abroad. But, for the most part, censure was distinctly underwhelming and echoed only an obsession with a normalisation of the domestic economic system in order to ward off further popular resistance or instability. Established during 1976 the Urban Foundation was perhaps the pre-eminent player in this field. Touted as an 'alliance-builder' it sought to win black allies by pressurising the government into allowing the development of a pro-capitalist black middle class, thereby intending to wean this group away from any revolutionary alliances with the working class.[92] Despite massive investment in housing and education projects, the influence of the Foundation faded with the deteriorating relationship between government and business during the mid-1980s.

What did emerge in the decades leading up to the negotiated political transition was an unprecedented breakdown in the coherency of the nationalist alliance and hegemonic project. At the heart of this degeneration lay the issue of the NP government's priorities: the irreconcilable tension between an accumulation (economic growth) imperative and a legitimation (wealth and power redistribution) imperative that afflicts all modern governments.[93] Failings in the nationalist project translated easily into the nationalist alliance and vice versa. Stretched too far the regime was unable to build upon the consensus and legacy of the project's formative decades. The strategic alliances that propped up the nationalist edifice could only hold as long as the ideological consensus articulated by the nationalist project held. When this began to fail, the wheels fell off the entire project and most tellingly Afrikaner capital revealed itself to be driven by the same motives as its English speaking counterpart.

At the close of the apartheid era, Afrikanerdom was not so much coming apart at the seams as embarking on a fundamental process of restructuring. In the remainder of this study, attention will be directed towards the 'genuine conceptual revolution in Nationalist thinking'[94] that proved a factor in the onset of negotiations during De Klerk's administration, and thereafter influenced the role of particular Afrikaner constituent parts within this process. The proceeding chapter will show that the political sea-change was not matched by any real 'realignment in the structural underpinning' that sustained capital accumulation,[95] leaving the door very much ajar for certain constituent parts to exploit opportunities within both the transition and the hegemonic project which followed. Ultimately, Afrikanerdom's nationalist project failed because successive apartheid governments were unable to settle upon a credible project of reform. And just as rival interpretations of Afrikaner nationalism and identity dogged the nationalist project during the apartheid years, so the grouping today remains subject to a divergent ideological, economic and political consensus represented within the body of the ANC's hegemonic project and against the wider structural backdrop of the globalised political economy.

3

THE NATURE OF CONSENSUS IN THE 'NEW' SOUTH AFRICA

Both this and the subsequent chapter provide an analysis of the ANC's hegemonic project and global regime with particular regard to contemporary Afrikaner identifications. Preceding chapters have explored the changing social composition of the Afrikaner grouping initiated under the *ancien régime*. Using Gramsci's concept of hegemony as a point of departure, the shape of the profound political, ideological and less marked economic transformation currently underway in South Africa will be sought. On the empirical front a Gramscian frame focuses attention upon the ambiguities which go to the heart of the ANC hegemonic project. Essentially, this framework provides a structural understanding of how consensus (in all the political, economic and ideological aspects of the ANC's hegemonic project) is being manufactured, and thus how wider structural shifts impact upon the character of contemporary Afrikaner identifications.

In order to explore the broader structural context and character of this hegemony, this chapter will focus upon two central claims. Firstly, it is suggested that the consensus building that coloured the negotiated transition also dictated the shape of the ANC hegemonic project so that the political settlement deferred any fundamental economic transformation. Thus the structural shifts in South African society (and thereafter the changing composition of Afrikaner identifications) should likewise be analysed within the wider context of the globalised political economy. Secondly, from its roots as a resistance movement to its contemporary populist appearance, the ANC hegemon cooperates with a range of constituent parts to maintain a semblance of unity. That is, the historical development of the ANC and its hegemonic project has ensured that existent ideological discrepancies on the level of ideas and material forces have become more pronounced with the advent of government and onerous demands of transformation.

It is beyond the reach of this study to disclose the implications of these openings for the majority of the ANC's electorate. But for the Afrikaans speaking grouping it will be contended that the dirigiste direction of old-style Afrikanerdom has been replaced among important constituent parts by a hegemonical common sense understanding of the role South Africa is supposed to play in the new global order and political economy. Emboldened by the nature of the transition and particular policies, certain constituent parts have been dealt a far better hand than others. Whilst some have settled for a truce with the ANC hegemon,[1] it is asserted that a significant few have been able to recast the character of this hegemonic project because of their position within the leading historic bloc. In order to trace the evolution of an Afrikaner identity project within the uncertain consolidation of the liberal project in contemporary South Africa, this chapter proceeds in three sections. The first offers a broad overview of the shape and depth of the hegemonic project. The second reviews the nature of the consensus that has marked the economic settlement. Here the strategies of both international and domestic capital during the transition are touched upon. Finally, the third section summarises nation-building tactics in order to examine how the liberation promise of a non-racial nation has progressed since 1994. As a consequence, it is possible to analyse the openings for particular constituent parts by addressing the level of hegemony (the nature of a post-apartheid consensus emerging from the connections between local and global structures of social forces) as an empirical question.

Consolidating dominance? The shape of the new hegemonic order

The comprehensive social revolution initially prescribed by the ANC liberation movement and later government has faltered. Indeed, the task of building and maintaining a new political economic order has been uneven. There has been no radical split with the apartheid past nor with the inequalities promoted by earlier, racially driven economic policies. The post-apartheid growth path and distributional regime has ensured that overall levels of inequality have changed only slightly so that whilst interracial income inequality has continued to decline, intraracial inequality is growing.[2] Instead it is contended that the impact of 'collusive illiberal capitalism in South Africa is to reproduce and reward racialism'.[3] Understanding these continuities requires an investigation of both the global and domestic constraints upon the shape and depth of the ANC hegemonic project. For the divisions that continue to plague the articulation of ANC hegemony are multiple and profound, relating as much to delivery problems and policy choices as to the wider structural environment, prevailing neo-liberal economic consensus and the character of its historic bloc.

During the negotiations process and the uneven consolidation of the liberal project that has followed, the transformation scenario promised by ANC elites has been systematically dismembered via a process of compromise which was begun in the later years of the struggle. It was the ANC's stress on emancipatory rhetoric and populism whilst addressing several audiences simultaneously that initially brought:

> 'the party into confrontation both at the domestic front with formerly sympathetic groups such as liberal whites and on the international front with global actors such as the international banking community that regards profligate spending to redress socio-economic injustices as bad economic policy. The party is thereby forced to act like Janus – it placates its internal constituent parts with promises of betterment and Africanist or socialist slogans but plays quite a different tune when confronting international bankers and political leaders from the G-7 countries.'[4]

This same emphasis ensured that neo-liberalism became the new orthodoxy. It is a logic that favours the free market and the 'relentless discourse of competitiveness', driven by policies including wage restraint, the deregulation of labour markets, tariff reduction and privatisation.[5] As an ideology it espouses a distinctive position for the state so that the market takes precedence: the delicate balance between state and market rests with a state's ability and/or choice to regulate particular components of the international economy.[6] With the relatively vulnerable position of the domestic economy, an urgent undertaking for the then Government of National Unity (GNU) was the support of capital in order that business confidence and thereafter investment should intensify to fund economic growth. Against this backdrop the interdependence of global and national capital diverted a globalised neo-liberal agenda down to the very grass roots. Privileging this economic orthodoxy has effectively divided the ANC's electorate. The customary alliance between the state and domestic capital promised in early ANC economic policy has faded. Restraint on expenditure and the pressure to attract investment, coupled with demands for low levels of inflation and taxation, backed the government into a corner whilst simultaneously affording domestic capital elites (and their global counterparts) considerable and enduring leverage.

The terms of engagement after 1990 actively pitched the forces for status quo (and economic orthodoxy) against the ANC's decades-old redistributive economic ambitions.[7] Yet the ANC's leadership was not simply stifled by the ambitions of capital. The vagueness of the Freedom Charter on economic matters and the lack of any sound economic blueprint prior to the negotiations, in tandem with the end of the Cold War and the ideological defeat of the socialist economic strategy, meant that the writing was on the wall for the left-leaning elements within the ANC virtually from the start. The NP government came to the negotiating table having reached an informal 'triple alliance' with private local capital and international financial institutions,[8] and wielding considerable clout given the parlous state of investor certainty. Moreover, the shift of the economic debate from the ideological to the technical terrain further stunted the ANC's transformative ambitions,[9] with the years of exile hindering the search for eligible policy initiatives.

Each of these issues has taken its toll upon the coherence of a new historic bloc. The success of such a union resides not only in the economic sphere but similarly with a persuasive ideological and political mandate. The leaders of a historic bloc must develop a worldview that appeals to a wide range of other groups in order that their agenda represents wider social interests.[10] And the strategic alliances that support hegemony must be continually fine-tuned. Thus whilst ANC hegemony has advanced in some spheres, the consolidation of the project has proved uneven. From the beginning, the inclusive consensus-building of the settlement was costly to once definitive populist promises of transformation. The process began prior to 1990 in the stalemate that existed between a regime that could govern only through coercion, and an opposition that fell short of the coercive capacity necessary to surmount the state.[11] Subsequently, transformative ambitions were sharply curtailed by the manoeuvrings of particular constituencies, an onus that has come to bear heavily on the condition of an ANC hegemony.

Many of these contradictions have been buried beneath the rhetoric of non-racial unity and reconciliation. Indeed, this discourse has come to represent an attempt to forge a new basis for the social consent pivotal to the quest for social restructuring.[12] By stressing inclusivity – equality, reconstruction and societal development take precedence – ANC claims mark a notable first in South African history.[13] Yet beneath this meta-discourse the hegemonic project rests on two central tenets that, whilst competing for the backing of dissimilar populations, are themselves fundamentally opposed on a number of issues. Both tenets have evolved from the necessity of appeasing the demands of different constituent parts within the historic bloc. The first economic pillar advances an export-orientated growth path that entails economic restructuring chiefly through market mechanisms. The following section will explore the implications of this neo-liberal macro-economic strategy in the development of ANC hegemony. It will demonstrate that the terms of a strong and often acrimonious economic debate in South Africa since the early 1990s have revolved around whether growth should precede redistribution or vice versa.[14] The government's stance, imitating the line of business on market liberalisation and deregulation even whilst pushing a redistributive agenda, has seen macro-economic policy making become increasingly circumscribed within the narrow confines of ministerial and business circles during Mbeki's administration,[15] affording international and domestic capital elites genuine sway.

The second ideological pillar represents an attempt to maintain older allegiances and quiet the fears of a privileged and largely white minority. It will be contended below that the ANC government's reliance upon the construction of this ideological project is becoming increasingly pronounced as disillusionment among traditional constituent parts mounts. There has been significant improvisation in this field, with an opportune and timely oscillation between reiterations of non-racialism and the two nations thesis – black and poor against white and prosperous – amongst other racialised themes.[16] This exploitation of the race card may go some way towards silencing some of the ANC's traditional electorate, but in the longer term it risks dissolving the myth of national unity that was at one time the ideological cornerstone of the ANC's hegemonic vision.

The ambiguities of the popular hegemonic project are readily apparent in the fragmentary and often dissentious roots of the ANC hegemon itself. That is, in the different components and agendas of the organisations that constitute the governing tripartite alliance that was first convened as a formal collaboration during 1990, although the association stretches back far longer. Policy positions have shifted considerably within the alliance since its conception. Initially, COSATU took the upper hand in economic matters whilst the bulk of the ANC leadership involved itself with negotiating the transition.[17] COSATU's adoption of the Freedom Charter in 1987 – viewed as little more than a set of 'minimum democratic demands' – was accompanied by an announcement of its continued commitment to looking beyond the initial stage of national liberation to economic transformation based on its working class constituency.[18] The institutional premise of the transition, however, channelled these inclinations into what was to become a historic class compromise between government, organised labour, business and civic organisations.

Since the onset of democratic rule, the ANC has served as the senior partner and political axis of the ruling alliance, whilst the SACP and

COSATU have undeniably proved the junior players. Although organised labour has capitulated to government and business pressure in key areas including labour legislation,[19] the divisions which surround the succession crisis may well signal a new phase in the alliance. Indeed, despite reservations on the left, there are signs that the government is beginning to clamp down on 'ANC inc' and switch its focus from internal division to building the party and improving service delivery.[20] Mounting opposition to privatisation in the form of national strikes and bluntness against the government's developmental priorities has been orchestrated by these increasingly vociferous partners.[21] Nevertheless, the alliance was not intended to be a concrete arrangement. The 'veneer of unity' that oversees the broad partnership has been consistently overstretched as the ANC has vacillated between business and its older political allies.[22]

Whilst recent years have demonstrated genuine qualifications to the loyalty of the hegemon's junior if more progressive partners, there is little probability of a total collapse of the coalition. Instead these machinations demonstrate the precarious nature of ANC hegemony in crucial policy areas and a ruling party vulnerable to a number of internal as well as external influences. Preserving unity through internal diversity as an organisational ethos is a clear historical spillover. Within the ANC an activist and popular democratic culture coalesced about a 'common strategic outlook': the eradication of the apartheid system, the full-scale transfer of political power from the white minority to the black majority, and the redress of grievances.[23] Liberation politics was characterised by several stages during the later decades of the struggle, building various ideologies that were eventually accommodated beneath the ANC's broad canopy in the form of an essentially non-racial and multi-class coalition. Yet these inclusive tendencies camouflaged deeper class divisions that were for the most part outflanked by nationalist dogma. Even the working class and their organisations found it hard to resist the nationalist pull.[24] With the advent of negotiations, and in efforts to present a united front, avoidance of economic discussion was in ebullient form in the ANC's privileging of the political over the economic sphere,[25] and its inability to build a viable economic consensus. During the years of exile and even after its unbanning in 1990, the ANC necessarily relied upon the administrative ingenuity of these partners and their disparate support bases.

History then has indelibly tempered the long march of ANC hegemony and healthy remnants of these pluralist tendencies remain. There has been a marked decline in the democratic organisational culture which marked the grass roots of the ANC and labour movement.[26] One reason may be the uncomfortable fit between 'the ANC's tradition as a liberation movement and the organisational requirements of effective parties in a liberal democracy'.[27] Another may rest with its readiness to discipline members and attitudes to democratic participation that are marked by a preference for 'intra-elite level' decision-making.[28] Either way the drift towards oligarchic and technocratic government apparently heralds a newly anti-democratic tradition with an emphasis on popular unity at all costs which may well have critical implications for the consolidation of the liberal project. Until the late 1990s, a 'methodological convergence' within the ANC, apartheid state and capital upon the requirement of redrawing political and ideological bases of state power effectively silenced much of this argument and ensured remarkable continuity in the economic sphere.[29] However, debate has continued to fester within the ranks of the alliance, in more recent years bearing upon even the leadership succession itself.

Solving the political emergency likewise hindered progress on economic and social transformation. Michie and Padayachee contend that during the negotiation process:

> 'certain concessions were made by the ANC in respect of economic issues which, however important they may have been to the political settlement, did serve to blunt the movement's economic weapons, close down certain policy options, and slow down the process of transforming the institutions, structures and personnel so crucial to a successful economic transition. Some of these [stemmed] from the constitution itself, others from what may be termed the "culture of compromise and reconciliation" which characterised political negotiations.'[30]

This has been most apparent in the steady repositioning between the Reconstruction and Development Programme (RDP) which was introduced by COSATU for the market-orientated strategy promoted by the Growth, Employment and Redistribution strategy (GEAR). The ANC government's track record has only cemented this trend, typified as it is by 'the ease and the speed with which numerous ideological "holy cows" have been led off to the slaughterhouse'.[31] Nonetheless, reworking a political hegemony without systematic economic restructuring has not served to create the necessary foundations for a new national-popular collective will. The consensus-building of the transition was begun largely outside the ANC caucus, as certain elements sought to pacify the demands and adept manoeuvring of the NP camp and its powerful business backers. These high level compromises in effect watered-down not only the ANC's populist emphasis, but also the making of an entirely new hegemonic order. Indeed, their impact amongst key constituent parts and interest groups, many of whom are represented within the historic bloc itself, is maturing in an economic climate still dominated by racially skewed inequalities. In effect, the ANC government is caught between external dissent and mounting suspicions of a neo-liberal sell-out from both its alliance partners and core constituent parts.

The crux of the problem lies in the continued delivery failures and deteriorating social infrastructure that have been brought into sharper focus by the government's neo-liberal development path. Not only has it failed to substantially alleviate poverty among key constituent parts, but these neo-liberal imperatives are acknowledged to be a source of massive job losses, increased income inequalities and marginalisation despite the dramatic growth of a black middle class.[32] Moreover state capacity has fallen conspicuously, most evidently in its ability to fulfil social, economic, health and housing needs where the state is 'struggling to re-establish governance after apartheid'.[33] These failings have not been experienced evenly so that those who have the most to gain from poverty reduction projects and state service provision have benefited least, even as an elite band of politicians, bureaucrats and businessmen have made significant material gains. It is not merely the shape of the ANC's hegemonic project which is important then, but more specifically its depth, the nature of consensus and the manner of the societal transformation it has initiated. The broad constellation of partners and the conditions of the negotiated settlement might yet prove to be its undoing. The ANC's dominance of each of the political, economic and social arenas depends to a significant extent upon the support of social forces over which it exercises comparatively little control. In attempting to win the consent of these diverse social forces the ANC government began by formulating two hegemonic projects: the first represented the confluence of both global and modernising forces, whilst the second constituted a popular transformation project.[34] Over a decade later, however, what it has wrought is the uncertain consolidation of the liberal project in a country riven by serious political, economic and social divisions.

Neo-liberal orthodoxy and the capital transition

Within the parameters of this project an economic hegemony initially premised on orthodox foundations and a faith in the 'magic of the market',[35] and which is now apparently shifting towards a 'post-stabilisation' or 'post-GEAR phase'[36] is considered more advanced than that in the politico-ideological sphere. In the period since 1994 a predominant economic hegemony emerged that indulged the imperatives of local and global capital, similarly resting on:

> 'measures that are hospitable and beneficial to a range of other layers – among them the broad middle classes, the African *petite bourgeoisie* and, to lesser extents, the organised working classes and sections of the African poor. Crucially, this "balance" has not been unilaterally and coercively imposed: it is made possible by the resolute cultivation of consent.'[37]

What has emerged is a relatively mature, class-orientated and apparently non-racial economic coalition broadly adjusted to the prerogatives of neoliberal global capitalism with the potential of adaptation to embrace 'massive social interventions' by the government.[38] The Gramscian concept of hegemony most accurately captures this dynamic process of marshalling popular support, giving rise to what has been termed the tendency to 'talk left and act right',[39] most recently evidenced by Mbeki's warning against the worship of material wealth.[40] Similarly, this focus exposes the wider structural context as well as the strategic decisions of various leadership and capital elites apparent in the process of macroeconomic compromise and more contemporary adjustments. The 'pragmatism' of these policy adaptations was invoked by the pre-emptive economic reforms of the NP government, the growing connectedness of domestic and global capital and, most significantly, the increasing globalisation of the world economy coupled with the comparative openness of the South African economy.

The ANC government's reliance upon neo-liberal orthodoxy to foster economic growth and thereafter wider societal transformation has afforded capital elites considerable leverage in policy-making circles. Nonetheless, in historical terms, the maturity of South Africa's capitalist class, and the tremendous amount of political influence it wields, is widely acknowledged.[41] What has received little attention is the contention that these capital elites – Afrikaner business alongside its English counterpart – have played a substantial role in fostering a neo-liberal economic hegemony under the aegis of an ANC government. Rather than the exclusion of the 'great majority of businessmen'[42] from decision-making under ANC rule, many Afrikaans speaking capital elites are pursuing opportunities that have taken them outside the borders of any clearly delineated ethnic business group or class. Marais contends that both black and white business leaders have come to broadly share a set of ideological principles – the need for austere fiscal policies, lower company taxes, capital account liberalisation and a flexible labour market.[43] Business leaders and government officials meet regularly within a variety of forums including Mbeki's Big Business Working Group,[44] whilst an 'inner core' of leading Afrikaner businessmen and academics have maintained a relationship with the president stretching back to discussions with ANC exiles in 1990.[45] The well-trodden path between ministerial posts and the private sector is perhaps indicative of the salience of this tacit consensus.[46] Despite disagreements over some issues,[47] in this atmosphere both government and business can be magnanimous in their support of each other's efforts. It is this constructive engagement with the hegemonic project that has furnished capital with considerable scope for manoeuvre, and cemented a globalist and neo-liberal ideology within the post-apartheid historic bloc.

The shift in economic policy from the ANC's socialist foundations to a wholesale purchase of neoliberal orthodoxy, and what has been termed a voluntarily imposed and self-styled Structural Adjustment Program (SAP),[48] was nothing short of profound. The narrowness of the debate that preceded this paradigm change was equally marked. Neo-liberal, market-orientated growth and development strategies held the upper ground, together with the realisation that the old power apparatus within South Africa was not threatened with a substantial likelihood of collapse.[49] From the outset the challenge was to develop a strategy capable of reconciling the needs of a historically disadvantaged majority with the imperatives of a predominant neo-liberal development paradigm. Indeed, of the considerations believed central to socio-economic transformation, building a stable environment for economic growth and the confidence from both local and international capital that this required was foremost.[50] In pursuit of the so-called economic 'holy grail'[51] – the securing of growth *and* redistribution – ANC policy-makers were pushed into a series of social pacts that have collectively been termed 'social contract capitalism'.[52] In this equation, both domestic and international actors (in particular the business community and banking sector) were able to influence the terms of a limited policy debate away from alleviating socio-economic injustice and redistribution to a discussion of economic policy and the mechanisms of growth.[53]

A series of compromises effectively derailed the ANC's transformation scenario. From the start, capital treated the political and economic settlements as one even whilst they were pursued as distinct arrangements. Marais suggests that:

> 'A negotiated political settlement . . . could serve as the gateway for an ongoing bid to revitalise South African capitalism. For the

democratic forces, a settlement could usher in a transition that heralded – but did not guarantee – far-reaching adjustments aimed at undoing the patterns for the allocation of power, privilege and opportunities.'[54]

Buoyed up by a favourable global balance of forces, capital was willing to take something of a back seat on the political front. Business leaders were broadly content that the ANC serve as the political axis of the new ruling bloc, and it was hoped that the terms of a preferential political settlement would restrict radical economic posturing.[55] For their part, the ANC was more than willing to salvage the terms of a political compact that might enable it to preserve the upper hand. The ploy was so successful that far from the transformation liberation rhetoric had promised, the transition has come to represent nothing less than 'an almost imperceptible realignment in the structural underpinnings that sustain capital accumulation . . . intertwined with a sea-change in surface appearances on the terrain of politics'.[56]

On the economic front, the ANC had been lax in building viable initiatives and subsequently was never to regain the high ground it retained in the political arena. Just prior to his release from prison in 1990, Mandela had affirmed the ANC's unchanged commitment to nationalisation and other tenets of a broadly socialist development path, insistent that any moderation of these views was simply 'inconceivable'. Early policy-making only served to underline this assertion. For example, the 1990 'Discussion Document on Economic Policy' unveiled in Harare displayed COSATU's signature in its pursuit of a 'sustainable and progressive economic policy', and the 'irresistible' theme of growth through redistribution facilitated by investment principally from domestic savings with a minimal level of FDI.[57]

Nonetheless, policy shifts were not long in coming. During 1992 the official line was already changing to embrace macroeconomic stability, the result of 'defensive adjustments' to business, government and foreign pressures,[58] combined with an increasing awareness of the so-called realities of the global economy. The vastly altered perceptions of FDI and the role of international financial institutions in reconstruction and development policies were to become ever more apparent.[59] Indeed, Mandela himself subscribed to the investment imperative during a speech to the United Nations during September 1993. To all intents and purposes then, surrendering the decades-old socialist mantra had appeared relatively painless.

Capital was able to trace its influence back to the assimilation of the South African state into the globalised political economy under a faltering

NP regime. The foundations of a development path that comprise a 'modernised class project of considerable sophistication and likely longevity'[60] were laid in the last decade of the apartheid era by an NP government that, dedicated to promoting the cause of Afrikaner business, had simultaneously created a policy climate favourable towards rapid capital accumulation in all sectors.[61] The real volte-face came during De Klerk's presidency, and the unveiling of the explicitly neo-liberal agenda of the 1993 Normative Economic Model (NEM).[62] The apartheid government mounted an outright challenge to ANC ascendancy within the economic policy-making field, careful to attack and disparage any of the latter's ideas that ran counter to neo-liberal orthodoxy. The then administration threw its considerable weight behind the concerns of the majority of South Africa's big business sector, as well as the tools of macroeconomic orthodoxy to iron out the decades-old economic decline. In this way:

> 'the NP [became] the organising and structuring political mechanism for capital, posing a resolution of the national question totally out of character with Afrikanerdom's ideological and political past and certainly at odds with apartheid.'[63]

The NP had effectively set itself up as the party of business, relying on 'the rhetoric of disinvestment and White flight' to boost this negotiating position.[64] At the same time, it pursued a series of strategic alliances with all manner of allies outside its traditional constituent parts. Even before the start of negotiations, the legacy of these reforms was effectively to anchor the ANC to a neo-liberal paradigm, thereby sidelining social inequalities and establishing a 'working compromise' that would serve to maintain 'the ongoing economic system within South Africa whilst de-racialising and deconstructing the more odious aspects of apartheid'.[65]

The ability of the informal government-business coalition to take advantage of its opponent's weaknesses was most apparent during the negotiations process. From visibly opposing starting positions both parties were able to form a broad consensus. On the part of the ANC it stemmed from the 'strategic perspectives' that developed in the aftermath of the signing of the Record of Understanding in September 1992, and the bloody violence that prefigured it. Thereafter the overriding necessity to promote tactical compromises and a new consensus took precedence, even if the ANC itself believed this to be an interim measure only. Thus, the 'political/ideological project of nation-building became paramount and supplanted – or at least overshadowed – the socio-economic features of the crisis'.[66] It broke the back of the ANC's hopes of forging an entirely new hegemonic project in the economic sphere and, together with the climate of consensus which oversaw the development of the interim constitution, ended the likelihood of anything but a compromise between economic growth and genuine transformation.

Even as economic policy-making progressively leaned towards neo-liberal orthodoxy, the capitulation of the ANC and its more progressive allies was incomplete. Nonetheless the pressure from all directions, including from within its own ranks, as internal power shifts took hold was intense. The demands of technical as opposed to ideological policy-making drew a heavy toll, especially of the organisation's activist wing and in the light of the failure of socialist development models in the Soviet Union and Eastern Europe. At no one point, however, did the balance tip definitively towards global or national capital or the apartheid government itself. Instead, the negotiations and transition process were distinguished by a process of cumulative drift. The period between the first and second democratic elections, when the dearth of macroeconomic policy debate signalled just how far the ANC's neo-liberal economic course had come to be accepted as 'common sense',[67] constituted the crux of this process.

Only in the last few years has Mbeki started to address some of the extensive disquiet concerning the government's economic and development paradigm.[68] It is not yet clear how substantial this focus on rebuilding the party and improving service delivery will prove to be. Certainly antagonisms continue to fester between the government and a more progressive alliance of labour interests. No one factor can explain the improbable attraction of the dominant economic discourse to the ANC's leadership. But as the government has continued on this trajectory, the bargain struck by the old-guard which traded exclusive political power for 'continued economic advantage'[69] has witnessed different interest groups and classes mired within a compact where the distinction between the economic winners and losers is becoming ever more readily apparent.

Connecting with the global consensus

The alliance between local and international capital has proved crucial in this fundamental detour in economic policy. Since the 1990s the influence of international institutions and western governments in South Africa's domestic economic debate has been profound, ensuring that the government is now increasingly 'obliged to weigh carefully their welfare, fiscal and monetary policies against the interests of investors', an ideological line which has significant policy implications.[70] The uneven consolidation of the globalised liberal project within South Africa has narrowed policy alternatives, preserved shameful apartheid inequalities and nullified transformation initiatives. Thus key figures including Reserve Bank governor Tito Mboweni have repeatedly warned against not 'staying the course' with market-friendly economic policies, at the same time chastising other African countries to 'put in place appropriate policies to improve macroeconomic fundamentals and financial market operations'.[71] This alignment between important economic actors in government and international and domestic market actors has led to the emergence of what has been termed 'predatory liberalism' in contemporary South Africa whereby 'neo-liberal restructuring of the economy is combined with an increasing willingness by government to assert its authority, to marginalise and delegitimise those critical of its abandonment of inclusive governance'.[72]

Nowhere is the position of Africa in the global economy better illustrated than by the levels of FDI that reach the continent.[73] Economic liberalism here has proved to be as much a curse as a blessing. For South Africa, the most economically advanced country on the continent, integration within the globalised economy has been a long-term process barely interrupted by patchy financial isolation in the later years of apartheid. It has proceeded on three narrow pillars, namely: as a primary product exporter, an importer of capital goods and technology, and a net recipient of indirect portfolio investment and direct foreign investment by multinational corporations.[74] Subsequent to the mid-1980s debt crisis the country became an exporter of capital. This volatility has lingered under the present administration with continued capital outflows placing pressure on reserves, inflation and future interest rate hikes.[75] Indeed, coupled with a crippling dependency on key imports and appetite for foreign goods, it has ensured that South Africa has continued to exhibit considerable impotence in the face of international financial flows.

The arrival of genuine multi-racial democracy placed South Africa firmly in the international spotlight and with the occasion for a redrafting of the conditions of its incorporation into the global economy. It represented an incomparable opportunity to buck the more unfavourable elements of global orthodoxy, an advantage that was rapidly squandered by the new government. Instead, the ANC was to fall victim to this same orthodoxy utilised by business and certain sections within the government itself that 'casually connected liberalisation to increased foreign investment and, consequently, economic growth'.[76] As soon as the new regime had undone the shackles of apartheid it was thrust into a policy matrix informed by 'disciplinary neoliberalism', associated with policies of market monetarism and a 'new constitutionalism' that delivers considerable economic dominion to a raft of international institutions.[77] The custodians of this particular ideology are international financial institutions including the International Monetary Fund (IMF) and the World Bank who have a long if checkered history of involvement on the continent since a new era of structural adjustment programmes was initiated by the World Bank's *Berg Report* during 1981.[78]

The political, economic and social consequences of this restructuring process across the continent are well known. Conditionality has come to define the neo-liberal regime whereby:

> 'both individual states and multilateral institutions attach formal, specific, and institutionalised sets of conditions to the distribution of economic benefits in order to press (mostly) developing countries to adopt particular kinds of domestic policy.'[79]

Coupled with a propensity to economic openness, South Africa's substantial investment requirements mean the purported link between liberalisation and economic growth has implications for the entrenching and even deepening of the apartheid era's racialised inequalities.[80] These requirements have artificially inflated the standing of capital in macroeconomic policy-making, handing hopes of overcoming endemic marginalisation a massive blow. That said, the Washington Consensus does not automatically condemn its adherents to a fixed development path.[81] Nonetheless, a strict adherence was apparent as:

> 'between 1990 and 1995 ANC international financial policy and strategy was systematically stripped of all commitments, or even significant reference, to the regulation or shaping of the nature and character of South Africa's relations with the international financial institutions and foreign investors of all kinds, as part of its national development strategy of reconstruction and development in the wake of the political victory over apartheid.'[82]

Even the social objectives set out by the RDP, the most progressive of the government's policy instruments, demonstrated clear signs of this consensus prior to its sustained modification by a series of sectoral White Papers and budgetary shifts over the last decade.[83]

The IMF and World Bank have remained influential in domestic policy-making since the negotiations process when they were invited in by 'powerful bourgeois forces'.[84] At the outset of the transition process, however, the World Bank offered a unique mix of 'restrained neo-liberal directives that were offset by incorporating aspects of progressive thinking'[85] even whilst the IMF persisted with more conventional prescriptions. But it is questionable whether by the mid-1990s the IMF or World Bank had any real, direct leverage over the government,[86] although their influence has made itself increasingly felt thereafter in the spectre of high-level endorsements of the country's economic programmes,[87] and the presence of senior ANC figures in high ranking positions within these forums.[88] Exceptionally for a developing country, South Africa has a 'formal economy equipped to participate in global economic competition'.[89] Regardless of these advantages, the post-apartheid, neo-liberal turn of macro-economic policy-making has witnessed the ANC government succumb to economic dogma, seeking the approbation a rapprochement with this orthodoxy would bring from the global capital regime and its national adherents.

Compromise on the domestic front

If the reach of global capital and international financial institutions is readily apparent, the interests of its domestic counterpart have been no less pivotal. The ANC's evident sensitivity to the dynamics of the global economy has contrived openings for local capital elites that, given the historical longevity of a monopoly capitalism dominated by six conglomerate groupings,[90] have easily been turned to their advantage. Southall claimed that big business was never unaware of the 'intimate connections between South Africa's external linkages and the character of its internal political arrangements'.[91] Indeed, long before the negotiation process proper got underway, the trek to Lusaka indicated the 'political reawakening'[92] and thereafter willingness of capital to take the resistance movement seriously.

Nonetheless, throughout the negotiations process, South African business clung to the salience of neo-liberal orthodoxy. Never shy about expressing their concerns including most prominently a market economy, social and political stability, continuity in state institutions and restraint from 'radical' redistributive programmes,[93] capital whipped up support for its game-plan, pursuing black businessmen, intellectuals and politicians – cannily offering them directorships and shareholdings – whilst at the same time contracting ANC leaders into a set of scenario-planning exercises and workshops.[94] In so doing, it was able to 'exert influence over the thinking of important leaders while simultaneously facilitating their entry into the ranks of the bourgeoisie'.[95] The success of these strategies was so marked that one scholar has contended that the 'highly concentrated corporate sector'[96] became the major obstacle to the achievement of economic transformation.

Anchored by a flourishing détente between ANC elites, multilateral institutions and international capital, domestic business leaders were able to manage much of the rightward progression of macroeconomic policy. The process of building this elite compromise was begun in the adroit series of corporate scenario-planning procedures which attempted to identify an enduring social pact between all the major players, thus derailing ANC economic policy planning and sidelining the more progressive voices of dissent. The whole exercise was nurtured through a kind of 'coerced harmony' in order to promote what was labelled a rearranging of the deckchairs on the SA *Titanic*.[97]

Nonetheless, as the remit of the major corporate scenarios demonstrated, capital elites were not entirely in agreement on many of the smaller details of their policy proposals. However, on key scores – that economic policy had to become grounded in relations of 'trust, negotiation and consensus-building' and macroeconomic stability; and, that future macroeconomic policy must be laid in a 'mutually reinforcing dynamic of growth and redistribution'[98] – there was unanimity. Thus, Nedcor/Old Mutual's 'Prospects for a Successful Transition' was somewhat less doctrinaire, whilst SANLAM's 'Platform for Investment' and 'Mont Fleur' scenarios were more unequivocal in their recommendations. Later documents, including the South African Chamber of Business' (SACOB) 'Economic Options for South Africa', and the then South Africa Foundation's 'Growth For All' veered more strongly to the right of the spectrum. In practice, the scenarios were floated with two audiences in mind:

> 'The first was White opinion-followers whose fight-or-flight reflexes were equally to be discouraged. Their superstitions – the potential collapse of public order and the coming worthlessness of the Rand – were given starring roles in most scenarios. The second audience was a hypothetical one in the ranks of the ANC: rabid populists with an ideological commitment to nationalisation were imagined by many businessmen to dominate the exile movement, and White political leaders saw them as genuine threats to the country's future.'[99]

To varying degrees, each of these 'games of chicken'[100] employed florid language and smacked of alarmism in order to plug the message of capital, signalling the 'evolution of the scenario plan from corporate survival strategy to social contract parable'.[101]

Certain aspects of these scenarios, for example the feasibility of combining a social welfare state in the developmental sphere with neo-liberalism in the economic sphere,[102] have survived in current policy instruments. Indeed, a social contract capitalism has taken precedence with social compacts virtually an inescapable prelude to development initiatives. Significantly 'compromise rather than consensus' was cited as the hallmark of the RDP.[103] From the start the ANC was all too aware of the ambitions of its electoral promises, and funding issues were to confound initiatives including the 1994 RDP White Paper itself.[104] This is a fact reflected in the strict fiscal and monetary policies that characterise both the RDP and GEAR. Far from the original intent of the RDP, a manifesto that had its roots in the Freedom Charter itself, the symbolism of this shift has not been lost on either the ANC or its alliance partners. As early as 1999, Max Sisulu (formerly the ANC's chief whip) needed to insist that the RDP remained 'a very popular concept and still exists in the hearts and minds of the people'.[105] Likewise the ANC's election manifesto of the same year was declaring it to be 'the only relevant detailed programme to carry South Africa to freedom and social justice'. The plan has long suffered from what has been whimsically termed the 'ignominy of suffocating love from newfound friends'.[106] Introduced as official ANC policy in January 1994, on the face of things the programme offered a comprehensive and sweeping transformation of South African society. Its ambitious goals included the provision of basic needs or alleviation of poverty and the reconstruction of the economy, both of which relied upon the realisation of substantial economic growth.

Whilst it was sold as 'an integrated, coherent socio-economic policy framework',[107] in reality the RDP represented a partnership between the state and private sector in targeting and redressing particular social development issues. Indeed, the RDP document was explicit that the 'democratic government cannot fund the RDP without support from the private sector'.[108] The problems had begun with the vagueness of the RDP White Paper, adopted in September 1994 as the central policy blueprint. Winning an electoral mandate necessitated cooperating closely with a wide array of players, and the programme was redesigned to broaden the ANC's appeal outside its tripartite alliance, and in particular with business.[109] Thus, Padayachee argues that:

> 'As a vision document the RDP largely succeeded in integrating and blending an emphasis on meeting basic needs and a state-led infrastructural investment programme and restructuring of financial, labour, land and external relations and institutions with the need to

be globally competitive, especially in manufacturing production in the context of a technology-driven world economy.'[110]

These ambiguities, together with the vagueness of the RDP White Paper, effectively left it open to politicking from the emerging corporatist alliance between state, labour and capital.

Whether or not the real failure of the RDP rested with the government's failure to adopt its more progressive sections,[111] there were certainly significant implementation and delivery failures even whilst there has been progress in many sectors.[112] Ironically the RDP has become an emblem of the ANC's hegemonic project where the 'variegated interests of capital and of the subaltern classes are not only blurred, but *made to appear contingent on each other*'.[113] At the heart of this shift rests the uneven consolidation of the liberal project whereby the government's main partners have opposing views on 'desirable' macroeconomic scenarios which has entailed ministers pitching to different audiences simultaneously.[114] Whilst the introduction of GEAR on 14 June 1996 was presented as an 'integrated' strategy for 'rebuilding and restructuring the economy' and 'implementing the RDP in all its facets',[115] it could be distilled to a logic which dictated that 'promoting the interests of capital (in the sense of creating an "investor-friendly" environment) is necessary for growth, and ultimately also good for the poor and unemployed – and hence will promote equity in the long run'.[116] Indeed, whilst the original objectives of the RDP have been in part superseded:

> 'Clearly there is a complex process of new packing of old promises; housing, water and sanitation live on in the commitments of the social cluster of the government's programme of action, although timelines on basic services taken over from the RDP are either dropped or extended forwards. The executive can be seen to be capitalising on its service-delivery strengths and relying heavily on continued performance by the more efficient national institutions. Inputs and strategies are highlighted, and when there is a reference to outcomes, there has to be good reason for confidence around achieving the outcome.'[117]

A far cry then from early, heady promises of fundamental societal restructuring.

The hapless progression of GEAR – annual GDP growth, the rate of private sector investment, savings, exports, the current account deficit, and formal sector job gains have all been substantially below projected targets –

has doubtless contributed to this shift.[118] This has been most evident as the ambitious social objectives established in the RDP were replaced by the neo-liberal proclivities of GEAR and then, more recently overtaken by a new set of expanded priorities; these new goals are now part of a much larger schema.[119] Government rhetoric continues to insist that the RDP retains primacy even whilst some key targets vis-à-vis housing for all by 2003 and expanded public works programmes have sunk without trace. In the first decade of democracy, the ANC's fixation with the correctness of economic fundamentals saw the formation of a concord that handed capital significant and potentially deleterious sway over economic thinking in government circles. Until only very recently it appeared that the consensus that characterises the ANC's hegemonic project had succeeded in consecrating the growth and investment imperative whilst simultaneously reversing a sacrosanct and long-term objective of redistribution. Nevertheless, the most recent indications from the highest circles of government that the country is leaning towards 'a procapitalist, interventionist state'[120] signal that GEAR's position as the ANC's principal macroeconomic charter may well be under threat. What this means for the role of the state and recent initiatives such as the Accelerated and Shared Growth Initiative for South Africa (Asgi-SA) which was launched by Mbeki during the 2006 State of the Nation address remains thus far unclear.

An African Renaissance?

The development of consensus has not been relegated solely to the economic sphere, and a similar if no less important and as yet unfinished project was begun simultaneously in the political arena. This project too has undergone significant change during the years of ANC government. The nature of this consensus was to be constituted by the overriding imperative of non-racialism and nurtured by a political project of nation-building intended to include all South Africans. Over a decade later, these sentiments have faded as a racially-tinged class project and new cultural nationalism have become visible, most prominently in the rise of Black Economic Empowerment (BEE) and a sizeable and growing black middle class. It has been contended that with the failure to undertake fundamental societal transformation the ANC government has become constrained by the lack of tangible delivery accomplishments. In order to retain at least some of the higher ground in an increasingly vociferous debate about the direction of the government and the lack of political economic enfranchisement, it is coming to rely upon various cultural rights and initiatives that imply a revision of these principles of non-racialism and inclusion in what has been termed a 'convulsive attempt' at nation-building.[121] At the centre of the political system of this post-apartheid society rests 'an explosive mixture of liberal and non-liberal politics'.[122] Paradoxically, it means that today, the basis of consent vacillates between the dictates of a liberal democratic politics and traditional cultural and group rights which may well prove contrary to the development of the liberal democratic project.

In the immediate aftermath of the apartheid era, the parameters of this accord were founded in the themes of unity, reconciliation and commonality. With the very real threat of ethnic and racial discord, the project of nation-building was indispensable to this new compact so that:

> 'The settlement and the launch of the transition depended on an activated awareness of "common interests" between the old order and the popular movement – on an acknowledgement that friend and foe have to pass through a gateway of concessions and compromises in order to avert disaster for their respective agendas. This principle of inclusion became the central ideological tenet of the new South Africa.'[123]

Using the juridical instruments rendered by the political settlement, it was intended that the narrow consent base of the former dispensation was to be replaced with a nation-building project which would serve as the basis of a similar transformation in the socio-economic sphere. That said, any 'historically effective' hegemonic project is multi-dimensional and advances on a variety of fronts simultaneously.[124] But, as in the economic sphere, the ANC's conceptions of a post-apartheid society were 'rudimentary' and 'impressionistic'.[125]

The 'fundamental political realignment' that followed echoed the compromises drawn in the economic realm,[126] but was more even-handed comprising a liberal democratic system and an interim Constitution that encompassed a wide-ranging Bill of Rights with a stress upon minority and property rights. Early in the negotiations the ANC had understood that garnering any consensus would involve a number of strategic concessions. Thereafter, a short-termism surfaced in their tactics that embraced compromise and the prioritising of a politico-ideological nation-building project over socio-economic restructuring.[127] With the ANC quick to emphasise its Charterist traditions, the very nature of its concessions – amnesty for human rights violators, no catharsis of the civil service, a qualified support for minority rights in the shape of local government seats, and language and education freedoms – all spoke to the transition myth of a one-nation coalition. Indeed, the rise of unity through diversity in the guise of the globally celebrated rainbow nation remains the success story of the transition even as it appeared but a 'romanticised representation of the Charterist interpretation of the South African nation'.[128]

At the forefront of the instruments intended to assist in the building of this scenario were the Constitution and the Truth and Reconciliation Commission (TRC). Formally adopted in 1996, the Constitution partners the introduction of universal suffrage with a simultaneous protection of the liberal model of individual rights over collective claims. Nonetheless, the principle of equality before the law is exalted in the same document. These blatant ambiguities and the refusal of the Constitution to grant absolute rights in any direction stems from the extensive deliberation concerning minority rights and vetoes that dogged the drafting of the earlier, interim Constitution. In spite of this, the Constitution Bill was launched with much fanfare before Parliament during 1996, with the then Deputy President Mbeki's 'I Am An African' speech providing the obligatory rainbow rhetoric. True both to the letter of the Constitution and the Freedom Charter itself, Mbeki affirmed the non-racial ideology which buttressed the ANC's hegemonic project, declaring that:

'The Constitution, whose adoption we celebrate, constitutes an unequivocal statement that we refuse to accept that our Africanness shall be defined by our race, our colour, our gender or our historical origins. It is a firm assertion made by us that South Africa belongs to all who live in it, black and white.'[129]

His speech was to effectively mark the first high point of this particular conception of non-racialism.[130]

In turn, the TRC was tasked with serving as the arbiter of this discourse. It sought 'to extend into the social sphere the consensual (or, at least, conciliatory) dynamics nurtured in the political sphere' and was 'burdened with the hope that the exposure of truths can reinforce a basis for reconciliation and, ultimately, help forge a united nation'.[131] A product of the negotiated settlement, the Commission was part of the same discourse that endeavoured to foster consensus across the political spectrum.[132] Most problematically, the accent on the individual perpetrators of crimes as opposed to the countless beneficiaries, as well as the failure to properly address historical and continued structural inequalities, perhaps critically compromised the reconciliation process. Perhaps the most significant omission was the role of business in apartheid despite a special three day hearing, and recommendations in the TRC's final report that government impose a once-off wealth tax on business and industry because voluntary contributions to the Business Trust had totalled a mere R800m.[133] Praiseworthy though it was, the whole exercise smacked of the sacrifice of justice in favour of reconciliation so that any public discussion of apartheid as a system was neatly circumvented.[134] Indeed, in its aftermath, enormous variability remains in terms of the levels of reconciliation across the country's various racial and ethnic/linguistic groups.[135]

Whilst the TRC's mission to build a genuine and wide-ranging process of reconciliation floundered, former President Mandela maintained overwhelming support for this cause which he sought to make the overriding objective of his presidency.[136] The status of Mandela remains roughly comparable across the populace, and especially positive among Afrikaans speaking capital elites.[137] This mandate effectively enabled him to create:

> 'a temporary recess in which a sense of unity or nationhood could sink a few tenuous roots. Mandela's historic feat was not only to steer South Africa away from the brink of catastrophe but to have carved out a breathing space where pulses could settle, enmities subdue and affinities become recast. The grand authority and mythic stature attained by Mandela enabled him to "float above politics" largely unencumbered by the realpolitik of his party and the attendant need to shore up power bases and juggle trade-offs.'[138]

The so-called Mandela factor has offered profound incalculable support for a rainbow nation and its spectre of a shared and inclusive future. Nowhere was this more evident than in his gestures towards Afrikaans speakers – appearing in a Springbok shirt during the 1995 Rugby World Cup, taking tea with Verwoerd's widow – and his broader assurances as to the grouping's position and cultural rights in the new South Africa.

Nevertheless, by late 1996 these overtures to non-racialism were weakening to be replaced with a somewhat ambivalent Africanist discourse which climaxed with Mbeki's famous speech on reconciliation and nation building during May 1998.[139] Since the late 1990s, the multiracial pact has been steadily if unevenly dissolved in favour of the so-called 'two nations' thesis and a blossoming attachment to the politics of race in ANC rhetoric. Situated in the enduring friction between non-racial and race-conscious discourse so prominent in both the ANC liberation movement and government, this Africanism has historically bisected every other ideological confrontation.[140] Yet it resurfaced as the government's failure to significantly ameliorate the marginalisation which continues to define the post-apartheid polity opened the economic aspect of the hegemonic project to widespread popular and continued dissatisfaction so that race has come to matter once again as a means of political mobilisation and redistributing power and wealth. In such a climate, the inclusion promised by the political settlement and interpretation of citizenship have become the most obvious victims.

Under the previous dispensation, a profound instability was apparent in the nation-state whereby the relationship of the individual to the community was set by two different criteria, namely: citizenship in the state and membership in the nation. The first formulation dictates an equal and formal participation in the political nation whereas the second, more complex construction depicts a particularistic belonging in the cultural nation. These inherently incompatible interpretations of citizenship have been effectively renewed under the terms of the post-apartheid democracy. In fact, there are at least three distinct types of liberal projects in play, namely: a minimalist liberalism aimed primarily at the establishment of the rule of law and minimalist government; a juridical liberalism concerned with rights, justice and obligations; and, a communitarian liberalism concerned with cultural pluralism, communal values and group rights.[141] Amid these competing liberalisms, the government treads a careful line claiming equal citizenship rights for all citizens whilst at the same time defining the nation in cultural terms so as to give priority of some kind to those possessing the attributes of cultural nationhood.

This new cultural nationalism and the 'strategies of exclusion' necessary to promote it emerged as a more conciliatory ethos was replaced with a firmer oratory, just prior to the change in ANC leadership during 1999. Around the same time, an ANC discussion document entitled 'Nation-Formation and Nation Building' was released.[142] It was one of the first documents to directly raise the nationality question and, in a departure from earlier rhetoric, it spoke of a 'continuing battle to assert African hegemony in the context of a multi-cultural and non-racial society'. Whilst the old euphemisms concerning a 'new Patriotism' were still apparent, the rising momentum of Africanism and its definition of nationhood handed the government a useful political tool. In this sense, it has been argued that the ANC is being pushed towards culturalism and black embourgeoisement by entrenched economic power so that the 'virtue of culturalism (or racialism: the two are the same in South Africa) is that it exaggerates the good of burgeoning elites, provides ways of dealing with the ensuing political and ideological challenges and serves the ANC's purposes'.[143] Henceforth, a nationalist stance was promoted as providing a 'better political potential to the ANC than non-racialism, whether based on class solidarity or on "rainbow" all-inclusive nationhood.'[144] In sum, repercussions from the economic sphere and the ANC's ideological traditions were making themselves felt.

From the start, this conversion bore the inestimable stamp of the new regime and would have been inconceivable under Mandela's presidency. Mbeki's standing is intimately connected to his popularisation of the idealistic notion of an 'African Renaissance' to which this shift has been neatly equated.[145] In truth, these continuities have offered Mbeki space for manoeuvre and a mandate that, unlike Mandela, he conspicuously lacked. The challenge for the remainder of his presidency will not only be to reconcile these divergent currents, but also to refine the Africanist debate within the ranks of the tripartite alliance and the wider system of hegemonic alliances with the growing realisation that black embourgeoisement has singularly failed to address wider poverty and inequality. No less a figure than Mandela himself has expressed his outrage at the increasing polarisation between racial groups.[146] One of the historic strengths of the ANC has been the Freedom Charter that compromises an 'ideological bedrock' and key 'hegemonic instrument'.[147] Even whilst maintaining a tight rein, the ANC has thus afforded itself considerable ideological breadth and latitude whilst safeguarding a heterogeneous range of interests. Nevertheless, it would appear that the symbolic resonance and legitimacy afforded by this one document and its ideal of non-racialism has not provided the government with a sufficient mandate to address the shortcomings of structural changes within society.

Confronted by international and domestic constraints, the Africanist discourse has allowed the ANC government to answer a number of issues, functioning as a:

> 'local response to domestic as well as international conditions and fundamental dislocations. It represents a local strategy to cope with profound domestic and global change, with constraints on the process of transformation, and with the process of dealing with South Africa's past. It is also a debate concerning present conditions and the future. Emancipation as defined by the ANC takes place not only in the social, political and economic arenas but also in the cultural and psychological fields. While the constitution provides equal human

rights, guarantees of equality of opportunity, education and training, housing, affirmative action, and labour laws to protect dignity and income, it is clear that the playing field is still far from level. The communist challenge is not a viable one to the neoliberal global and local paradigm, but the Africanist response certainly is.'[148]

Whilst Mbeki's willingness to assume the populist mantle is increasing, dependence on this rhetoric as burying conflicting interests beneath the broad church of reconciliation is becoming ever more complicated, the policies of his government are leading to the deracialisation of the first nation, whilst the second marginalised, poor and overwhelming black nation is effectively stranded.[149] As a result, the ahistoricity of Ubuntu is paired with the dehistoricisation of its counterpart Western materialism:

> 'Public discourse in post-apartheid South Africa is marked by the taboo that has been placed on racism, while at the same time racism has been separated from the cultural nationalist and ethicist discourses that were always closely connected with it. In this way, cultural nationalism has been liberated from the racist connections it had during the apartheid era, and has become available once again. Social problems in the 'new' South Africa are, increasingly, viewed through a nationalist lens.'[150]

This new mandate then has become prized as a means of transforming the dangers of rising inequality and class struggle into cultural and ethnocentric differentiation.

Nowhere has this politicking been more evident than in how capitalist globalisation is wheeled out time and again by the ANC leadership as a justification for redistributive and other shortcomings.[151] The Africanist treatise and the African Renaissance with which it is equated have been linked to a grandiose diversion from serious domestic issues. On this stage, it is viewed as an 'updating' of the African-nationalism variant conspicuous during the middle of last century to conform with contemporary South Africa's racial divisions and the inequalities of the global capitalist order.[152] In many respects the African Renaissance represents an 'empty policy vessel' promoted by a government that faces a number of domestic and international challenges.[153] Yet it is a genuine if certainly ambitious and romanticised attempt to build a new, progressive and modernised Africa at the centre of the globalised political economy,[154] and to redress the conceptual basis of the continent's relations with a non-African world.

The point is that the meaning of the Africanist discourse is vague and thus inherently flexible, managing 'to nod in numerous directions at once' so that:

> 'the circle of inclusion drawn is tensile, offering entry to others as well. It offers a pliant ideological framework for inclusion and tolerance but at the same time contains a basis for censure and exclusion.'[155]

It is perhaps then best conceived as an ideological device, a method of improvisation with which to obscure the worsening discord between the government and a disaffected majority. Mbeki has repeatedly demonstrated his political deftness on this issue, balancing signals to the business community with grassroots interests, which reflects certain hegemonic ambitions without placing too deleterious an emphasis on the ongoing and serious problem of racism.[156] The harder direction on race and attendant tactical alignments is pliant enough still to reproduce the necessary measure of consent from critical constituent parts, even as it deliberately scores a line about certain racially defined groupings. Nonetheless, and in the longer term, the continued omission to substantially convert the social and economic condition of the majority of South Africans poses a serious risk to the long-term success of the hegemonic project as it currently stands.

4
CONTEMPORARY MANIFESTATIONS OF AFRIKANER IDENTITY IN AN ERA OF INCREASING GLOBALISATION

It has been contended above that a profound paradigm shift has dominated the Afrikaner grouping since the 1994 constitutional settlement and the formal loss of political power. Prior to that, Afrikanerdom was able to shift the direction and gear of its nationalist project to preserve the necessary measure of cohesion. Today the grouping is in transition; whilst the material gains of the apartheid era remain and have been consolidated, the foundations of any revised nationalist or group ethos, or ideological, political or programmatic axis, are in flux. During this chapter, the dynamics of identity adjustment will be examined more closely by illuminating how key constituent parts (capital elites and a cultural intelligentsia) behave in real historical conditions. Whether these constituent parts are able to comprehend the wider connections and prospects between national and global structures, and thereafter to discern new spaces or openings (whether economic, cultural or political) in which to act and rearticulate a new identity or identities, will comprise a particular focus.

To this end, the extent to which certain constituent parts are initiating a politico-cultural dialogue and thus rejuvenating a community (and the terms of inclusion therein) will be evaluated. Given that leading constituent parts including capital elites and to a lesser degree elements of a cultural intelligentsia have lent their support to the government's neo-liberal agenda, these openings must be outlined from within the parameters of the post-apartheid consensus. The chapter focuses firstly on the parameters of the constitutional settlement and the implications of transformation for the nature of contemporary South African citizenship, and thereafter a new cultural agenda. A specific focus will highlight the new discourse of minority group and consequently language rights. The second part explores the manner in which an increasingly globalised Afrikaans speaking middle class and capital elites are linked to the globalised political economy. Thus, the chapter investigates whether the development of a new cultural agenda exhibits the potential to overcome the ideological and material consensus compiled by the ANC, its hegemonic allies and connected global social forces, and even to find common ground with a wider range of social partners and issues.

Rethinking the cultural: The future of the Afrikaner past

Afrikaner cultural activists are today faced with a very different task from that which confronted their predecessors. Long past the apogee of a cohesive ethnic identity, cultural politics has become the new battleground and the yardstick by which the success of any post-apartheid grouping is to be measured. That said, the terms of the debate have altered paradigmatically and the challenge is formidable. The crisis of cultural politics stretches not only to minority rights and nation-building, but also the global hegemonic consensus itself: the triumph of a neo-liberal economic regime and its adjunct liberal democracy. Notable divisions are evident in the multi-dimensional nature of contemporary Afrikaner identifications. On the economic front, these have been interrupted by the success of Afrikaner capital and the continued rise of an increasingly globalised middle class under the new dispensation.[1] By contrast, in the cultural arena, the old foundations of cultural identity are no longer credible and consideration of an 'Afrikaner problem' remains disputed if it is considered as a problem at all.[2] Even a 'more liberal Afrikanerbond with a new approach' is battling to find a suitable niche.[3] Nonetheless, among white Afrikaans speakers, stronger ethnic identification is associated with active involvement in cultural organisations and activities that involve mostly in-group members,[4] suggesting cultural politics could perhaps represent the base of a new programmatic axis for an Afrikaans grouping.[5]

A new round of Afrikaner identity politics then looms large. With the issue of material resources or entitlement virtually obsolete despite rising white poverty levels,[6] there is an increasing focus on more abstract and intellectual disputes concerned with perceptions of marginalisation, entitlement and belonging, as well as clashes over institutional and symbolic power. The basis of both inclusion and exclusion is now concerned with the drawing of cultural boundaries although these boundaries remain the subject of considerable debate, most especially with regard to race. The groundwork has been laid for a broad and inclusive national consensus that enshrines the communal rights that could potentially undermine this very consensus.[7] In terms of global cultural politics this divergence between group and individual rights traditions is similarly pronounced.[8] Just as the ANC's hegemonic project and its global counterpart has supplied openings for components of Afrikaans capital and an increasingly globalised middle class, so a repositioning of cultural politics has the potential to supply space for elements of Afrikaans intellectual and cultural capital. That said, the terms of any new cultural dialogue remains far from settled. Whether these constituent parts can secure an identity receptive to other minority groups and aligned with new global hierarchies, or whether a retreat to a more exclusive and parochial vision transpires, remains to be seen.

As both a system of meaning and a basis of social identity, culture is integral to any understanding of the dynamics of identity politics. In processes of identity adjustment a new cultural basis for the community, a means of redefining boundaries and even the identity project itself, must be authenticated. The explicitly political dimension of culture has come to the fore during an era of increasing globalisation that has forced a reconsideration of the relationship between culture, identity and national or territorial solidarity. Cultural globalisation is 'transforming the *context* in which and the *means* through which national cultures are produced and reproduced'.[9] Contemporary globalisation has stimulated cultural reinvention through the production of localities and a new Other which is most apparent where economic and social turbulence has implications for a redefinition of citizenship.[10] It offers a fertile ground for the reproduction of communal identities. Indeed, contemporary identity movements must be capable of adapting to this new globalised order, and the dislocation of previously solid relations between identity, place and meaning.

Certain group interests have been well served by this overt politicisation of the cultural domain and the multidimensional redrawing of global space,[11] and the revitalised relationship between the local and the global has sponsored a voice for localities. The concept of community has become far more complex in this new geography and hybrid identities often rooted in post- or non-national traditions have flourished. Hall anticipates a shift in the cultural politics of minorities to a 'politics of the relations of representation'. Not only does contemporary globalisation then contest national cultural boundaries, but it also has:

> 'a pluralising impact on identities, producing a variety of possibilities and new positions of identification . . . making identities more

positional, more political, more plural and diverse; less fixed, unified or trans-historical.'[12]

Thus, external linkages and a commitment to the globalised political economy can serve as a springboard for particular minority group aims.[13] Nonetheless, the impact of globalisation on communal identities in terms of cultural resources is ambiguous. For a once highly territorialised and culturally distinctive Afrikaner identity, the implications of this restructuring are as yet unclear. Language has become a focal point, and whilst the spectre of race remains new components are likewise evident.

The politics of transformation

Post-apartheid South Africa is perhaps an unlikely site for the consolidation of liberal democracy. The key remains the constitutional settlement and the paradigm shift delivered by way of an inclusive accommodation of disparate communal identities. Yet the ANC's quest for a 'national democracy' that 'equalled procedural democracy plus economic egalitarianism'[14] was crudely stymied by a mix of global and domestic factors. International financial institutions including the IMF and World Bank tied loans and debt repayment agreements to a set of political values and principles that advanced a set of 'procedural democratic political arrangements'.[15] In negotiating circles, the then NP government was resolute in its support of this particular vision of democracy, albeit with significant consociational adjustments including minority protection clauses. This same ideology remains the source of a fundamental ambiguity within the ANC's leadership circle where globalisation is both 'accepted but also resisted'.[16] But by the close of negotiations and the adoption of the interim constitution in late 1993, a new model of consensus democracy had been established.

The nature of the constitutional settlement and the majoritarian democratic system it enshrined is a significant achievement. As with any liberal democracy, the protection of property and political rights – historically in the hands of a privileged few within South Africa – figured highly. The instruments of the new democratic regime were broadly majoritarian with universal suffrage for a unitary South Africa at the heart of the settlement. At the same time, the 1996 constitution included a number of instruments to counter this trend including a federalist structure, a proportional representation electoral system, and a selection of watchdog institutions to monitor the power of the executive.[17] Nonetheless, South Africa's constitutional liberal democracy betrays certain ambiguities. Most importantly, there is a fundamental rift between the principles of equality and diversity which have been given equal billing in the constitution, and to varying degrees in ANC rhetoric.

A tension between a Western-orientated mode of democracy – a commitment to capitalist modes of production, a particular set of norms concerning the rights of individuals, and a neo-liberal position on the role of the state[18] – and an Africanist tradition of communal group rights and duties has prevailed within the constitution itself. Indeed, the preamble proclaims that the country 'belongs to all who live in it, united in our diversity',[19] fêting the two principles of equality and diversity as the 'central axis' of political and social relations. During the negotiations process, recalcitrance on the part of the apartheid government concerning property and education (single-medium schools) confronted the ANC's determination that certain socio-economic rights were vital to the rectification of apartheid-era inequalities. What followed was a considerable climb-down on the part of the ANC and its coalition partners in the face of some very cynical politicking from De Klerk's administration.[20]

In the months that followed this brinkmanship a new national consensus stressing unity and inclusivity was nurtured. Yet the ambiguity of the constitutional definition of civil society comprised both of individuals and communities has never been reconciled. Community is at the core of the state's interactions with civil society but even this interpretation is fraught with ambiguities, alluding to both traditional and indigenous categories as well as those defined by self-determination or the right to seek economic, social and cultural development.[21] At the heart of the government's liberatory legitimacy lies its claim to act as the representative of all communities, regardless of ethnicity or race. Treading the fine line between populism and a genuine, inclusionary citizenship project means that a tension between race-conscious and non-racial perspectives, what has been termed a dual connotation of citizenship as moral conception and a legal category, is explicit.[22] The racialised distinction between citizen and subject that bedevilled the apartheid era is held by a vocal minority to be omnipresent today, in the spectre of a nation-building project and dual citizenship philosophy that promises a single hegemonic culture. The concern is that the persistence of populist sentiments might mean that solidarities to the group or nation will overwhelm the wider citizenship project, so that the struggle to achieve unity from diversity will be sacrificed for political expediency.

The new discourse of minority rights

Citizenship has historically been the signifier of membership within a national and sovereign collectivity. Previously, class was understood as the 'principal axis of inequality' over and above other dimensions including gender, race and ethnicity. Until recently, this same basis of exclusion was practised throughout liberal democracies despite a concession to individual rights. The practice of a universal and national programme of citizenship was instigated largely in the West during the postwar years, and was consolidated by national assimilation and the introduction of the welfare state as an instrument for building equity among citizens. More recently this model has given way to a new citizenship that draws upon categorical equity and privileges differences in order to grant a set of rights. It is a shift that signals the birth of what has been termed the 'cultural politics of citizenship'.[23]

Citizenship thus has come to be regarded more as a matter of cultural distinctions or rights rather than similarities. It represents part of a trend towards the globalisation of liberalism, paralleled by the rise of various supranational citizenship options and protections that have had consequences for popular meanings of citizenship.[24] However, Kymlicka promotes the significance of cultural membership within this liberal tradition of rights – the accommodation of ethnocultural diversity – by drawing a crucial distinction between national minorities including indigenous peoples (distinct and potentially self-governing societies incorporated into a larger state), and other minority ethnic, cultural and social groups (immigrants who have left their national community to enter another society).[25] The importance of Kymlicka's variety of multiculturalism is that it provides for differing rights for different minority groups. As a riposte to the assimilationist model of citizenship, it has become a well-accepted solution to culturally differentiated claims which has the kudos of the global liberal establishment firmly behind it.[26]

Whilst the South African constitution does not affirm a policy of multiculturalism per se, it does preserve significant equality for various cultural, linguistic and religious communities. This recognition is strengthened by particular passages in the constitution that allow for nothing less than the 'constitutionalisation of ethnic politics'.[27] The stakes here are inordinately high despite the increasing codification of these rights in international law,[28] and considerable 'concessions to Afrikaner chauvinism and conservative African traditionalist forces' have been held guilty of prolonging the 'lifespan of politicised ethnicity'.[29] Nonetheless, since the fall of the apartheid regime, the majority of Afrikaans speakers have hesitated to label themselves in a minoritarian style, even whilst a vocal and largely self-appointed cultural intelligentsia are keen to 'work within certain [formal] registers',[30] perceiving there to be a 'merit in appealing to the constitution'[31] in order to protect certain of these rights.

The advocacy of minority rights and a culturally differentiated citizenship was intended to provide protection for vulnerable minorities vis-à-vis the dominant majority. Yet, in the case of the former leading minority grouping in South Africa, several sections including the *Federasie Afrikaanse Kultuurvereiniginge* (FAK), the revamped *Afrikanerbond* and other cultural organisations play the minority card.[32] Former President De Klerk put the minorities case at an *Afrikanerbond* conference to mark Human Rights day in 2001,[33] and continues to champion this 'national accord' via the FW de Klerk Foundation.[34] It is a point that has been similarly and consistently argued by other scions of the former Afrikaner establishment. But it is contended that this marginalisation rhetoric is all too frequently not matched in reality. Instead, it has progressed unevenly among different constituent parts amid the multiple and often contending cultural agendas open to Afrikaans speakers today including the propagation of genuinely liberal, postmodern, non-hegemonic and multiple forms of identity.

Defining majorities and minorities within electoral and legislative politics as well as constitutional principles was a critical factor in the negotiations process. Here a number of sections of the constitution and Bill of Rights are particularly significant including articles 181(c), 185, 186 and 235. Each of these stem from the constitution-making processes both prior to the 1994 election, and the later deliberations within the Constitutional Assembly that included key clauses relating to education and a general freedom to one's culture and language.[35] South Africa's rights system is secured both within the constitution and a comprehensive and extremely progressive Bill of Rights. Thus, article 30 of chapter two expressly states that all persons have the right to 'use their language and participate in the cultural life of their choice'. Expanding on this proposition, the following article declares:

(i) Persons belonging to a cultural, religious or linguistic community may not be denied the right, with other members of that community –
   a. to enjoy their culture, practise their religion and use their language; and,
   b. to form, join and maintain cultural, religious and linguistic associations and other organisations of civil society.

(ii) The rights in subsection (i) may not be exercised in a manner inconsistent with any provision of the Bill of Rights.

The constitution also provides an equal footing for 11 official languages and the first official recognition for a number of indigenous languages. All the same, agreement on this new conceptual framework required hefty concessions, and shaped an uneven equilibrium between the imperatives of minority and majority rights, diversity and equality.

Chief among the concessions won by the outgoing administration was the inauguration of a Commission for the Promotion and Protection of the Rights of Cultural, Religious and Linguistic Communities. It was a highly politic development on the part of the Constitutional Committee who agreed to the formation of the body during April 1996 in order to placate highly vocal and fractious elements of the Afrikaner right wing, as well as elements of the apartheid establishment. Effectively it represented a corollary of the 34th constitutional principle that first ceded concessions to the right wing in order to secure its participation in the 1994 elections. This manoeuvring was revealed in the alterations to the Commission's mandate which, as expressed in the 1996 constitution, lost any prerogative to promote either self-determination for cultural communities, or supply any significant or instrumental meaning to the group rights project. Indeed, the primary objectives of the Commission include the promotion of respect for and between those communities on the basis of national unity and equality. Further, those responsibilities only stretch as far as those 'necessary to achieve its primary objects, including the power to monitor, investigate, research, educate, lobby, advise and report on issues concerning the rights of cultural, religious and linguistic communities'.[36]

Despite these final adjustments the Commission is named as one of the state institutions charged with strengthening constitutional democracy in the new republic,[37] and is not easily defined as a sop to minority interests. In fact, the ambit of the Commission extends far beyond self-determination for self-styled ethnic or linguistic communities. Instead, as part of the new constitutional ethos, it has sought to revise the cultural debate to address all groups seeking 'cultural expression', to create an officially-sanctioned framework for the resolution of related disputes, and therein to guard the integrity of the democratic transition. Indeed, the Commission was expected to take the 'major responsibility to manage diversity as part of the nation-building process'.[38] It proved an onerous task, complicated by the phrasing of its powers as well as a general distrust of its mandate. However, the Act was passed during July 2002 and 18 commissioners were appointed by the government after public nominations the following year.[39] Most recently, alongside other Chapter 9 institutions, the Commission was the subject of the country's self-assessment report which was handed to the African Peer Review Mechanism secretariat during July 2006.

This same politic dexterity was apparent in the reinvention of Afrikaner cultural or territorial self-determination, a creation both vindicated and emasculated by the constitution. Prior to the 1994 elections, self-determination had proved a highly emotive issue advanced by direct negotiations between the ANC and prominent figures from within the ranks of Afrikanerdom in the body of an 'unsigned agreement' during December 1993. This was followed by the 'Accord on Afrikaner Self-Determination' signed by General Constand Viljoen, Mbeki (in his capacity as National Chairman of the ANC), and Roelf Meyer on behalf of the then government and NP on 23 April 1994. It comprised the backdrop for an ambiguous recognition of cultural-national autonomy and conceivably an independent Afrikaner *volkstaat* initially agreed upon in the Interim Constitution of 1993, and later enshrined in section 235 of the 1996 constitution.[40] A number of mechanisms including a *volkstaat* council were established to support the constitutional principle. Yet the First Interim Report of the *Volkstaat* Council only highlighted the polarities of the various organisations pursuing the *volkstaat* dream. Former Council chairman Hendrik Robbertze identified a further impediment to separate statehood as 'the growing number of Afrikaners' who are 'willing to accept a form of cultural autonomy which falls short of independent statehood'.[41] It was a trend that Viljoen anticipated in his later repackaging of self-determination as akin to a cultural crusade.

Consensus on self-determination was steadily watered down both by the right wing's entry into constitutional negotiations and legitimate electoral politics. Moreover, it faded because, as Viljoen himself surmised, after 1996 'most Afrikaners didn't experience the new South Africa that negatively'.[42] Successive democratic elections have levelled the playing field further and made any genuine ethnic politics a far harder proposition. At the national level and in intellectual circles the emphasis has largely been on toeing the narrow line on communities advocated in the constitution, even as a new set of challenges has surfaced in the uneven consolidation of the liberal project, rising inequality and Mbeki's enthusiastic courting of the Afrikaans business constituency. The *volkstaat* issue has been forced onto the backburner, countenanced largely as a local issue as evinced by the municipal-level bickering over Orania's boundaries.

If the old model of self-determination has been abandoned in the political mainstream, minority rights remain conspicuous within the constitution itself. Even the most avowed of minority parties the Freedom Front Plus is careful to exploit these constitutional safeguards, as evidenced by the debate over the name change of Potchefstroom to Tlokwe during 2006.[43] Using this same idiom the government has been more or less able to direct the debate via the constitutional rights protocol. It has continued to deflect deliberation into rigid channels tackling orthodoxies including language and schooling, whilst at the same time preserving relations with select constituencies from within the Afrikaner old guard.

This shrewd political footwork was perhaps most evident during the special parliamentary debate regarding Afrikaners on 24 March 1999. The debate marked the culmination of months of discussions between both ordinary and elite Afrikaners and the then Deputy President Thabo Mbeki, Mangosuthu Buthelezi, Essop Pahad and Matthews Phosa amongst others. As it unfolded:

> 'Mbeki's initial strategy was to neutralise and win over the Afrikaner establishment by acknowledging its power and sympathising with the "predicament" created by its reliance on racial domination. In the new South Africa, this strategy could only be continued by re-consolidating that establishment. But this had the effect of fixing Afrikaner identity in the patterns of the past, and marginalising once again the dissident Afrikaners who had never defended apartheid power, nor shared the predicaments of its apologists . . . [Instead] Mbeki now sought to block this salvation, by making the defeat of apartheid acceptable to the establishment which had grown up to defend it. In the process, this re-consolidation of the Afrikaner establishment threatened to end the challenge of those Afrikaners who had struggled to free Afrikaner culture and the Afrikaans language from the matrix of apartheid.'[44]

Indeed, the proclamations contained in the government's final report on euphemistically titled 'Afrikaner question' essentially went no further than the raft of protective measures established by the Constitution. It concluded that: '[The government] therefore commits itself continuously to address their concerns, as it must address the concerns of all communities.'[45] In retrospect, the report has come to represent the virtual exhaustion of the minority rights regime in government circles.

With the political endgame reached, dialogue between elements of the former Afrikaner establishment and government has continued. During the ANC's National General Council during mid-2005 it was evident that the so-called 'national question' remains to some extent on the government agenda.[46] Much of the early impetus came from within the ranks of the ANC itself. Prior to and during the transition period both Mandela and Mbeki relentlessly courted key figures from different Afrikaner constituent parts.[47] The trend has continued with President Mbeki regularly meeting certain Afrikaans constituencies for 'quiet exchanges of views'.[48] Elsewhere, a new wave of cultural dissent somewhat less avowed of constitutional norms is discernible. Unlike that of the old guard, this politics has little to do with protecting a sullied ethnic hierarchy, and everything to do with the so-called 'interests' of Afrikaans speakers. It is this contest between a traditionally drawn and bounded minority, and a new if somewhat looser association that chooses not to emphasise structural means of redress, as well as the multiple and often contradictory agendas represented therein, that will be elaborated below.

The culture industry

Large tracts of the intellectual realm then are currently embroiled in a long-running internecine dispute over not only institutional, but to a lesser extent symbolic and material power. Perceptions of insecurity and marginalisation are paramount because sovereignty is understood only in terms of power and territory, and not currently in terms of other impulses such as artistic or charitable deeds.[49] As a result, this often regressive and insular dialogue has been termed 'an Afrikaner debate among Afrikaners',[50] akin perhaps to a new cultural nationalism with its defence of minority language rights and attempts to reconstruct tradition to better meet the demands of modernity.[51] Even so this remains a period of widespread ferment as certain constituent parts within the grouping struggle with cultural authenticity and reinvention, and efforts to cultivate a place for the Afrikaner in the new South Africa and an era of increasing globalisation. Whilst the shape of any reconfigured linguistic or wider cultural hegemony remains very much in its infancy, cultural spaces are perceived as being one of the few remaining areas where Afrikanerdom is intact or can at least be recreated.[52]

A series of revised cultural projects are taking shape among a younger generation of activists asserting a 'post-nationalist' or 'new Afrikaner' identity within the Gauteng-based journal *Fragmente*,[53] on the web pages of *Litnet* and within the weekly newspaper *Die Vrye Afrikaan*, as well as at the margins amid a growing literary and musical revival represented within the plethora of Afrikaans festivals which have emerged over the last decade. These quite different currents are engendering an imperfect if 'radical critique of globalisation' within a grouping associated by 'accident of their language'.[54] Some are content to dispense with special protections, believing that:

> 'Afrikaans literature, music and theatre are among the most vibrant on the continent. The language and its users have been enriched by their liberation from the shackles of apartheid and previous attempts at standardisation and entrenchment. The more Afrikaans celebrates its Africanness, it seems, the more it flourishes. And the more the language is re-appropriated by groups marginalised in the past, the more exciting it becomes.'[55]

But on the other side of the divide a prominent, increasingly vociferous if motley group of academics, intellectuals, authors and journalists have drawn their line in the sand about the subtext of minority rights. By and large, this task has fallen to a range of rejuvenated and new cultural organisations including the *Stigting vir Afrikaans* (Foundation for Afrikaans), *Afrikaanse Taal-en Kultuurvereninging* (Afrikaans language and culture society), the Group of 63 and,[56] most recently, the Federasie van Afrikaanse Kultuurvereiniginge. Language has become a more legitimate means of defending these rights so that a formal defence of group rights and language as cultural survival within the spirit of the constitution remains the overwhelming priority. However, the ambivalence of these claims to cultural protection illustrates an ongoing and complex:

> 'shift from racialised claims of supremacy to ethnicised claims to protection, in so doing deracialising whiteness and reinscribing difference through the language of culture in the form of the volk.'[57]

It is a debate that signals an entirely new cultural odyssey driven by a self-styled culture industry.

With linguistic concerns increasingly central to the feasibility of culture as a new system of legitimation, Afrikaans has become very much a language-centred culture, albeit commonly synonymous with race. But whether or not a cultural movement/s can provide a programmatic axis for a new group ethos is unclear. The status of the Afrikaans language and the protection of cultural diversity remain contentious issues. There is no clear indication as to how different divisions and antagonisms within any community could be overcome within a new cultural dialogue. Whilst language and identity may be close political bedfellows, the relationship invokes a wide spectrum of attachments: language can act as an ethnic marker, but similarly a high level of linguistic sentiment does not always translate to increased ethnic consciousness. Perhaps most problematically in this regard, there is no singular or widely accepted definition of Afrikanerness beyond that of language affiliation. The most common definition retains strong links with race and a European heritage, even whilst a leading member of the cultural intelligentsia maintains that an Afrikaner is 'someone who wants to be an Afrikaner'.[58]

From the earliest decades of the nationalist phenomenon, the manufacture of an Afrikaans literary culture was a crucial terrain upon which nationalist ideologies were shaped and normalised.[59] And with language once more a prime focus of Afrikaner identity politics there has been an 'increased acceptance of the legitimacy of minority nationalism'.[60] The contemporary debate has many nuances, spanning the range of sympathies from those advocating an active defence via the mother-tongue educational and language protections afforded by the constitution and subsequent legislation,[61] to others wanting an emphasis on 'self-sufficiency' with the concern being that 'the moment you stress only rights, you make your interests in accordance with those rights' and undercut your autonomy,[62] to those satisfied with the role of Afrikaans as a literary language and a means simply of everyday communication whose survival as a vernacular is assured by its status as the mother-tongue of the growing Afrikaans speaking coloured community.[63] There is genuine disquiet among certain cultural elites that a 'strong distinction needs to be made between a culture of rights and a democratic ethos' in this environment, with a preference for the non-reactionary creation of an ethos to create and protect 'spaces in which the Afrikaans language can be vibrant'.[64] The nature of these spaces is less certain. Yet the process of linguistic differentiation should be set within historical and political economic context as an entirely political activity contingent on both subjective factors and particular political circumstances, varying widely among individuals and groups depending on *the degree to which we define ourselves by it*'.[65] Whilst language can be of critical importance to many ethnic and national groups and certain component parts therein, to others it is far less significant.

This is nowhere more evident than in regard to expectations of the government vis-à-vis its responsibilities for language preservation that has broadly polarised opinion among Afrikaans speakers. Widespread disquiet over language rights among the white Afrikaans speaking population has not been so apparent among coloured Afrikaans speakers or other linguistic populations. Regardless of perceptions of marginalisation, any support for a mandate as to the official protection of language and cultural interests was endorsed only by a few, a trend crosscut by class and religious affiliations.[66] Indeed, it has thus far been this most privileged of the minority language groupings – interest groups among white Afrikaans speakers – who have campaigned on the language issue, a response which has been described as a progression 'from apartheid to multiculturalism in its most conservative form'.[67] This strength of attachment to language and its perceived importance for the community is most significant where its cultural significance heralds its political prominence, reflecting the legitimation and institutionalisation of a particular language by the state, usually to the detriment of other languages.[68] With the institutionalisation of formal language equality by way of the constitution alongside the hegemony of English in the public sphere, Afrikaans has been afforded legal protection alongside a range of other indigenous languages. It is a markedly different situation from the previous regime of linguistic purity and protection.

Nonetheless, few minority languages diminish where residual and growing material resources are manifest. There is not necessarily a link between the maintenance of a minority language and cultural and linguistic stasis – cultural and linguistic continuity and change are always and inevitably entangled.[69] Given that adaptation and management are central, the Afrikaans grouping has had something of a head start by way of a healthy resource base and its African, constructed and readily adaptable linguistic roots.[70] However, the ongoing campaigning for the reaclimatisation of Afrikaans has done little to advance the more disempowered of South Africa's language communities despite this being a commonly stated aim of empowerment initiatives.[71] Nor, despite a number of high-profile public debates between coloured and white Afrikaans speakers on this very issue, does *die groot Afrikaanse debat* (the great Afrikaans debate) appear particularly representative of the wider Afrikaans grouping. Several prominent coloured intellectuals including Hein Willemse, Neville Alexander and Jakes Gerwel have expressed their scepticism about the mobilisation for an Afrikaans language struggle.[72] Indeed, the campaigners themselves are by and large drawn from a self-appointed intellectual core and their focus is equally restricted so that many of the nuances of the debate have been sidelined or lost.

Given the importance of ideology to developing hegemonic and counter hegemonic projects, the role of an Afrikaans intelligentsia in the articulation of such projects, the building of a group awareness and the nature of ideological leadership are key concerns. Yet the depth of antagonisms within this intelligentsia and the wider grouping are considerable and readily apparent within a series of long-running, arcane and often vicious contests.

These range from the so-called *Boetman* debacle during 2000 whose inauspicious beginnings were in the book '*Afrikaners: Kroes, Kras, Kordaat*' by Willem De Klerk,[73] an exploratory treatise concerned with the continued existence of the Afrikaner and the dangers of identity withdrawal,[74] which was roundly condemned on the letters pages of *Die Burger, Beeld* and *Volksblad* and within another book,[75] to the furore which surrounded the awarding of an honorary doctorate by the University of Stellenbosch to the deceased communist anti-apartheid activist Bram Fischer during 2004. It is striking that much of this cultural dialogue is now occurring within the pages of the Afrikaans print media, with various publications including *Die Burger* in particular playing a reactionary role 'protecting Afrikaans for moral reasons' as a means of retaining their readership;[76] issues of language and culture have become a lucrative business. Even relatively obscure opinion pieces on these issues excite considerable and undeserved attention.[77] Significantly this dialogue remains far from any community-wide or national conversation, taking place almost exclusively within narrow intellectual circles.

One area which does serve both as a rallying point for the vocal Afrikaans *taalstryders* (fighters for the Afrikaans language) and a microcosm of the often vicious antagonisms within this intelligentsia is the *taaldebat* (language debate) and associated 'moral panic'[78] which underscores conservative ideas and interests. In recent years, the debate has taken on a new energy as the tensions between the necessity of raising diversity through more access in the higher education section and the survival of Afrikaans as an academic language with higher functions has overwhelmingly come to centre upon the University of Stellenbosch as 'the last, best hope'.[79] Whilst the Higher Education Act of 1997 was intended to promote diversity as well as address past inequities, the National Plan for Higher Education in South Africa released in March 2001 stated that Afrikaans continued to 'act as a barrier to access' at some universities.[80] At that time, the need for the existence of at least two predominantly historically Afrikaans universities – Stellenbosch and Potchefstroom – was recognised within the Plan. Nonetheless, the government and the then Minister of Education Kader Asmal were concerned that language should not act as an obstacle to transformation initiatives.

Under a clear obligation to provide dual medium instruction, the University of Stellenbosch became a focal point of the growing debate in part because of the unique population and language demographics of the Western Cape province, but also because of the arrival of a new rector Chris Brink during 2002, who chose to strongly advance the cause of diversity. For

Brink, diversity within the university included not simply a focus on Afrikaans as the 'natural language', but likewise diversity of race, gender and ideas. Indeed, his attempts to reform initiation ceremonies in the residences were to pitch the new rector against the full weight of the influential alumni networks. A new language policy and plan were finalised by a special task group before December 2002 for implementation during early 2003.[81] Keen to stress a commitment to 'being language friendly, with Afrikaans as a point of departure', the report exhorted that the university should meet this challenge 'creatively' and 'in keeping with the Constitutional prescription that practical and positive measures must be used to raise the status of indigenous languages and to advance the use of these languages'. Afrikaans was to remain 'the language medium as well as the primary language of instruction', but the university's language policy and language plan now explicitly aimed to comply with the National Plan for Higher Education, particularly in the manner in which it serves transformation.[82] Brink's efforts to move beyond what he termed a *'volkstaat* of the mind'[83] in order to overcome the essentialism of group rights saw the debate change character quite considerably, with the latest fracas centring upon the A- and T-options in the Faculty of Arts and Social Sciences.[84] Perhaps as a parting gesture, the departing rector requested that a number of his leading opponents conceive of an alternative language policy. Were a revised language policy to be agreed, the current date for implementation would be 2008. That said, it is Russell Botman, the incoming rector appointed during December 2006, who will decide the fate of Stellenbosch as an Afrikaans university at this critical juncture.

Perversely, it is the influence of certain constituencies among the cultural intelligentsia who have exerted considerable influence upon the *taaldebat*, with most university academics generally supportive of the proposed changes. Deep-seated fears about the future of the language and a 'hidden [government] agenda' against Afrikaners led Freedom Front leader Pieter Mulder to declare 'a new energy in Afrikaner circles' at the height of the diversity debate at Stellenbosch during 2002.[85] Among the various self-appointed guardians of the Afrikaans language and culture, a continuous stream of initiatives has been launched. In this vein, *Die Afrikaanse Oorlegplatform* – a group representing 15 cultural organisations – sent a document entitled 'A strategy for an equitable and efficient language and culture framework for South Africa' to the then Education Minister Kader Asmal during March 2001. Leading light Hermann Giliomee sent a similar plea for the universities at Stellenbosch and Potchefstroom.[86] And one of the most outspoken of their number, Dan Roodt, acknowledged for his very public deliberations as to the 'complete destruction of Afrikaans culture and the Afrikaner identity' and similar commentary,[87] chose to vilify Asmal to make his point:

> 'To the dismay of Afrikanerdom, an intellectual from Natal, himself a member of an ethnic minority, but thoroughly anglicised and inculcated with the universalist spirit of Milnerism, Education Minister Kader Asmal has been given power of life and death over Afrikaans culture. No one is more hated today by Afrikaners than Asmal, who has patiently set about undermining the ultimate repository of Afrikaner identity: their education system. In the past weeks, Stellenbosch University has been at the centre of an acrimonious clash over language policy, but so has every other Afrikaans university. Once at the centre of South African identity, Afrikaners now find themselves on the scrapheap, and prone to the same old identity crisis that used to haunt them throughout the 19th century under British rule, and which was only resolved by the suffering of the Anglo-Boer war.'[88]

Much of the public debate tends to be dominated by this self-styled cabal. What is not so clear is whether these strong sentiments are shared by even a minority of Afrikaans speakers outside *taalstryder* circles.

Defending Afrikaans today among the cultural intelligentsia then is based very much on maintaining the status quo, on working within the constitution and concomitant global attention to minority rights to regularise the status of Afrikaans. Yet the authority of the *taalstryders* to voice the concerns of Afrikaans speakers and their implicit interpretations of Afrikanerness are rarely addressed. Consideration of diversity has stretched barely as far as the coloured community, and often only superficially so that much of their reasoning is unreflective of the many and contradictory identifications among contemporary Afrikaans speakers. Thus their concern at incremental anglicisation and monolingualism has come to be framed so that the best chance of 'bridging the gap between white and coloured Afrikaans speakers is at Stellenbosch'.[89] The *taaldebat* then becomes about reconciliation, restitution and a 'responsibility to coloured people who have acute developmental needs'.[90] In this regard, one of the foremost intellectuals driving the debate favours siphoning funds away from the university's research institutes and efforts to build a world-class institution towards providing for previously disadvantaged coloured students as if both aims are simultaneously unachievable. Given historical events, this newly discovered sense of responsibility is an interesting development.

If certain constituent parts have hijacked the *taaldebat* it has equally proved an easy target. Whilst several intellectuals are keen to stress the historical intellectual tradition of dissent from within Afrikaner nationalism, 'democratic impulses' and the 'republic tradition' the fewer voices of dissent have been progressively crowded out. The noted author and academic Marlene van Niekerk made a courageous stand to exclude activist Dan Roodt from the Stellenbosch *Woordfees* during 2005 for which she received little peer support. Her vision of 'undogmatic and purely academic endeavours to construct an avenue for developing and keeping and holding open the ability of Afrikaans to formulate ideas and critical theoretical work . . . clean of any nationalist or ethnic legacy' is resolutely outside mainstream dialogue.[91] This and other dissent within the intelligentsia is vulnerable to the reach of Afrikaans elite pressure groups, cultural organisations and in particular the Afrikaans print media. Almost daily, the two principal Afrikaans newspapers of the Western Cape devote much of their letters pages to the role of Afrikaans in public life.[92] Many intellectuals have availed themselves of these 'narratives of marginalisation' so that in the case of Naspers, the company has been able to cleverly 'straddle the different strata and transformation itself . . . whilst retaining the identity past'.[93] It comes back to a narrow, zero-sum understanding of sovereignty fuelling a stifled intellectual debate that currently has 'no other recourse to any other notions which could build a feeling of sovereignty'.[94]

In other quarters, and most especially among the younger generation, the elaboration of a new collective sentiment is slowly assuming shape. One of the catalysts behind this regeneration is the globalisation regime. Whilst this qualitatively different defence of Afrikaans represents a dramatic political deviation it is:

> 'located firmly in the context of the new South Africa, and takes non-racial democracy as its explicit starting point. It is explicitly concerned with the interests of Afrikaans-speakers without regard to their ethnic background. Second, unlike the initial proposals of the NP in the constitutional negotiations, it is not concerned with formal means for securing political power for ethnic and other minorities . . . Third, the version of Afrikaner culture defended by this politics is itself far less conformist than that defended in the apartheid era. It assumes cultural diversity among Afrikaners, and is easily compatible with elements of Afrikaner life . . . which Afrikaner cultural authorities previously sought to suppress or exclude. [Finally], it depends on a new political style – drawn largely from the youth

culture and new social movements of the West – which opposes hierarchy and dogma, and encourages delivery of opinion and spontaneity of expression . . . Its philosophical ideas and idiom are drawn from the postmodernism of Derrida rather than the neo-Calvinism of Dooyeweerd.'[95]

That said, this 'new collective intellectual project' adheres to a vernacular that is barely transgressive of the normative ideology of globalisation,[96] so that their logic has come almost fully about to 'defend the self-conception provided by liberal constitutionalism and the capitalist market'.[97] The most salient examples of this intellectual revival are the philosophical journal *Fragmente* founded in 1998 and more recently launched newspaper *Die Vrye Afrikaan*. Both publications engage critically if selectively with the neo-liberal project, its logic of 'cultural homogenisation', and thereafter a limited measure of social justice. Indeed, the editor of *Die Vrye Afrikaan* is keen to underline the fact that there is 'a small minority of thinking Afrikaners who do realise that globalisation is a much bigger challenge to their community than state-centralism'.[98]

The nature of this challenge is viewed in terms of the isolation of the individual by the modern project which 'redefines him as a consumer' so that the 'concept of community itself is under pressure'.[99] This tendency to individualisation is problematic to certain cultural elites for the reason that there are increasing numbers of Afrikaners 'who are withdrawing from public life to a private existence' which is most marked in terms of high consumption and emigration.[100] Increasingly, the debate is painted in terms of a community disintegrating in the face of globalising neo-liberal forces. This then might explain the situation whereby during regular debates with other South African intellectuals, representatives of the *Federasie van Afrikaanse Kultuurvereiniginge* have met with Jeremy Cronin of the SACP and Moeletsi Mbeki has invited Rossouw to co-author an article on poverty. Rossouw himself perceives there to be clear common ground due to the impossibility of separating 'the class struggle from the struggle for identity'.[101]

There is certainly merit in opening new channels of debate and even tentatively addressing these structural inequalities. Paradoxically, just as this global regime remains the source of great disquiet within the ranks of the tripartite alliance, critical Afrikaans constituent parts demonstrate similar disquiet about the pressures wrought by contemporary globalisation. Goosen contends that the 'real engagement with Mbeki and the government is only happening within this small circle of people', whereas the closeness between Afrikaans capital and the ANC only 'maintains the status quo'.[102] However, the parameters of these promising dialogues have been hobbled by a steadfast refusal to critique the role of the neo-liberal variant of globalisation vis-à-vis the legacy of apartheid, as well as the continued enrichment of Afrikaans capital and embourgeoisement of an increasingly globalised Afrikaans middle class. In the other corner the position promoted most vigorously by Dan Roodt veers closer and closer towards 'old-style defensive apartheid'.[103] Both the narrower, group rights focus and the more progressive frame share a more or less uncritical understanding of the uncertain consolidation of the liberal project in a country riven by profound political, economic and social divisions. As the economist Sampie Terreblanche suggests 'there are much larger issues [than Afrikaners]'[104] at stake in a post-apartheid South Africa.

Some of the most internecine splits within the grouping rest closer to home. Grappling with issues of guilt, reconciliation and justice for the crimes of the apartheid era, tantamount to a re-evaluation of Afrikaner history,[105] has been a central plank of nation-building initiatives that has impacted on all whites often endorsing a deep-seated sense of alienation and even betrayal. Rossouw claims that there is a sense that what 'really bedevils political progress is [that] the stereotypes of the past are being maintained, and there is an interest in maintaining them'.[106] Yet in the new South Africa, the defence of Afrikaans 'more often rests on denying the possibility of collective responsibility for the past, or on the view that "what is past is done with."'[107] At the heart of this open sore lies the axiom, promoted by the Truth and Reconciliation Commission (TRC), that reconciliation must come before any real measure of justice in order to inaugurate a united nation, 'buttress political stability and help engineer a "psycho-social catharsis"'.[108] The process has taken on a deeply divisive cast so that:

> 'Although white South Africans may be committed to nonracialism and transformation, their commitment is one based on the abolition of apartheid practices. To white South Africans the concept of reparation and reconciliation does not imply accepting some form of collective guilt and shouldering the financial burdens of compensation. Yet it implies precisely that for many Africanists in the ANC.'[109]

Numbed by the machinations of the amnesty process, and ambivalent toward more widespread prosecutions against those who originally refused amnesty or did not apply, the wider white community has kept largely quiet in this debate.

Substantive racial divisions continue to mar opinions toward the TRC and the business of reconciliation.[110] Within the Afrikaans grouping in particular, this revival of the politics of memory has been traumatic indeed. Yet here too, a focus on the Afrikaner nation defined by a widespread feeling that it represents the 'scapegoat of apartheid'[111] ignores many contending perspectives ranging from moral ambivalence, recalcitrance, to more laudable sentiments. A number have signed the 'Home for All' initiative, acknowledging the profound damage done by apartheid, the 'white community's responsibility', and committing themselves to 'redressing these wrongs'.[112] Among this few number several Afrikaans speakers – Antjie Krog, Carl Niehaus, Wilhelm Verwoerd – who talk of a large number of South Africans still 'battling to find space in the new South Africa'; a problem put down to denial and the failure to deal properly with 'the historical facts of our past'.[113] Krog's commitment to reconciliation is generally perceived as 'owning up on their behalf'.[114] But these 'apologists' or 'self-denialists' have largely failed to connect with wider community sentiments although they have gained some very public praise from Mbeki.[115] More recent acts of atonement have thus far proved similarly limited in impact even whilst provoking considerable public debate.[116] One former scion of the nationalist establishment is outspoken in his opinion that 'there is a real need to re-educate the Afrikaners so that those who are currently uncomfortable can adapt to the changes in South Africa'.[117] It is not a judgement that currently carries much weight outside certain limited circles.

Whilst it may be possible to speak of a nascent group ethos in some small quarters of the grouping, it is an ethos that currently lacks any central programmatic or legitimatory axis. Despite some patently retrogressive motives, the main thrust of intellectual disenchantment has found its strongest voice in a movement of the 'other or new' Afrikaner; post-nationalist Afrikaners with a strong if largely uncritical and ahistorical sense of community. Presciently, it is exactly this divide between proponents of a post-apartheid minority rights dispensation and a growing number keen to dispel the impression of a 'white minority *kraal*' or '*boere laager*', that continues to ensure the greatest tensions. The early days of the transition which revealed genuine flux and debate about the meaning of Afrikanerness vis-à-vis race and historical privilege, perhaps the greatest tests of any new ethos, are now apparently long past and the label has hardened. Only a few of these initiatives continue and there is apparently little space in which a more inclusive refashioning of Afrikanerness can resume. Indeed, in these times of racialised inequality the failure thus far of the cultural intelligentsia to build a common project not only with the range of Afrikaans constituencies but also the majority of other South Africans is a failure indeed.

The rise of a globalised capital consensus

The development of the Afrikaner identity project demonstrates that there is a distinct, historical union between the structure of capitalism and the Afrikaner community. Previously various capital factions comprised a crucial group within pax Afrikaner.[118] Today the position of these same elites must be reanalysed in light of both the dominance of a globalised neo-liberal hegemonic consensus, and the engagement of elements of an increasingly globalised middle class with a new globalised division of labour and power (GDLP). This contemporary restructuring of global capitalism, production and social relations means a core workforce of highly skilled people able to take advantage of opportunities afforded by the global economy rest at the top of this new hierarchy.[119] Moreover, the hegemony of neo-liberalism in terms of policy in contemporary South Africa ensures that certain national, as well as global, capital elites are able to maintain considerable influence over state policy.[120]

It is contended that in contemporary South Africa the inequalities of this new globalism have exacerbated those of the apartheid era,[121] so that many Afrikaans speakers are among the best positioned to take advantage of the new GDLP. Despite policies aimed at transformation, contemporary South African society remains in large part distinguished by these 'inequalities of apartheid' which significantly include those relating to the distribution of economic power, of property and land, economic, entrepreneurial and educational opportunities and experience, and the share of income and per capital income of the different population groups.[122] The foundations of this position were laid during the apartheid era when a new post-industrial middle class with high levels of education and a strong skills base was born within a unique racial-capitalist context. Even whilst the education system has changed quite markedly, it remains 'a story of the reconfiguration of dominance in relation to race, class, gender and language dominance'.[123] School performance is highly variable with disparities closely mirroring economic position and race,[124] most especially in the key arenas of science and mathematics. Indeed, the impact of this apartheid legacy is such that there remains a strong correlation between being postmodern and being part of the country's highly skilled, most white or Indian (professional, managerial, information and financial) post-Fordist sector.[125]

With the loss of political control, it has become evident that many Afrikaans speakers are now 'concentrating their efforts on business' most especially within sectors of the new economy including information technology and electronics.[126] Elsewhere the presence of Afrikaners on the

JSE is most evident in the IT sector: 42 per cent of listed companies were headed by Afrikaans speakers in 1999.[127] Indeed, with the launch of the Accelerated and Shared Growth Initiative for South Africa (AsgiSA) during July 2005, and with government reviews of black economic empowerment (BEE) and protective labour legislation in an attempt to implement this accelerated growth plan, the position of these skilled workers at home and abroad has been strengthened. Coupled with the persistence of racial differences in human capital attributes and the possible continuation of discriminatory practices within employment, it means that the racial wage hierarchy will remain and may yet worsen,[128] especially as skills shortages inevitably result in pay pressures. Certain capital constituent parts including 'Afrikaner captains of industry' and a younger generation of entrepreneurs have been able to optimise their position within the new capital consensus,[129] replacing a division of capital most closely associated with the ethnic pact with a different stratum that owes comparatively little or no allegiance to any nationalist economic coalition. Although individualistic materialism and consumerism are raised time and time again as genuine concerns by a range of Afrikaans commentators,[130] there has been little backlash against social concerns including widening intragroup inequality which is coming to define the post-apartheid consensus. Currently only a few organisations such as the trade union Solidarity are attempting to address the needs of working class Afrikaans speakers.

Paradoxically then, neo-liberal globalisation and the post-apartheid capital consensus have afforded the white middle class opportunities to participate in the globalised economy which were not conceivable during the apartheid era. The most visible indication of the strength of these opportunities is the number of largely white South Africans working overseas within the United Kingdom on a working holiday visa,[131] as well as the white professionals, managers and graduates who have emigrated on a permanent or indeterminate basis.[132] Whilst there has certainly been a dramatic increase in white poverty and unemployment levels since 1994,[133] so too has there been an enrichment of the white middle and upper classes.[134] Among both these beneficiaries and the more marginalised of the past 12 years there are strong perceptions of disillusionment and dissatisfaction vis-à-vis legislative initiatives such as affirmative action which has contributed to the changing racial composition of the workforce, particularly at its highest reaches and within the previously white-dominated public sector. Nonetheless neither affirmative action nor BEE has significantly altered the overall patterns of income distribution,[135] which depend more on the broad growth path of the economy, shifts in the labour movement and patterns of social expenditure.[136] It is these and continuities from the *ancien régime* including the structural inequalities of education and privileged access to the labour market which continue to afford these opportunities to the white racial group.

What is not so obvious, given the elevation in capital circles of a hegemonical commonsense understanding of the role South Africa is to play in the new global order, is how cohesive Afrikaans capital has been in positioning itself to take advantage of these material openings. This consensus has certainly afforded capital elites a voice and genuine leverage in economic policies and practices. There is widespread recognition within elite circles, including many from within the business community of which an 'increasingly internationalised Afrikaner elite' is indelibly a part, that the ANC's agenda of social transformation has been curtailed by the financial markets.[137] White capital has not proved to be as vulnerable as was initially suggested, and many of these elites have understood the need to make 'fundamental adaptations' in order to continue to operate successfully under majority rule.[138] However, tentative moves towards an industrial policy driven by an interventionist, developmental state would provide a new set of challenges for capital, which has shown itself to be increasingly comfortable with investing overseas, in Britain, the rest of Europe, the United States and also in Africa.[139]

Thus far the terms of this engagement have been conducted largely within the parameters of the neo-liberal economic consensus. Mbeki was quick to commit his government to substantial and ongoing dialogue with the business sector of the Afrikaner community which has been touted as nothing less than the 'reconsolidation of the Afrikaner establishment'.[140] There is little evidence of any attempts by Afrikaner capital to reintroduce any remotely dirigiste direction or innovative, counter-hegemonic strategies that might in any way tamper with or transcend this consensus. In fact, the evidence points quite to the contrary. The Executive Director of the Afrikaanse Handelsinstituut (AHI), Jacob de Villiers, the only chamber of commerce in South Africa directly associated with Afrikaner capital, has emphasised that despite areas of difference, in general he believes that:

> The support of the Afrikaner capital elites for the government's macro-economic policies is widespread and runs deep. There is a genuine appreciation and enthusiasm for the economic cluster's approach to adhere to strengthening the market drivenness of South Africa. Yet, when government spokespersons do not understand the impact of short sightedness, regarding for example redistribution, the

impact of costs/levies on profitability or the brittleness of confidence in the economy, it blunts open support and creates cynicism. Any interventionist action of government, which harms the free market, is suspect and creates doubts. However, we are here for the duration, so we can agree to disagree on some issues. The joint intention is to promote growth and development and our acceptance of each other's integrity, bring us together again and again.[141]

De Villiers contends that the AHI's approach to the government is one of 'constructive engagement' which is very much 'valued' by his counterparts in government. Indeed, in keeping with the hegemonical commonsense understanding of the relations between government and capital, the AHI has devoted its energies towards the goal of allowing 'the economy the scope to build its competitive ability and to maintain the confidence of investors', at the same time as securing the best environment for members to participate constructively in the economy.

A historically high degree of concentration of both ownership and activities has favoured big business in particular since the transition. In its aftermath, the major policy-related influences on corporate restructuring comprised the liberalisation of tariffs and exchange controls, privatisation and black economic empowerment.[142] According to the economist Sampie Terreblanche, capital has survived a variety of storms since the advent of ANC government 'by adapting like a chameleon'.[143] Indeed, these restructuring patterns have not unseated corporate performance or effected dramatic changes but rather consolidated certain trends. For example, the most successful Afrikaans group Rembrandt has flourished by maintaining interests in different sectors of the national economy, consolidating international interests and 'engaging earlier and in a more integrated way with major BEE players'.[144] It is similar story at the biggest Afrikaans media empire Naspers, formerly Nasionale Pers, where developments have similarly been driven largely upon their own terms. Restructuring was far more muted among the Afrikaans media and the shareholding base remains smaller so that Naspers was able to consolidate by diversifying its varied media interests both locally and increasingly globally.[145] The main responses of this media can be grouped into three processes – mobilisation, privatisation and ideological repositioning – whereby the sector:

> 'played a paradoxical role in this refashioning of identity and cultural citizenship. While on the one hand drawing on international discourses of group rights in multicultural societies and an insistence

on acknowledgement of minority cultural rights on the level of the state, Afrikaans media also embarked on an increased commercialisation where culture was privatised and commodified, within reach of those that are able to pay for it.'[146]

These adroit balancing acts between a strong material position and distinctive cultural legacy typifies the means by which certain Afrikaans capital elites have capitalised on the liberalisation of the domestic economy to reposition themselves in the new dispensation.

With a strong reliance on capital investment to drive economic growth, the terms of this tacit bargain show no signs of abating despite the government's publicly expressed belief that there has been no 'quid pro quo' from business in the form of increased investment and job creation.[147] Whilst capital has been quick to counter any government proposals that might restrict profit margins or political influence, it has been careful to hedge its bets. Indeed, legislative initiatives serve as a useful example of the continuing efforts of Afrikaans speaking and white capital elites to cement their historically advantageous position. Ironically, it was the Afrikaans insurance conglomerate SANLAM and Anglo-American who first cooperated to create formal opportunities for black business.[148] Black economic empowerment remains the principal policy for the sustained transformation of the domestic economy, vesting the African capitalist class with a key role in the 'uneven deracialisation of inequality'.[149] Levels of compliance have been influenced by the shift from a largely voluntary process between big business and black entrepreneurs to a more 'interventionist posture' following the Black Economic Empowerment Commission (BEEC) Report of April 2001.[150] At present, however, it would seem that capital elites are discussing more 'the details of implementation' as opposed to 'expressing total opposition' to the strategy itself.[151]

Historically the record has been mixed. Early empowerment initiatives focused on co-opting black investors, effectively as investment trusts, using special purpose vehicles, a strategy which ran foul of a troubled domestic and global economic climate.[152] Until early 2001 then, the government took a more restrained role, apparently content with the enrichment of a small number of individuals and demonstrating very real ambiguity at disturbing the terms of the hegemonic consensus. In the aftermath of the BEEC Report, however, a more assertive version of empowerment has begun to take shape. Building on the report's recommendations, a new strategy founded upon a broad-based approach to the empowerment project taking in a growth accord between business, government and labour, as well as targets for the public and private sectors under the auspices of the Broad-Based Black Empowerment Act (53 of 2003). The onus has been placed squarely on all sectors of the economy in this regard, including the key mining and financial services sectors. Whilst different empowerment codes are still being drafted, a number of transnationals and larger corporates, including Old Mutual, Absa and most recently De Beers, have announced empowerment deals.

To date, it has been suggested that progress has been 'uneven and difficult to quantify'.[153] Empowerment initiatives have done little to change the market capitalisation share of black-controlled companies on the JSE which totalled only 3 per cent as of December 2003,[154] whilst 98 per cent of executive director positions of JSE-listed companies in 2002 remained in white hands.[155] At the same time, a very public spat between Mbeki and Archbishop Desmond Tutu over criticisms that empowerment appeared to benefit only a small 'recycled' elite surfaced during late 2004. For the most part, however, reaction from business itself has been muted. Reddy and Ritchken have suggested that:

> 'While business and government are in agreement that a process of integrated historically disadvantaged people in the mainstream economy is essential for the sustainability of both our democratic system and a market economy, there is much debate as to how to achieve this goal. Central to this debate is the issue of ownership – in particular, the question of how to facilitate a sustainable transfer or redistribution of the ownership of the economy without destroying the basic incentive that drives a market economy – the ability to make profits for shareholders and accumulate personal wealth.'[156]

Prior to the legislative changes, reaction was limited to those of economic expediency, poaching and the widespread practice of fronting in particular – the 'price of doing business' according to one prominent businessman[157] – as well as sustained pressure against the redistributive ethos of legislation including the controversial Mineral Development Bill. This was despite the fact that the majority were agreed that black ownership should be encouraged and state licensing had become inevitable.[158]

Just how far the terms of this consensus vis-à-vis the government's economic transformation policy will alter is unclear, more so because of new speculation about a revised industrial policy driven by an interventionist, developmental state. More visible and global corporations have taken the initiative in empowerment deals,[159] at the same time as mining companies are expanding overseas operations with the likelihood of disinvestment in

South Africa over the longer term.[160] In fact, disinvestments occurred largely in the mining sector and grew to more than R34bn during 2006.[161] Nonetheless, it has been contended that 'white capital is beginning to wake up to black empowerment as a political and economic imperative'.[162] Mbeki recently praised the empowerment initiatives pursued by Old Mutual and Anglo American, although ANC spokesman Smuts Ngonyama maintained that there are concerns about the 'division between the political and business leadership' which is undermining the 'capability of the developmental state' in South Africa.[163] At the same time, according to Reg Rumney of BusinessMap, the revolving door between government and business in empowerment deals is 'unpreventable'.[164] By publicly supporting these policies, white capital has enhanced its position and continues to exert considerable leverage within government circles and the boundaries of a globalised neo-liberal consensus. It remains to be seen what shape corporate innovations and a growing strategic awareness will take, but all the indications are that the influx of global as well as domestic capital will continue to adapt to a transformed playing field.

It is too early to identify fully the extent of the transformation that is occurring among Afrikaans speakers as a result of this consensus. What is clear is that a metamorphosis of sorts is underway. The reconfiguration of power associated with contemporary globalisation has driven particular political, social, cultural, ecological and gender outcomes.[165] This brief focus on the emergence of an increasingly globalised middle class, as well as the participation of capital elites in the prevailing hegemonic consensus, has demonstrated that ethnic and other affiliations which previously assumed great significance are being eroded as other, different affiliations such as class are growing in importance. Whether this is a continuation of the conflict within Afrikanerdom as a whole on the merits of economic growth begun in the 1970s remains to be seen. Playing the government at their own economic game has proved a considerable achievement for certain sections of white and Afrikaans capital in South Africa. However, it is highly questionable whether the latter represents any longer the old-style ethnic business grouping per se. What this means for the salience of ethnic feeling within the wider grouping must, for the present, be a moot point.

5

THE 'LOGIC OF THE LOCAL' IN CONTEMPORARY AFRIKANER IDENTITY POLITICS

The local level has proved one of the most enduring components of Afrikaner identity politics. At this level of analysis, Afrikaans speakers in contemporary South Africa exhibit the greatest variety of identification or absence thereof, to the extent that it is necessary to examine not only how local actors respond to global and hegemonic forces, but also how these responses differ depending on local circumstances. Introducing a subjective element of group identification makes it possible to address the increasing plurality of constructions of Afrikanerness. For whilst a pervasive sense of 'being Afrikaans' exists, habitually expressed in terms of language and less commonly descent, the meanings and significance attached to this self-understanding are so varied, at the local level in particular, that it is problematic to speak of an Afrikaner nation or ethnic group in any formal sense. This careful balance between the subjective and objective elements of identification does not imply a distinct, bounded group or exclusive identity. Instead it accepts that there are major discrepancies among Afrikaans speakers in South Africa today which are part of a historical legacy and structural change that continue to be very much a contemporary reality.[1] Within this study, the local logics of geographic location, generation and provincial politics assume significance when explaining these broad variations.

By looking to substantive developments at the local level, the increasing salience of both historical and contemporary subnational forces within popular cultural developments and the process of identity adjustment will be explored. It is argued that the richness and variation in identification are influenced by a complex number of factors that include not only ethnic descent and culture, but also multilevel structural change. The question to be answered is the extent to which, if at all, the process of identity adjustment has renewed these identifications on the local level on the basis of consensus in the common pursuit of material, cultural and political interests? This chapter begins by briefly analysing the tenacious provincialism that has dictated the historical and continued importance of the local tradition in Afrikaner nationalist politics. Diversity will be tackled firstly on a cultural level by tracing new directions and dialogue at the literary and artistic edges of the culture industry. Here the emergence of a burgeoning if as yet fragile Afrikaans pop culture among the younger generation takes precedence. To end, the outline of politics at the provincial level and the possible resurrection of a nationalist agenda is investigated to determine whether institutional shifts have endorsed a new, cohesive group politics, or rather represent the best means of maintaining material security. By using the local prism, each theme is meant to raise awareness of the huge diversity in identification among Afrikaans speakers and its implications for the future of any grouping and communal ethos.

The local tradition in Afrikaner nationalist politics

Although the years between 1910 and 1948 laid the foundations of a new Afrikaner nationalism and national consciousness, substantive work was required before the highly polished political ideology that surfaced during the Verwoerd era was properly finished. Regionalism or a persistent provincialism has proved an important factor in the continued evolution of Afrikaner nationalist politics. From the start, communities in each of the three principal regional Afrikaner groupings – the Cape, Transvaal and Orange Free State (OFS) – matured at very different speeds as economic development, migration, unification and quasi-proletarianisation all took their toll.[2] Uneven economic and industrial development, as well as the unequal returns drawn from NP rule by different Afrikaner constituencies, served only to intensify regional (and class) differentiation among Afrikaans speakers.[3] During the middle years of high apartheid, fierce internal conflicts raged about the true definition of Afrikanerdom, its constituent forces and agenda; much of this conflict took the shape of regional discord.

Over the course of the last century provincial tensions ebbed and flowed. Within the NP conflicts flourished within a sectarian political atmosphere where provincialism prevailed. Comprised of four, relatively autonomous party structures, the federal party was riven by an innate inclination towards provincial competition, scheming and intransigence. The persistence of this regionalism made a strong federal structure a troublesome proposition.

Moreover, these tensions – most prominent within the body of the Cape and Transvaal parties, initially *verligte* and *verkrampte* respectively – worsened dependent upon the provincial pedigree of the national leader. Verwoerd was a case in point. Rising to power without preset provincial allegiances, he was forced to build bridges to bring the unruly provinces into line.[4] It was a tendency that remained throughout successive NP governments, comprising a troubled inheritance for an increasingly besieged nationalist coalition.

Indeed, the electoral triumph of 1948 revealed the very different social bases of the provincial wings of the NP. The winning class alliance, albeit with distinct ethnic appeal, was constructed about the Cape, Transvaal and OFS farmers, certain categories of white labour, the Afrikaner petty bourgeoisie and the rising financial and commercial capitalists of the *reddingsdaad* movement,[5] all cemented by a nationalist ideology and more pragmatic material concerns. Yet, the election was won for the most part in the Transvaal where the NP broke out of its petty bourgeoisie straitjacket to win the support of two constituencies – Transvaal maize farmers and Afrikaner workers on the Witswatersrand – who had previously voted for Smuts' coalition.[6] Prior to the victory, vicious internal contests had dictated the shape of Transvaal nationalism as the NP, *Ossewa Brandwag* and a number of smaller nationalist organisations fought for ideological supremacy. Later an immensely influential *Broederbond*, although proclaiming neutrality throughout these early *broedertwis*, came to exert supremacy over the Transvaal nationalist apparatus by stressing a 'rigid "Christian-national" vision of the Afrikaner *volk*, stressing its "anti-imperialism" and the interests of the Afrikaner "small man" against what were seen as the "imperialist-orientated" monopolies which dominated the economy'.[7]

It was a very different story in the Cape where the NP machinery was patently uneasy with the 'anti-capitalist rhetoric' of the north; the *Broederbond* never carried the same clout in Cape circles. Indeed, the social base and content of Cape nationalism:

> 'had long rested on an economic and political alliance between the wealthier capitalist farmers, particularly of the Western Cape, on the one hand, and a small group of financial capitalists in the SANLAM (and later, Rembrandt) companies on the other. The moving spirits in Sanlam had in fact themselves formed the Cape NP in 1915. They dominated the party machinery and controlled its press. What can be called the nationalist Cape establishment was composed of Sanlam and Nasionale Pers, complemented by bigger wine farmers and the NP leadership and party machinery.'[8]

This more liberal nationalism was also eschewed in turn by the NP apparatus in the OFS where, like its northern counterpart, the petty bourgeoisie and rural capitalists comprised the most consequential social forces. Here too the *Broederbond* played an important role, although this was tempered by the size of the province.

Perhaps the most visible aspect of these regional struggles was the rancour between the regional NP leaders which frequently reached the federal stage. This similarly reflected the very different (personal and provincial) interpretations of the nationalist project that also beset the NP; indeed, the '*gesuiwerde* (purified) and *herenigde* (reunified) brands of Afrikaner nationalism had always been marked by sharp provincial tensions'.[9] Even the much eulogised 1948 watershed came at the expense of huge animosity between the Transvaal leader, J G Strydom, and the NP *Hoofleier*, D F Malan, that was to become a running political sore upon the event of Malan's retirement. As successive leadership contests demonstrated, provincialism was to set the tone of the struggle for nationalist hegemony until Verwoerd finally brought the more unruly elements into line during the early 1960s. By which time, deeply held conceptions of Afrikaner nationalism had pulled all three major provinces and nationalist organisations,[10] including various *Broederbond* and party apparatuses, into the mêlée and scarred the cause of unity irrevocably.

The *broedertwis* of the late 1960s and early 1980s proved the point. Ideological battles for predominance of the NP spilled over into virtually all the organisations of Afrikaner nationalism.[11] Whilst the character of the *volk* and that of the nationalist alliance formed the core of the debate, the strains of provincialism added another dimension and considerable fuel to the fire. For the *verligte* and *verkrampte* wings of the NP were broadly represented by each of the warring 'liberal' Cape and 'conservative' Transvaal provinces respectively. Although the issues remained largely similar, by the time of the second and more profound round of *broedertwis*, the old provincial tensions were more or less represented within the Transvaal NP and the *Broederbond*: those organisations where Andries Treurnicht did command solid support. An intra-regional brand of ideological warfare had surfaced:

'The overwhelming majority of the MPs and MPCs close to Treurnicht were Transvalers representing rural constituencies (particularly in the Northern Transvaal), or those urban areas populated by state officials and/or Afrikaner workers. Their complaints with the 'liberal' P W Botha reflected those of their constituents who generally made up those strata of the Afrikaner population which had not shared in the thoroughgoing embourgeoisement of their urban Afrikaner confreres.'[12]

Not only did it recreate the old and familiar quarrels within a new and local paradigm, it also signalled, during the 1981 general election, the start of the right wing as a significant force in mainstream Afrikaner politics.[13]

The end of nationalist government did not, however, signal an end to these deeply entrenched traditions. The history of the Afrikaner nationalist project and its hegemonic project is characterised by the changing composition of the *volk* and the social transformation occurring within Afrikanerdom's relatively short-lived social coalitions.[14] Here a regional prism will be used to introduce shifts in each of the material, symbolic and institutional realms of Afrikaner nationalist politics from a local angle. There is no question that 'large numbers of Afrikaner workers, farmers and civil servants in the lower-income groups [became] disaffected'[15] by the systematic fragmentation of the nationalist alliance. But what is deserving of further attention is how, behind this hard-won consensus, all manner of conflicting national, provincial, rural and urban interests fed into the manifold ideological and institutional alignments that today have made reclaiming any genuine unity beyond the local level a tough proposition indeed.

At this level, the economic element of nationalism's hegemonic project had been very much a mixed blessing in so far as the material security of the farming sector and Afrikaner workers were concerned. Economic upliftment favoured different constituencies in very different ways. On the one hand, there was a massive increase in the numbers of an urbanised managerial middle class and Afrikaner financial and commercial entrepreneurs. On the other, Afrikaner workers and farmers bore the brunt of these remarkable economic developments as their star within the nationalist alliance faded fast. Rapid socio-political change during the 1980s had a real and detrimental impact on wage levels, the unemployment rate and bankruptcies among the white population. Most markedly:

> 'the "protective racial shell" which apartheid structures had maintained around urban whites broke down as state controls on African mobility dissipated . . . exacerbating white fears about physical and economic security.'[16]

The state was in the process of retrenching, pulling back from Afrikaner interests per se in its efforts to deracialise and expand its support base and concerns.

No one group was worse hit by these uncertainties than the farming sector. The national economic emergency was only exacerbated by natural factors including drought as profits fluctuated dramatically during the early 1980s. Indeed:

> 'Farmers became increasingly reliant on borrowed capital and by 1984 an estimated 22 700 farmers (33 per cent of the total) had overwhelming debt burdens. Most of these were in the Orange Free State and Transvaal, and many were younger farmers. At the same time, the government, under budgetary pressure, began to cut back on state support to smaller and poorer white farmers. In the 1980s it shifted agricultural policy towards a greater market orientation. Prices rose, subsidies and credit facilities for farmers became scanter and scarcer, and the interest charges on farmers' debt escalated.'[17]

The government's efforts at economic liberalisation and a change in budget priorities which included increased spending on security and black education had obvious consequences in the agricultural sector.[18] Disillusionment set in, and those most disaffected by the reforms deserted the NP in droves. In many respects, the unthinkable had occurred: a former mainstay of the 1948 nationalist alliance had jumped ship. The electoral achievements of the CP in the rural areas of northern and western Transvaal and OFS were ample testimony to a burgeoning sense of alienation among these voters.[19]

Similar tensions in the cultural and institutional realms were manifested as Afrikanerdom's ideological compass came gradually unstuck. No bastion was immune with even the guardian of Afrikanerdom's spiritual values, the Dutch Reformed Church, falling victim to these schisms; the *Afrikaanse Protestante Kerk* was established by conservative dissidents during 1987. In this way politics was also roughly cast on a local level as establishment ideologies were challenged and steadily dismantled by the growth of an intellectual and popular activism. In the Cape, the publication of *Die Suid Afrikaan* by a group of liberal Afrikaner intellectuals 'promoted not only a more open polity but also a more flexible and de-politicised understanding of Afrikaner identity which could extract Afrikaner culture from its entanglements with state and race'.[20] Similar sentiments were echoed by the populist and Transvaal-based weekly newspaper *Die Vrye Weekblad*. More localised if short-lived initiatives were appearing all the time: a small, iconoclastic counter-cultural musical movement led by Johannes Kerkorrel and the *Gereformeerde* Blues Band emerged in the rural Transvaal. But each association was as much circumscribed as sustained by its local origins and the irregular liberalisation of mass opinion; longevity and unanimity proved all but impossible.

The real winners during this tumultuous period were the plethora of right wing groups who emerged to take advantage of these stirrings of discontent. In the period immediately following the 1982 NP split, this new political culture was variously represented by the HNP, CP and NP. The first was something of a Calvinist throwback, 'unashamedly and exclusively an Afrikaner party whose programme insisted that Afrikaans should be the sole official language, [it] personified the anti-monopoly and anti-English strand of labour-orientated Afrikaner nationalism'.[21] In contrast, the CP sought to draw upon the support of all lower income whites, and 'owed more to the openly petty-bourgeois strand of Transvaal Afrikaner nationalism . . . [and] represented instead the more conservative middle groups of Afrikaner rural and urban communities'.[22] Despite these somewhat eclectic political messages, however, neither party made their mark on the national scene, support being primarily concentrated among poorer rural and urban constituencies in the northern provinces.

What this small-scale political renaissance demonstrated was that, despite the many inconsistencies of the right wing, there remains a gap for an identity-based politics of a sort. Local elections during the 1980s and early 1990s confirmed this resurrection, despite the limited appeal of mobilisation based upon security concerns and later, confused notions of self-determination. The movement mobilised:

> 'through a grass-roots strategy which exploited the organisational weaknesses of a NP now more pre-occupied with state power, and which fostered a sense of cultural betrayal within "traditional" community organisations based on a perception that the state was no longer theirs.'[23]

Indeed, the last apartheid election of September 1989 was a highpoint for the right wing which won a majority of Afrikaner votes in the Transvaal and OFS. Bekker and Grobbelaar convincingly argue that, post-1987, Afrikaner nationalism laid the foundations of a new political, social and geographical home in these northern provinces.[24] Joining and sustaining the link between material interests and cultural politics has become the very real dilemma for this new, locally orientated political movement that draws on a wide range of influences.

An alternative Afrikanerdom?

The nature of the link between (national and provincial) politics and culture – the definition and very essence of Afrikanerdom – was a cardinal issue of

Afrikaner nationalism. Today it remains at the centre of the debate regarding the interpretation and defence of Afrikaans language and culture in the new South Africa. There can be no question of the dense and profound connections between these spheres during NP rule, inasmuch as the 'protection and advancement of the Afrikaans language was perhaps *the* most important raison d'être for the NP's existence'.[25] Although culture was nominally the domain of civil society, the *Broederbond* and other nationalist organisations in fact very closely regulated cultural issues. The real consequence of this symbiosis was brought into the open during the cultural wars of the 1960s, and in the intellectual ferment and popular debate that gathered pace in the decades which followed. In the rigid, traditional version of Afrikaner nationalism, political power was viewed as indispensable to the conservation, advancement and durability of Afrikaans language and culture. The nationalist establishment thus was seen to provide the sole and authentic voice of the Afrikaner community.

In practice, this veneer shielded a cornucopia of expressions of Afrikanerness and a diversity of cultural forms and identifications that continue to flourish. As Figes has remarked of Russia, Afrikanerdom was too complex, too socially divided, too politically diverse, too ill-defined geographically, and perhaps too big, for a single culture to be passed off as the national or group heritage.[26] Yet the character of the link between culture and both national and provincial politics – and the significance of political power (and its loss) to this link – continues to exercise the minds of many of the best and brightest among Afrikaans speakers. The role of an intellectual elite and cultural activists in a new cycle of identity politics within the auspices of the constitutional settlement and a majoritarian democratic system has been concerned with the rights of a minority community inside a new national consensus which stresses unity and inclusivity; one scholar has described it as nothing less than the 'constitutionalisation of ethnic politics'.[27] In contrast, at the local level there is some evidence of the development of an alternative Afrikanerdom; the development of novel, divergent and manifold cultural agendas that variously promote liberal, postmodern, non-hegemonic and multiple forms of identification outside any reconsolidated Afrikaner establishment or community. Perhaps even outside any identification with Afrikaans as an identity marker whatsoever.

The local logics of generation, geographic location and provincial politics are pivotal in establishing the lack of any fundamental homogeneity among non-elite Afrikaans speakers. Identification is formed by the three global, national and local logics, extending along a highly mobile spectrum that runs from *verloopte* (walked away) Afrikaners to white Afrikaans speakers who identify strongly with their ethnic group, and all colour (including black and coloured Afrikaans speakers), shape, and manner of identifications in between. The younger generation is very much a case in point. From among their number, perhaps the 'most lively, focused and sustained' collective intellectual project in the new South Africa has taken shape.[28] They might be heavily politicised, but their politics is frequently highly skeptical of nationalist or group values as the anti-authoritarian agenda of the independent satirical comic magazine *Bitterkomix* demonstrates. From tackling many of the taboos of Christian nationalism and ridiculing Afrikaner stereotypes, today the founders admit to a changed publication that aims to consider the 'many issues [which] are difficult to address within our political context'.[29]

Generation then comprises one of a number of key concepts necessary for an understanding of identifications among contemporary Afrikaans speakers. Although internal dissent has long been an integral part of Afrikanerdom, it has maintained a relatively restrictive focus. Any sense of an albeit fractured counterculture over the decades has been particularly strong amongst the young. Heterogeneity among Afrikaans speakers should be understood not only in historical context, but also in terms of social and economic change. Generation is of significance here in conceptualising changes in identification, as a marker of broader and changing patterns of employment, roles and responsibilities, mobility and new patterns of inequality in the restructuring of social relations. Alongside the logics of geographic location and provision politics, the dimension of time is crucial in that it presents a means of better investigating the processes that shape shifts in identification.

The Gramscian frame used in this study has made it possible to trace the rival interpretations of both Afrikaner nationalism and its hegemonic project within the ranks of Afrikanerdom in each of the material, institutional and symbolic realms. It has demonstrated that 'the very notion of 'Afrikanerdom' was always an ideological construct',[30] always in a state of becoming. What is also evident is that for so much of NP rule, and most markedly during the 1960s and 1980s, struggles over ideology and what O'Meara has termed the 'desperate search for *eie*',[31] overwhelmed the Afrikaner cultural pantheon. By the early 1990s, any sense of a collective ethnic identity had disintegrated along with most remnants of an official culture. What remains are hugely diverse sentiments and identifications expressed by former anti-apartheid dissidents, proponents of Afrikaner group self-determination, capital elites, and a younger generation freed of the political and intellectual constraints of apartheid amongst others.[32] A generation that is increasingly different from their parents not merely in terms of material well-being, but also their willingness to engage with their moral inheritance.

Making sense of these identifications requires looking carefully at each of the cultural, economic and political spheres. Identity is meaningful in terms of how it manifests itself in behaviour so that:

> 'What makes up a culture is not simply works of art (or literary discourse), but the unwritten codes, the rituals and gestures, and the common attitudes that fix the public meaning of these works and organise the inner life of a society.'[33]

As many a cultural history of Afrikanerdom has demonstrated, 'authentic Afrikaner cultural values' have long been at the heart of internal divisions. Prior to the watershed *Silbersteins* incident:

> 'the overwhelming majority of Afrikaner writers had always identified with the political struggle of their volk – whatever their sometimes acute personal struggles of conscience and retrospective horror at some of the policy turns of Afrikaner nationalist politics and ideology. Much of the mainstream writing until the 1960s grappled with issues of the individual and collective identity, with the struggle of the new language to establish itself, with the perceived history of oppression by the British and with the devastating impact of urbanisation. With a few exceptions, mainstream Afrikaans literature had become particularly sterile by the 1950s, provoking frequent calls for its renewal.'[34]

In its aftermath, seeking cultural authenticity came to involve a certain activism against the face of the traditional nationalist establishment. This rich history of internal dissent was begun by the *Sestiger* (Sixty-ite) writers during the 1960s – Andre Brink, Breyten Breytenbach, Jan Rabie, Ingrid Jonker and Bartho Smit were among their number – who were 'revolted by the smug, provincial materialism of the newly emerging Afrikaner urban middle class'.[35] Indeed, the remains of the decade witnessed nothing less than open warfare for the *eie* of Afrikanerdom and its cultural institutions.

The *Sestiger's* riposte to the establishment was echoed during the mid-1980s in the contempt of the more radical *Voëlvry* (Feel free) music movement, *grensliteratuur* (border literature) and cultural activism against the politics, ideology, language and identity of Afrikanerdom itself; in short, 'perhaps the most eloquent statement of the historical failure of the once-sacred ethnic mission'.[36] What is most evident is that this relentless barrage of ridicule, disillusionment, malaise and creativity was,[37] and in many respects continues to be, virtually an entirely internal affair, part and parcel of the grouping's broad cultural pantheism. Any idea of an official Afrikaner culture was very firmly laid to rest during these critical decades. Expressions of dissent became far more open, even as the dissenters themselves were embraced in part by the very establishment they derided. Indeed, a tradition of dissident activism was entrenched that not only borrowed from Afrikanerdom's recent past,[38] but also, by tampering with and stretching the Afrikaans language, elevated its resonance as an instrument and expression of this activism in political and cultural circles.

As disillusionment and dissent intensified, the cultural crisis deepened and debate reached more mainstream circles so that the importance of dissident critics of apartheid in this development became undeniable. Figures such as Breytenbach, Brink and Van Zyl Slabbert became prominent household names, at once fêted and reviled by their audience. But amid this dissension, the 'tradition of dissident solidarity' was in many respects very narrow. That is, it produced a fiercely critical quantity of publications and activity on the grounds of resistance to Afrikaner nationalism and the privileges it wrought. Yet it did not develop an especially creative or constructive intellectual project despite the onset of such rumblings on the campuses and in certain literary works and papers. Although non-white communities did sometimes enter the equation – Degenaar tied the liberation of Afrikaans with that of South Africa's black and coloured population, and Breytenbach's lecture to the UCT Summer school during 1973 likewise referred to this project of liberation in order to 'speak Afrikaans: one of the many languages of Africa' – the model of capitalism and its inequalities venerated by apartheid and the global hegemonic system did not. Analysis of Degenaar's argument reveals that it is:

> 'conducted strictly at a normative level. That is, it proposes a single norm for "the Afrikaner", regardless of whether that norm should be adopted by all Afrikaners, or by none, or some number in between. The argument never reflects on the likelihood that Afrikaners differ with one another on apartheid, or on the need to preserve political power. It does not consider the differing ways in which Afrikaners (or others) could align themselves with the aspirations of the oppressed majority, nor how the meaning of their political choices may change over time. It takes no account of how Afrikaans culture and language has been formed by the context of racial domination, nor of how this

legacy would be contested in a post-apartheid context. Within this perspective, the burden of the past could be shaken off through a simple normative choice. The "sins of the fathers" would not be visited upon the generations to come.'[39]

Nonetheless, the project did open the way towards an acceptance of different philosophical and moral themes in Afrikaner political and intellectual life.

The price of this conformity has exacted a high toll of the 'new politics of Afrikaans'. It is coloured by a 'peculiarly selective continuity' with these Afrikaner dissidents:

> 'It derives its legitimacy partly from the record of Afrikaner critics of apartheid and its association with them. At the same time, it brushes aside a theme which was essential to their critique of apartheid: that of the need for Afrikaners to demonstrate their solidarity with the majority of oppressed South Africans by upholding common principles and values.'[40]

This became evident in a letter signed by several dissidents to *Die Burger* on 20 March 1999 that disputed any 'reconsolidation' of the establishment which might settle Afrikaner identifications firmly in the apartheid past. At the same time, however, the message of these same figures is ambiguous. Most prominently Breytenbach has come almost full circle from preaching indifference to the fate of Afrikaans, to speaking out strongly in its defence. It is claimed that he has identified himself with 'arguments which quite uncritically assume the framework of global capitalism and liberal constitutionalism, and turn a blind eye to the inequalities created by apartheid and now perpetuated by a non-racial capitalist order'.[41] Yet this dissident old-guard continue to carry considerable and perhaps disproportionate clout in the very public debate about 'the Afrikaner'.

To understand the significance of these contradictions it is necessary to revisit the parameters of this debate. In the media and official circles it centres broadly upon language and identity issues, as well as the symptoms of so-called Afrikaner alienation. There is a fundamental assumption concerning the homogeneity of the Afrikaner or Afrikanerdom. One prominent commentator has spoken of 'the current sense of crisis among Afrikaners' which is 'compounded by crime, farmer murders, affirmative action and Asmal's anglicisation policies';[42] the 'only way the Afrikaner will escape the destruction of the ANC's revolution is by launching a counter-revolution of its own'.[43] These issues are then addressed wholly in this context as Afrikaner problems: that is, economic, political and cultural forms of marginalisation that are to be found only within the Afrikaner community. Certainly this is reflected in the efforts of the ANC government to confer with a range of Afrikaner organisations that perhaps reached a high point prior to the 1999 parliamentary debate about Afrikaners. It continues to a lesser extent with Mbeki's overtures to Afrikaans business and academic leaders. The question of who has the (moral) authority to speak on behalf of Afrikaners, as well as a fitting definition of 'who or what the Afrikaner is'[44] is far from resolved. Nonetheless, the defence of Afrikaans culture and language in the new South Africa has, for the most part, fallen to a number of cultural and nationalist organisations – the culture industry – as well as the same band of dissidents who spoke out against the *ancien regime*.

At the margins of this debate are important groups of non-elite Afrikaans speakers who do not identify, or identify only in a very limited manner, with the language and/or group as a category of identification. It is difficult to conceptualise the broad variety of identification among these groups without considering the local logics of generation and geographical location in particular.[45] For here, outside the constitutional settlement and establishment circles, a novel politics and new agendas are slowly taking shape. The influence of postmodernism has been a vital development in this plurality among the younger generation. On the ideological plane, it has opened up a space for the contemplation of multiple identities that reaches beyond the corruption of race that characterised modernity in South Africa. During the 1990s, postmodernism was most pronounced in Afrikaner literary and cultural life where it:

> 'played two main roles: first, it provided a world-historical framework within which arguments for pluralist politics could be developed and extended; second, it provided a challenge to conservative ideologies – particularly within the sphere of culture – which were either resistant to modernity, or at best ambiguous about it.'[46]

Latterly, it has been absorbed into an embryonic post-nationalist identity that is potentially more tolerant, plural and porous than its earlier, nationalist counterpart. It represents the climax of a process begun as a 'coming of age' (*mondigwording*)[47] that has culminated in a political and philosophical outlook that seeks to protect Afrikaner cultural values and minority rights.

Although it represents a break with the ideology of Afrikaner nationalism as a means of ensuring the survival of Afrikaans language and culture, it nonetheless operates squarely within the hegemonic ideology of the neo-liberal global capitalist system. Certainly it is committed to 'pluralism in politics, culture and religion', albeit one that is 'never developed into a larger programme of social change, nor engages in any sustained way with actual historical struggles'.[48] What this means is that although the connections between politics and culture today might be somewhat more oblique, hegemonic and global forces still play a critical role in the alternative project offered by postmodernism and its commitment to pluralism. All the same, the 'local and particularistic character' and generation feature of this alternative is evident as an intellectual current within the journal *Fragmente* (*Tydskrif vir Filosofie en Kultuurkritiek*) and more recently the weekly newspaper *Die Vrye Afrikaan* which are based in Gauteng and the Western Cape respectively.

The historical context against which this project is set is highly significant. It seeks to protect 'cultural diversity and *local forms of community* against the homogenising pressures of capitalist globalisation', and to defend '*local forms of autonomy*'[49] in order to create an 'anti-hegemonic position against the powers that be'.[50] Only certain forms of community and political marginalisation are addressed. In this way, its concerns are narrow and limited to a defence primarily of marginal cultural values and language, and without a wider agenda or outlook it has most appeal within localised pockets or groupings. Its targets might appear extravagant to the majority of South Africans – for example, a future Afrikaans university – but it is all about 'creating spaces in which the Afrikaans language can be vibrant', 're-imaging ourselves along radical democratic terms' and thus 'linking with democratic impulses in our past'.[51] A local framework is a readily acceptable means of assuring a future for Afrikaans language and culture within a democratic South Africa and emergent consensus. *Fragmente's* first editorial explained its purpose as being 'to lend a voice to the unique and exceptional'.[52] It offers the perfect platform for an elevation and celebration of the peripheral.

A similar bias and contradictions are to be found in the Pretoria-based trade union Solidarity, an offshoot of the whites-only Mineworkers Union, which has approximately 100 000 blue- and white-collar predominantly white members. The agenda here typically assumes the shape of a dialogue against state policies regarding not only language, but most prominently affirmative action (variously described as racism and new discrimination)[53] and empowerment initiatives. General Secretary Flip Buys denies that the union is racist:

> 'We are open to all races, but for historical reasons we have mainly Afrikaans members. Whites have joined because of job insecurity, they are not protected by the labour legislation any more. They are feeling

alienated ... About affirmative action we say inequalities must be rectified but this mustn't lead to new inequalities.'[54]

Nonetheless, the union has gained in popularity among the large numbers of non-elite Afrikaans speakers who exist outside the political mainstream but who cling to their version of the Afrikaner 'ideal', by consistently campaigning against policies such as affirmative action.[55] In recent years, the dialogue has broadened to encompass an end to rugby quotas,[56] jointly launching the Come Home Campaign during 2003 due to concerns about skills shortages, protests against crime, and a international tour during January and February 2006 which took in Belgium, the Netherlands and the United States where the delegation was fêted by a range of free market institutions and groups generally considered hostile to trade unionism.[57] Apart from a number of shared cultural concerns and a distaste for selective aspects of neo-liberal capitalism, however, there is as yet little common ground in the programmes promoted by the younger generation of cultural activists and the Solidarity trade unionists.

All the same, the development of strong sub-national identities is not a new phenomenon in South Africa. During the apartheid era ethnic and racial identities were institutionalised by various government organisations and legislation, an event no less marked in a post-apartheid South Africa where the local logic of geographic location in the elaboration of certain contemporary identities remains important.[58] An invigorated regionalist (Western Cape) coloured identity surfaced in the lead-up to the 1994 national elections, partly as a result of National Party tactics to spread tensions between Africans and coloureds.[59] Indeed, Cornelissen and Horstmeier contend that aside from their role as administrative regions, 'the provinces of South Africa can also be said to be *territorial microcosms* of the identity and legitimacy problematique represented by the nation-building endeavour'.[60] In this regard the Western Cape, with its political traditions, provincial power sharing and racial demographics, is somewhat unique in the country. Although the ANC is the dominant partner in a coalition government in the province with the Democratic Alliance (DA), closely fought local government elections during March 2006 saw DA candidate, Helen Zille, elected as major of Cape Town. Despite these political upheavals, the convoluted history and degree of dislocation between federal and provincial policies suggests that 'Cape politics' will continue to influence patterns of identification in the region. Whether the current solidarity between the national and provincial governments will weaken or strengthen such localism remains unclear.

As to the nature and extent of this connection, much rests with an interpretation of the political scene today. Historically, the then Cape Province was the largest of the four apartheid-era provinces. With the redrawing of provincial borders during 1993, the new Western Cape retained much of its distinctive character by dint of these boundaries. It is the best-developed province with a population which is highly urbanised (89 per cent) as compared to the national average level. The 2001 national census confirmed that the coloured population group is in a majority (61.1 per cent), preceded by the white population (19.4 per cent), and then the black African group (3.4 per cent).[61] It follows then that Afrikaans is the dominant home language within the Western Cape, spoken by 55.3 per cent of the population, with English (19.3 per cent) and IsiXhosa (23.7 per cent) considerably less popular; both Afrikaans and English speakers have fallen as a proportion of the population since 1996. Nonetheless, the character and significance of sub-national identifications under the new dispensation is largely unsettled.[62] For example, there is a suggestion that the reason why the New National Party (NNP) and DA were able to garner support during the 1994 and 1999 national elections was because there is 'a strong affinity between the coloured [population] and Afrikaans speaking white people, centred on notions of a common culture and value system, of which Afrikaans is one element'.[63] In contrast, a number of surveys of electoral motivation among different communities in the Cape demonstrate that language and population dynamics have but a very modest influence upon voting behaviour. Nonetheless, the coincidence of race and class in voting patterns remains unexplored in the scholarship even whilst it is touted as a likely explanation for the 'continuing racial polarisation of party politics'.[64]

Recent changes in the political landscape appear set to complicate this politics and the maturity of a distinct local identity and emergent sub-national identities in the region. Much has been made of the fact that up until November 2001 the Western Cape government was comprised of the NNP and, after December 2000, a merger with the DA. The coalition's ignominious slide into oblivion followed by the electoral collapse and then dissolution of the NNP during 2004 saw the ANC extending control over much of the province. With the DA currently governing the unicity in a multiparty coalition whilst the ANC controls the province, the 'decided activism' on the part of the former Western Cape government to use 'the leeway provided for in the national Constitution to enhance province-specific features', and to 'acquire more political power and independence', has surely faded.[65] Nonetheless, the 2006 local government elections and a subsequent by-election in Tafelsig in particular demonstrated the divisions within the coloured vote.[66] The winning candidate in the latter campaign, who defected to the DA in protest at the Independent Democrats' informal cooperation pact with the ANC in the Cape Town metropolitan council, declared:

> 'I'm not a racist, but under the whites we suffered and our people are still suffering. We're still not getting jobs; our voices are still not heard. I'm a coloured and we're marginalised – how can we align ourselves with a political party who will continue to disregard us?'[67]

It is clear there remains an overt concern among key provincial communities that certain national policies are affecting their economic opportunities.

Prior to the collapse of the alliance, an empirical investigation into an autonomous process of identity construction linked to the Western Cape showed that there were two 'contiguous flows' of identity formation, namely: 'identity construction as this is exercised by political actors who occupy positions of power (identity construction *from above*); and identity construction as it occurs within and among social groupings (identity construction *from below*).'[68] A series of unstructured and structured interviews with firstly provincial opinion-makers of political leaders and, secondly, community focus groups comprised the two stages of the research project. The findings are considered to be highly pertinent to this study. On the part of the opinion-makers, there was a 'concrete view' that there is a Western Cape identity that is 'historically grown, reinforced by natural elements, cosmopolitan, almost completely Afrikaans-speaking, constituted of 'whites' and 'coloureds', different from the rest of South Africa, economically stronger, and mainly rugby-playing'.[69]

This same conception of a definite provincial identity was not however reflected among the community focus groups.[70] Instead, they stated an 'overtly local orientation', often to their 'immediate dwellings or surroundings'. This translated into a 'powerful and pervasive dissatisfaction with local government and municipality structures that stretched across the province, and occurred in different types of residential areas'.[71] The subject of most antagonism was 'economic opportunities' relating to perceptions of being handicapped vis-à-vis affirmative action legislation. This meant that the concept of race surfaced significantly and suggests that race remains a 'principal identifier' for people so that:

> 'the investigation of identity among Western Cape residents shows a much clearer conception and acceptance of local or sub-provincial, rather than provincial or national, identities. These identities are

based on a loyalty to, and acquaintance with, residents' immediate surroundings or spaces. Where a conception of political territory does exist among residents, it is in relation to the old borders of the former Cape Province, or those of South Africa as a whole. This, along with the fact that residents lack awareness of newer political institutions, and that they choose to orient themselves to their local environments and local municipalities (even when asked about the Western Cape province), suggests that residents shape their identities around factors that are most familiar to them. Alternatively put, residents draw on long-founded bases of cognition in order to make sense of their own existence. The identities of Western Cape residents therefore seem to be a continuance of older identities. This explains the often starkly defined racial and class identities that coincided with residents' local identities. The fact that most people still reside in racially divided residential areas, secondly accounts for the strong racialised identities picked up during the focus group interviews. The separated spaces among the population groups perpetuate ignorance about 'the others' and maintain the category 'race' in the foreground.'[72]

Certainly, the shifting coloured vote demonstrates the complexity of a population delineated by a range of important cleavages that may be 'regional, religious, class-orientated, linguistic, ethnic or gendered, with shifting combinations of these at different moments'.[73]

Striking a balance between the diversity of concerns and identifications represented within this variety of Afrikaans constituencies has occasioned some eclectic and even regressive agendas. Indeed, unity has been a delicate issue and language has historically proved the most effective means of raising group sentiment and awareness among Afrikaans speakers. Much of the intellectual and popular activism in this quarter is motivated by national policies that are most visibly tackled as local and rights issues. But local spaces have yielded diffuse themes which, despite some common threads, have no singular ethos and have not translated well to the political stage. The deliberations as to the uneven consolidation of the neo-liberal project within organisations such as the FAK and Solidarity amply illustrate these contradictions, as well as the continued salience of class and other divisions including race. With the loss of political power, progress beyond Afrikanerdom demands a conformity that has so far proved elusive and demonstrates the very real limits to the safeguarding of an Afrikaans language and culture today.

Recreating the cultural: New visions of Afrikaans

A more telling evocation of new directions rests within the literary and artistic wings of the culture industry, and the spectre of a thriving alternative or counter culture. Its ambit is far wider, its content more innovative, and its outline far less settled than that sought by the more traditional cultural organisations. Moreover, these individuals are exploring 'an explicitly antiauthoritarian identity with fluid boundaries, *open to all kinds of global as well as local influences*'.[74] At the nexus between the local and the global, this broadly drawn and diverse constituency is articulating very different patterns of cultural identification. Members of the younger generation have historically been perhaps the most visible proponents of this new tradition. During the mid-1980s, whilst their elders and Afrikaner society as a whole were seized by a deep 'sense of malaise and self-doubt', younger Afrikaners 'rejoiced in a new anarchistic, angry and satirical Afrikaner punk rock music and poetry'.[75] Their rejection of many of the sacrosanct pillars of apartheid and the nationalist establishment so revered by their parents was blunt: 'We realise that many of the country's problems over the last 40 years must be laid at the door of the National Party and us Afrikaners. But we are angry about this. We are furious because our parents have fucked up everything.'[76] It was tantamount to a declaration of war from the Afrikaner campuses:

> 'The names adopted by some of these self-described 'Children of Verwoerd' systematically mocked all of the holiest cows of the nationalist culture and sacred history. Much of their work was a direct and deliberate desecration of the Afrikaner civil religion . . . These artists set out to change the outlook (and politics) of the Afrikaner youth.'[77]

In these heady days nothing was immune from censure or ridicule. *My nooi is in 'n nartjie, My ma vrees elke kommunis, My oom het 'n jacuzzi, En ek weet nie wie de fok ek is* (My girl is in a tangerine; My mother dreads every communist; My uncle has a jacuzzi; And I don't know who the fuck I am) runs the final stanza of Andre Letoit's poem '*Curriculum vitae.*' Few could have anticipated the intensity or depth of this wholesale rejection of Afrikaner hegemony and identity amongst the young.

Plays by Breyten Breytenbach (*Die Toneelstuk*) and Pieter Fourie (*Boetman is die Bliksem in!*) angrily chart the ways in which 'a once tightly controlled cultural and political Afrikaner elite – organised for so long on avowedly ethnic lines – is buckling under the strain of memory, of a past increasingly unpalatable to a younger, more open-minded generation'.[78] Younger artists are asking questions of this identity and the political situation in futuristic, satirical performances and even cabaret (*Skroothonde*, *Terre'blanche* and *Swartskaap*) so that little remains sacred. Nash is confident that for this generation:

> 'whose political and intellectual formation took place largely after apartheid had entered its terminal crisis, or after negotiations with the unbanned ANC had begun – the issues at stake have been very different. Too young to have a consistent and publicly-acknowledged record of opposition to apartheid during its darkest days, but associated with its atrocities through the accident of their language, this generation has to establish a "moral place to stand" in the new South Africa. Renouncing apartheid has no cost any longer, and no principle is served by disowning Afrikaans – except perhaps that of self-advancement. Among Afrikaners of this generation a collective intellectual project has taken shape, drawing much of its inspiration from postmodernism, which is perhaps the most lively, focused and sustained to have emerged in the new South Africa.'[79]

If the issues are distinct from those which confronted even their immediate forebears, the nature of the dialogue and directions within this age group is varied indeed. Nonconformity today does not entail seeking cultural authenticity. It does not denote any linear development, comprehensive or coherent agenda. Language remains unquestionably the focal point of cultural activities and identifications, but there is little common ground between individuals as to the significance of what singing, writing or performing in Afrikaans might mean.

Different Afrikaans speakers have responded very differently to the fate of the Afrikaans language and the younger age group is not dissimilar in this respect. Their identifications are similarly moulded by various patterns of integration within the three global, national and local logics. Indeed, the generation gap is most telling again of a local celebration against what are generally perceived as the homogenising tendencies of globalisation. Only within these circles, the local is more strongly associated with 'African influences'[80] and the 'Africanness implied by the very name of their mother tongue'.[81] Undoubtedly there are huge distances still between young black and white South Africans upon the legacy of the past, reconciliation, minority rights and economic imbalances. But there is certainly a high degree of awareness of being Afrikaans and a solid sense of Afrikanerness among young Afrikaans speakers that is to varying degrees far removed from traditional conceptions. Despite this contemporary cultural flowering, marked by a range of lineages and concerns which are indicative of difference as much as commonalities, there are as yet very few signs either of the emergence of a definitive subculture or of collective identity.

After almost a decade of stagnation following the high point of the 1988 *Voëlvry* Tour, and the advent of Afrikaans musical trailblazers including Anton Goosen, Koos Kombuis and Johannes Kerkorrel, a new Afrikaans rock music movement is gathering momentum. Once again young pioneers are using a far from *suiwer* (pure) Afrikaans in a profusion of different sounds that include metal, hip-hop, popular Afrikaner songs and African music. This resurgence does not so much challenge the establishment as celebrate their country and the language itself: this is a 'new generation of South Africans who believe *local is lekker* (best). They have disposed of their hang-ups about identity and language, in particular being Afrikaans. They speak it, they write it and they rock 'n roll in it.'[82] Consequently, there has been a move to 'more personal lyrics' among young Afrikaans bands that are not simply 'trying to write songs for a generation'.[83] Thus Paul Riekert of battery9 can comment that: 'The music is accidentally Afrikaans. We are Afrikaans speaking – at least half my day is. If we were Polish we would have sung in Polish. I love Afrikaans, but I am not on a [language] mission.' Similarly, Ryk Benade says '. . . we do not consider the language thing too much; in fact, not at all.'[84] Whilst these same artists might not wish to take up the gauntlet laid down by the *taalstryders*, they are fully aware of the artists who preceded them: 'Afrikaans *volk* heroes that broke down the doors of conservative crap.'[85]

Politics does play some role in their music in the sense that 'Afrikaans rock is about South Africa. It is unconditionally local, and it is unintentionally political.'[86] Bok van Blerk's elegy to Koos de la Rey, a song that became a popular if controversial national sensation during 2007, is not precisely apolitical. But nor is it indicative of any new or distinctive cultural shift or a longing for the past. The singer himself admits:

> 'The song wasn't written for [a political] reason. I'm a singer not a politician. I wanted to create something for people to be proud of. It's like "Flower of Scotland". There's a warm feeling inside and it's got that feel to it. My generation of Afrikaners wants to be proud of who we are, and where we come from, and our language, this whole Afrikaans things. We grew up with the guilt of apartheid, being told, "You are wrong – apartheid is on your heads." We don't want to say sorry any more. This is a democratic South Africa and we have moved on. We keep on being told that if we have a white skin, we can't get a

job. You walk into an interview and are told, "Sorry." People are fed up. The younger generation says "enough".'[87]

Whilst the innovation and creativity among this music is particularly marked, the space opened up by the establishment of DStv's MK89, the first Afrikaans music channel, as well as a burgeoning market for music in Afrikaans, has cemented this revival. Any political or social commentary is largely drowned out by themes including 'babes, booze and the places they love', a 'natural progression' from the protest lyrics of the 1980s, love songs of the early 1990s, to the songs about 'day-to-day' living in South Africa today. The De La Ray phenomenon is just one small part of the revival and Francois Blom asserts that this 'hand on the heart and brandy glass in the air' trip is not so much driven by his peers as the 'older people [who are] looking for identity'.[88] Indeed, this generation does not fit the iconoclastic cast of their predecessors, nor are they part of the musical mainstream. Instead, a unique voice is emerging which resonates with both local and global tensions: the lyrics of *Fokofpolisiekar* 'infuse the international punk sound with a local relevance and create hybrid anthems out of the Afrikaans suburban South African experience'.[89] Karen Zoid has in part reshaped the Afrikaans music scene with her overt political focus.[90] Although their audience base is increasingly diverse, there is little evidence to suggest that they are capable or even perhaps inclined towards disrupting the politico-economic status quo, or joining with wider national or even provincial concerns. Instead their remit is narrow if at times nonconformist and eclectic. Cultural currents flow both ways: the music of Pretoria-based Pieter Smit harks back to more halcyon and traditional themes, whilst the internationally acclaimed Springbok Nude Girls perform so-called 'macabre rock' – 'a dark and fantastic rip-off act of everyone and everything once considered holy in Afrikaans music.'[91]

Nowhere is this incipient diversity more apparent than upon a growing festival scene that has provided a platform for many such artists. A large number of these festivals developed from comparatively humble origins to annual events which have incited a new wave of arts festivals, appealing to a wider crossover audience of both Afrikaans and English speakers. Yet there is no one true centre of gravity to this renaissance which climaxes annually in the form of the *Klein Karoo Nasionale Kunstefees* in Oudtshoorn and which has deliberately tried to position itself as 'Africa's largest arts festival'. A fixture within a flourishing Afrikaans cultural scene, the festival has run for over ten years and draws more than 130 000 visitors annually. On only a slightly smaller scale, a myriad of local Afrikaans festivals are upstaging more traditional arts festivals to foster an increasingly inclusive, innovative and vibrant culture.[92] Once again the Afrikaans language is pivotal, with regional differences and local connections increasingly celebrated. Moreover, the local character of these festivals is starting to win through so that whilst attendance may remain resolutely white and largely Afrikaans, there is little question of the beginning of a genuine sea change in cultural identifications.

At the same time, the 'festivalisation of Afrikanerdom' also represents a changing consciousness about the meaning of Afrikanerness in post-apartheid South Africa. It represents a clear assertion of 'ethnic nesting' where 'time is in suspension' and Afrikaans speakers can 'step outside their everyday rituals'.[93] Perceptions of marginalisation and the language being under threat drive these overwhelmingly middle class festivals where creativity and originality in the form of visual arts, dance, classical music, theatre and even the intellectual debates which initially excited much comment are increasingly being sidelined for popular music.[94] Instead creativity is viewed in 'market terms' and as 'a form of interior decoration',[95] whereby the heavy influence of corporate sponsorship seeks to comfort that 'cultural sense of loss' which is so prevalent among the older generation.[96] Certainly there has been massive growth in the festivals sector, but it has been a growth in part driven by various business interests such as Naspers who are keen to fan the language debate and 'retain an audience',[97] even though their influence has been scaled back since the earliest days of the *Klein Karoo Nasionale Kunstefees*.

This crossover between a deep sense of marginalisation and the polarisation which disfigures the grouping is readily apparent in the new wave of radicalism among contemporary Afrikaans writers who are aggressively reinventing this cultural commentary. Hall's argument that globalisation brings the margins 'into representation', and into the very centre of cultural life holds considerable weight here.[98] Literature has long stood at the pinnacle of Afrikaans culture, with the community's favourite sons and daughters an inestimable part of this tradition. A key protagonist in this burgeoning and multitudinous cultural commentary is the poet and author, Antjie Krog. She dates the 'traumatic and dishonourable' Afrikaner narrative back to the days of the Boer War: the 'commando mentality'.[99] Her painful testimony to this tortured history comprises a seminal event in Afrikaans literature, an agonised questioning of an ethos and exclusivity that she attempts to reconcile with her beloved country and language:

> 'Was apartheid the product of some horrific shortcoming in Afrikaner culture? Could one find the key in Afrikaner songs and literature, in

beer and braaivleis? How do I live with the fact that all the words used to humiliate, all the orders given to kill, belonged to the language of my heart?'[100]

The responsibility of speech, assuming a culture 'to support the weight of a civilisation',[101] is not a responsibility taken lightly by a new generation of authors and poets keen to transgress traditional linguistic and ethnic boundaries.

There have long been suggestions of a new Afrikaans literary genre. The so-called 'post-apartheid novel' is concerned with the margins of Afrikanerdom: white trash and drop-outs in Marlene van Niekerk's anti-epic '*Triomf*' and a reinvention of the farm novel in '*Agaat*'; misfits and shattered illusions in Tom Dreyer's '*Stinkafrikaners*' and '*Equatoria*'. Changing the face of Afrikanerdom thus may thus have invented a new form for the Afrikaans novel; not so much magic realism as something closer to 'marijuana realism'.[102] Among their number, Dreyer is adamant however that his fiction is 'apolitical', lacking an 'ideological framework' or any 'moral compass'. He talks explicitly of confronting 'a void' and feeling 'very little sense of community'. Nonetheless, he asserts that being Afrikaans is 'still very important to me'. Whilst the older generation confronted the Afrikaner establishment, the challenge for this generation is positioning itself within a 'shared moral framework'. All the same, he sees a considerable gap between the intellectuals who confront why 'being Afrikaans matters' and the masses who want 'nothing whatsoever' to do with the past, and are typically ambitious and money-orientated: he senses a strong 'economic dimension' to the 'whole Afrikaans thing'.[103]

Whether this new generation is willing to become 'the voices of conscience' is far from assured. The notion of an 'organised community' no longer holds much appeal, and Dreyer is dubious about the 'sense of communion among the new millennium writers'. But then Afrikaner literature has become a 'concoction' that subsists within a postmodern frame: a theme common in Afrikaans writing is that the peoples of south Africa are a family under the skin, 'one people' linked in a long and brilliant narrative of voices.[104] At the same time, this fiction has become Afrikaans fiction. Even whilst there is a growing trend to seek new readers and larger markets by publishing in English,[105] it is expedient to publish in Afrikaans because the publishing industry is independent and far more vibrant. Anecdotal evidence suggests that the wealth of new local authors is matched by Afrikaans readers whose numbers have grown such that Afrikaans literature now sells better than English literature.[106] Stephen Johnson, the Head of

Random House SA, commented that there is nothing in the English media to compare with the 'space for book reviews in Afrikaans newspapers and on radio'.[107] These developments do not suggest the beginnings of a new, formal movement or any willingness to rebuild a culturally-based ethos, but indicate that Afrikaans as a medium of cultural expression is gaining in popularity. Whilst these margins may well represent 'part of the future',[108] it is early days and it would appear that there is no resolution here as yet to the many contradictions that beset similar initiatives among contemporary Afrikaans speakers.

Reorienting the local: Politics at the provincial level

The exact form and content of a local Afrikaner politics, as well as the possibility of a nationalist revival, is difficult to discern. There are few signs at present that these conservative political parties and fringe groupings display any more tangible cohesion or conformity than other group-based initiatives among Afrikaans speakers. Contrary to the popular image of a resilient and stable nationalist politics,[109] Afrikaner nationalism has yet to recover from the traumatic transition years and 'a political-cultural split which gave the right wing a massive presence on the political landscape *despite its political unity and incoherence*'.[110] Munro contends that:

> 'An analysis of shifts in the cultural politics of Afrikaner nationalism shows how the pivotal issue in Afrikaner group politics was the relationship of Afrikaner culture to the state and to state power. As a consequence of intensifying tensions between a race-based nationalist ideology, its institutional vehicle (the National Party), and its raison d'être (state power), political shifts in the 1980s came to be interpreted by Afrikaner conservatives as cultural betrayal and the very bases of group identity politics were thrown into disarray. Seen in this light, it becomes apparent that the emergence of a broad Afrikaner nationalist social movement in the mid-1980s has not reconstituted the basis for group politics but opened a new territory on which cultural politics will be played out. No-one yet dominates that territory.'[111]

Historically, a more conservative nationalism within the northern provinces was pitted against the more liberal brand of Cape nationalism. Whilst these geographical traditions remain, other local logics as well as various global and national forces also come into play in the shape of a resurgent nationalist politics, rejuvenating identifications in the common pursuit of group-based material and cultural interests.

The right's agenda is broadly phrased in terms of Afrikaner problems including issues of marginalisation and the objective of self-determination that have considerable appeal for a sizeable tract of lower-middle and working class, and even unemployed Afrikaans speakers. Parties and organisations continue to build upon a potent sense of betrayal and a common enemy, perceptions of alienation and a very real if fluid sense of disillusionment among their by and large non-elite membership. The Freedom Front Plus (FF+) is perhaps the political mainstay of the right wing. Under the leadership of Pieter Mulder, elected during 2001 following Constand Viljoen's retirement, the FF+ has moved inexorably closer to a new policy of 'more than just opposition', sold as 'a home to Afrikaners who love South Africa and who love its people, but who would like to see that democracy is entrenched to such an extent that South Africa will be seen as a community of communities, that offers a home and a place for all in the sun'.[112] Their platform is to represent the 'natural home' for those who desire to be modern and up-to-date and who think accordingly; cherish Afrikaans and wish to promote and protect the language; say crime must be tackled and corruption eradicated; aspire towards economic prosperity and progress; are proud of their Afrikaans identity and who work towards protecting their own culture, education and values; work towards a society based on true Christian values; and, promote regional autonomy for all communities claiming that right.[113] Although somewhat diffuse, there is little doubt that the crux of this programme centres upon 'self-determination and minority rights for those who want it [as] part of the South African political solution [which] must include cultural and territorial self-determination'.[114]

In terms of mainstream electoral politics, the Front's platform has yielded some very mixed outcomes. Balancing the *volkstaat* ideal, which first emerged as the defining principle of the right during Viljoen's tenure, with a constitutionally acceptable definition of self-determination, meant a great deal of indeterminacy in the 'new nationalism's' early political direction.[115] Nonetheless, the party won 2.17 per cent (424 000 votes) during the 1994 election to gain nine national seats in the northern provinces including Free State and Gauteng. Subsequent national elections have demonstrated that securing the votes of key constituencies requires a more expansive agenda. At the polls, the Front's share of the vote declined by nearly two thirds to hover at approximately 0.8 per cent of the electorate (127 217 votes) and 0.89 per cent (139 465 votes) during the 1999 and 2004 elections respectively. Again support was concentrated in the northern provinces, primarily

Free State, North West, Northern Cape, and Gauteng with increased support in the Western Cape during 2004.[116] Most pointedly the Front has come to place increased emphasis on minority rights. It now seeks to improve the 'prospects of minorities' with a drive to source skilled unemployed or underemployed citizens to ease the country's skills shortage, as well as addressing sound economic management and widespread concerns including the crime rate and other issues of marginalisation.

On a local scale the restrictions of such an agenda are readily apparent. Mulder himself is aware that the FF+ must effectively position itself so as to distance itself from the 'traditional image' of the 'white right', and take advantage of the fallout in the DA,[117] if his party is not to come unstuck entirely. There are some few signs that the political right is becoming crowded with Leon accusing the ANC of a 'waging a silent but determined war against minorities' whilst cautioning that his 'is not the politics of the ethnic cul-de-sac of the kind offered by parties like the Freedom Front Plus and the Minority Front'.[118] But there are indications that this new strategy is paying limited electoral dividends. The FF+ contested the 2006 local elections in all nine provinces and six metropoles, as well as approximately 141 municipalities in the hope of holding the balance of power in tightly contested seats. By winning only 1 per cent of the popular vote however, despite a record 79 councillors being elected, the party has not come to satisfying Mulder's earlier prediction that 'the Afrikaner's temporary flirtation with the DA is busy coming to its end'.[119] It is far from clear whether such a manifesto can endorse a new and cohesive ethno-nationalist politics. In voting terms the FF+ is undoubtedly the most consistent performer on the right and among many non-elite Afrikaans speakers, but the scramble for popular appeal means contending with the changing social profile of their key constituencies. Afrikaans youth in particular are concerned that the 'laager mentality' and 'an uncompromising objective of Afrikaner self-determination' simply represent 'pie in the sky'.[120] Right wing parties are widely perceived as being 'too divided to act as an electoral force', so that if 'we throw our eggs in their basket, we lose everything'.

A microcosm of this variety in observable behaviours, and the contradictory tendencies which continue to afflict any group politics or identifications, is to be found within the Afrikaans farming sector. Under siege from violent crime including a decade-long wave of farm murders,[121] a probe by the Human Rights Commission into human rights abuses in farming communities,[122] the renewed urgency of government efforts to meet land-reform deadlines to absorb greater numbers of the unemployed and unskilled,[123] as well as the economic pressures of state deregulation in 1992, rising debt and shrinking margins, there is a huge heterogeneity of political opinion within this community. Farming organisations including the provincial Agricultural Unions, Agri SA and the Agricultural Business Chamber represent this sector. Whilst there is some evidence that would suggest many white farmers have abandoned public or political activity of any sort,[124] recent years have seen an increase in tensions over 'artificial pressures' on land, language, culture and arms.[125] Agriculture has become far more competitive in the wake of deregulation, and farmers have had to reposition themselves as business-driven competitors in a free market that is far more volatile. Many will not survive this aggressive business environment and the new agribusiness model, suggesting that the fears within this community, previously a stalwart of nationalist politics, are as much economic as cultural or group-based.

This certainly seems to be the case in the town of Cullinan where more than one thousand white farmers, many of whom were members of the then FF, joined the ANC during May 2000. Many followed two prominent Front councillors believing that joining the ANC would 'help ward off the threat of Zimbabwe-style land invasions'. One of this pair became chair of the ANC's new interim branch in Roodeplaat and recalled his first overtures to the ANC in June 1999:

'There was a big fear among the white farmers following the propaganda by some parties that the country was going the way of [Zimbabwe]. There still is fear. Now we find out there is no such thing. It took us a few months to decide and we realised that the ANC was the only party which could hold the nation together.'[126]

To these farmers, the ANC's provincial structure was able to provide reassurance that there 'are no plans to invade your farms'. The biggest farming organisation Agri SA is working with the government to resolve land reform and other issues,[127] and there is certainly a growing pragmatism in the sector reflected in a series of land reform summits, bridge-building sessions initiated by provincial governments,[128] and plans by Afrikaans business to launch a top-level empowerment initiative for black farmers.[129] In economic terms, many local farmers have adopted well to the free market. Johan Van Rooyen of the Agricultural Business Chamber argues that for those farmers able to 'embrace the new agribusiness model quickly, there are even better opportunities than ever before to make money in SA agriculture and in the global economy'.[130] President Mbeki himself is keen to see agribusinesses flourish – the Trade and Industry Department (DTI) pays out money to agribusinesses for its incentive schemes – whilst improving the sector's global competitiveness and boosting black empowerment. Many signs point only to an increase in coordination between agribusinesses and the government, although the AgriBEE Charter may yet throw up some challenges most especially to the smaller and less profitable commercial farmers.[131] Even whilst there is a very considerable sense of alienation in certain farming quarters, deregulation has meant the more successful commercial farmers have become integrated into the dynamics of the neo-liberal global market, enthusiastic if circumspect advocates of the ANC's macroeconomic policies.

For those largely non-elite Afrikaans speakers who remain on the traditional right, fringe groups would appear to offer one of the only remaining political avenues. During October 2003, the CP and the *Afrikaner Eenheidsbeweging* (AEB) were absorbed by the FF+, although the latter retains its brand and image intact. Yet with the FF+ only slowly amassing voter support in preparation for a new style of political opposition, the options in mainstream politics remain to be seen. The spectre of a right-wing plot to recapture South Africa has loomed since the early 1990s, raising its ugly head once more during late 2002 in the shape of a plot by white militant extremists based in the northern provinces that was thwarted by the police. But these extremists represent a tiny minority and even staunch defenders of the *volkstaat* ideal have been swayed by the promise of constitutional safeguards.

In the traditional heartlands, the ideal of Afrikanerdom is still strong, if tempered by the widespread understanding that 'cultural or territorial self-determination can succeed only as the outcome of an internal settlement with the government that conforms to the constitution'.[132] The idea of a successful, sustainable *volkstaat* remains little more than exactly that; Orania is a prototype of Afrikaner self-determination that has only just got off the ground on a local level. The political ambiguities that flourish among contemporary non-elite Afrikaans speakers, reinforced by a variety of local, national and global logics, are such that the likelihood of any one political party being able to straddle such divisions is extremely low. Recent years have seen a number of issues which have cut across some divisions such as the widespread disquiet and protests over the controversial nation-wide campaign to change place names, even whilst here too a pragmatism is readily apparent with one march organiser claiming we are 'not protesting against the proposed name but the process behind it'.[133] Nonetheless, many of the policy changes of the last decade appear to have entrenched a deep sense of polarisation among certain Afrikaans constituencies. They have lent weight to the increasingly widespread language of minority rights centring upon affirmative action, economic empowerment and multiculturalism that has been borrowed by certain political organisations.[134] Despite these developments, the current versions of so-called nationalist politics resemble a messy and shallow compromise which does not stretch to any singular political agenda, and remains beset by class, generational and regional differences.

Incoherence remains perhaps the defining feature of the character of identifications among contemporary Afrikaans speakers. From Aardklop to Oppikoppi, a hitherto unprecedented exotic, local and African tinge is colouring expressions of Afrikanerness. Certain Afrikaans speakers are proving more adept at conversing with the historical Other. Different factions have found a different stage in multilingualism and a campaign against a revived Other: the 'Anglicising neo-imperialism' contained within the globalisation paradigm is pulling many local concerns and communities together. [135] Language then is the easy shibboleth which pulls the greatest number of Afrikaans speakers together, even whilst sentiments as to the interpretation and defence of this language and culture remain very diverse. Exactly who or what constitutes an Afrikaner is itself a highly contentious issue: inclusivity in some quarters stretches as far as coloured and even black Afrikaans speakers; in others, it does not. [136] Disillusionment and perceptions of marginalisation might be widespread, but there is no one organisation or grouping which is not still wrestling with a definitive definition of the *eie* of Afrikanerdom.

The lines of division which define these extremities are exactly those same global, national and local logics that dissect the entire spectrum of Afrikaans speakers from *verloopte* Afrikaners to their *taalstryder* brethren. Certainly the continued success of an increasingly globalised Afrikaans middle class has driven a wedge through much of what once represented the traditional Afrikaner electorate. The most vocal and visible proponents of an Afrikaner identity are these guardians of the language or cultural mafia for whom the nature of the link between politics and culture remains key. Many of these figures are prominent in more than one of the plethora of cultural and political organisations suggesting that linkages here are relatively deep.[137] As historical experience illustrates, the idea of a common enemy or threat has real purchase and is manipulated in order to right the propensity towards internal differences. Once this was the British imperialists, then *swaartgevaar*, and now not such much the ANC government and its neo-liberal turn as policies including affirmative action and empowerment, and a few select pillars of the global regime such as the English language and threat of cultural homogeneity. Outside these populist circles, there is greater emphasis upon the development of new and manifold cultural agendas which simultaneously advance a cornucopia of identifications beyond any renovated Afrikaner establishment or identification with Afrikaans whatsoever. It is early days as yet, but the character of any solidarity here is so rich, varied and malleable that it should be considered fragile if it is manifest at all.

6

RENEWING THE CONSENSUS IN A POST-APARTHEID ERA?

During the last decade, and to a lesser extent those preceding it, there has been a paradigm shift in the political economic context of identifications among Afrikaans speakers in South Africa. A wide range of factors informs contemporary Afrikaner identifications. The subjective experience of identity varies considerably in relation to the position of the constituency vis-à-vis the prevailing structure of power relations, and any objective reference has been dislocated by the many differences including class and race that divide contemporary Afrikaans speakers. Certainly the once sound link between an Afrikaner nationalist identity, regime and state which characterised the years of apartheid government, and that sustained a delicate balance of ethnic, racial and class forces, has been irretrievably damaged. Whether or not contemporary Afrikaans social identities can be described as derived solely from ethnic affiliations has been a central question of this work. For whilst a pervasive sense of 'being Afrikaner' exists, characteristically expressed in terms of cultural attributes and less frequently descent, the significance attached to this self-understanding varies considerably.

First and foremost, this book has attempted to understand the dynamics of the process of identity adjustment among an Afrikaans grouping, as various elite and non-elite constituencies have adapted to the loss of political power that has occurred in tandem with a rise in economic influence. The paradigm that has dominated much of the previous scholarship has insisted upon an autonomous ethnic dynamic. The scenario anticipated by this line of analysis – a bleak future for Afrikanerdom under an ANC government broadly opposed to Afrikaner interests – has not materialised. The complexity of the Afrikaner population, its changing social composition and internal stratification, is clear, as this book confirms. The shrinking population is beset by all manner of tensions and antagonisms that stretch far beyond any single ethnic, nationalist or other agenda,[1] even whilst such an agenda remains key to both the national economy and success of the government's empowerment initiatives.[2]

The principal aim of this work has been to evaluate the shifts within the globalised economy that have served to constrict or empower different Afrikaans constituent parts by analysing their responses to these wider structural renovations on a national and sub-national level. By looking at the opening up of spaces on the level of ideas and of material forces upon the local, national and global stages, the study has sought to discover new opportunities for a contemporary process of identity adjustment. The global character of the current world order has had a major effect on the political economy of post-apartheid Afrikaans identifications with the uneven consolidation of the liberal project in contemporary South Africa. Identity is both a structural and subjective condition determined by historic forces and the prevailing structure of power relations. What this means is that only by reaching a balance between these interconnected structural and subjective dimensions can a proper comprehension of post-apartheid identity politics be sought.

To this end, the critical insights of Antonio Gramsci were aligned with a global political economy perspective. This framework made it possible to address the link between ethnicities and related phenomena, and the reconfiguration of power associated with contemporary globalisation which has driven particular political, social, cultural and gender outcomes.[3] Employing this conceptual vocabulary demonstrated that the Afrikaner identity project has undergone several transitions. Here both the domestic and global hegemonic orders, as well as the so-called local logics, provide certain opportunities which impact on the process of identity adjustment. Rethinking the notion of difference so as to conceptualise a 'positional, conditional and conjunctural' politics recognises that social associations are, in effect, historically produced and intersect with specific and local contexts.[4] The concept of community cannot be accepted unproblematically. Through its recognition of power relations and the structures of inequality within social formations (both on interconnected material and symbolic levels) Gramscian theory relates diversity to contemporary conditions. Identifications encompass both a political economic and cultural dimension: ethnic (or nationalist) bonds may be rejected by members of the putative group; the essential characteristics of the group may be the subject of (political) contestation between dominant and subordinate members; and ethnic unanimity may be the result not the cause of historical process.[5] These wider tensions afflict the uneven process of identity adjustment. What matters then is linking community to context, for the 'political economy that links diversity [the conditions of locality production in a global era] to contexts is thus both methodologically and historically complex'.[6]

This work has emphasised the global political economy and closely associated ideology of globalisation as a major catalyst for change in Afrikaans identifications. Wider structural shifts were related to changes in identification within elements of the grouping by analysing connections between social forces in South Africa and the globalised economy. In this instance, the historical context of the transition and the uneven consolidation of the liberal project were evaluated. Since 1994, an economic hegemony that panders to the welfare of local and global capital has been in the ascendant. What has transpired is a class-orientated and superficially non-racial economic coalition that broadly fits within the neo-liberal genus of global capitalism. In this analysis, different connections between diverse local and global structures and agents prescribe a particular ideological consensus and directly influence the pattern of Afrikaans identifications. There are certain contradictions but '[the historic bloc] has to be equipped with an elasticity that allows subordinate classes to align themselves to the hegemonic project – and benefit from it'.[7] Not only does this mean that the affinities of white elites are complicated,[8] but that these inconsistencies can be exploited by certain elements within the bloc itself. The nature of the alliances at the heart of the ANC's hegemonic project and its global counterpart are of considerable importance in this account of the dynamics of identity adjustment.

The issue then was to address the openings that have anchored particular and historically important elements of Afrikanerdom within this historic bloc, typically to the detriment of any new system of legitimation or group ethos. More simply, this has required probing how power and consensus are reproduced in contemporary South Africa. The nature of consensus, how compliance was manufactured, as well as the ambiguities of consent, all comprised important issues. For Hall, the triumph of the global neo-liberal economic regime and its adjunct liberal democracy is about the 'remaking of common sense',[9] although it does not preclude parallel ideological, institutional and cultural agendas. A Gramscian frame made it possible to evaluate the openings for certain elements of Afrikanerdom in real historical conditions by focusing upon the level of hegemony (the character of the post-apartheid class-based consensus comprising ideas, institutions and material factors that materialised from the connections between local, national and global structures of social forces) as an empirical issue. Across each of these levels, the consensus that coloured the historic settlement was sought vis-à-vis prominent constituent parts such as capital elites and a cultural intelligentsia.

It was contended that among these critical constituent parts the dirigiste direction of traditional Afrikanerdom has been overtaken by a hegemonical commonsense understanding of the role South Africa should play in the new global order. Most significantly, these constituent parts have proved to be empowered to varying extents by the character of the transition and the neo-liberal turn which has followed. In this way, a significant number have been able to engage proactively with the ANC government so as to genuinely alter the character not only of particular policies, but also that of the hegemonic project itself, due to their privileged position within or access to the prevailing historic bloc. Indeed, despite recent government concerns about the nature of its relationship with big business, there is little sign of these close relations fading although ANC spokesmen Smuts Ngonyama maintains: 'It doesn't mean because we are meeting business people that they are going to influence us.'[10] The true measure of their influence is hard to estimate but, as has been shown, alongside their global counterparts, they have thus far proved a counterweight to particular (redistributory) tendencies within the ANC government.

Whether or not the acceptance of this neo-liberal consensus in the domestic realm has defeated the ethnic slant of the social coalitions that previously sustained Afrikaner solidarity, or rather signifies a new round of identity politics was the primary focus of the empirical chapters of this study. History suggests that these same social coalitions were persistently reformed so as to enhance Afrikaner material and cultural interests in chorus. More philosophical and intellectual disputes concerned with perceptions of marginalisation, entitlement and belonging, together with frequently parochial quarrels regarding institutional and symbolic power, have become increasingly prominent. A concentration upon the status of the Afrikaans language and closely associated contention of cultural space has bestowed an agenda beset by contradictions. On the one hand, a solid but narrow core among the intelligentsia is wholly committed to a narrow, linguistic and local focus that retains some ethnic undertones in spite of protestations to the contrary. At the same time, this is countered by another, patently more progressive, framework. In contrast to Afrikaner nationalism, the 'new politics of Afrikaans' aims:

> 'to ensure a vital and viable future for Afrikaans, which does not depend on white racial domination or Afrikaner political power. At

the same time, it seeks to prevent Afrikaners from disowning their lingual or cultural identity, or abandoning the sphere of the political in the new South Africa. It seeks instead to defend cultural diversity and local forms of community against the homogenising pressures of capitalist globalisation.'[11]

What it is impossible to ignore is that both share an uncritical understanding of the current milieu. Neither properly acknowledges the highly salient fact that the grouping today represents a minority that still retains a sizeable material *and* cultural inheritance, an aspect of apartheid's historical legacy that has only been reinforced by contemporary structural change.

It has been suggested here that there is a distinct, historical union between the structure of capitalism and an Afrikaner community. Applying a Gramscian frame it was argued that the uncertain consolidation of the project of globalised liberalism in South Africa mirrors the global hegemonic correspondence between international institutions and ideas where the ideology of neo-liberal globalisation is in the ascendant. Among these material forces, Afrikaans capital elites have a singular relationship with capitalism in the new South Africa. Indeed, the director of the AHI admits that the support of these elites for the government's macro-economic policies is 'widespread and runs deep'.[12] By very publicly supporting these macro-economic policies, capital has improved its position and equipped itself with considerable leverage within government circles. Nonetheless, since the severance of wholly ethnic linkages between big business and other divisions of Afrikaner capital under the NP government, a new group that has little or no obligation to a nationalist ethnic coalition is becoming increasingly prominent. How else to explain the scramble for Africanism – 'the price of doing business' according to one prominent businessman –[13] that has determined (white) capital's stance towards empowerment initiatives? Similarly, the continued enrichment of an increasingly globalised Afrikaans middle class prospering within a post-apartheid South Africa and the new global division of labour and power should be contrasted with the growing and largely unaddressed issue of white poverty.[14] Class and race are becoming ever more significant divisions within the Afrikaans grouping.

Where there is most enthusiasm in the form of a new politico-cultural dialogue is within the ranks of a flourishing cultural sector. There is certainly considerable empirical evidence as to the emergence and nature of a new cultural politics on the level of ideas that is involved in the preservation of an evolving Afrikaans language and culture. However, this new cultural campaign likewise reveals the tensions within the grouping, as well as the many and frequently diverse agendas contained therein.[15] Within the culture industry, engagement with the prevailing global consensus has been subdued both by these antagonisms and also the skewed reasoning that dictates recognition for minority cultural rights despite or because of a privileged material position. Although cognisant of the historic and contemporary rewards of a capitalist system which has long favoured the white minority in South Africa, few of this cultural intelligentsia have gone beyond symbolic attempts to tackle the broader ramifications of globalisation for *all* South African communities, and thereby afford themselves a legitimacy with which to begin to address a more lasting, non-formal promotion of an Afrikaans language and culture. The culture debate is countenanced largely within the intelligentsia and has made few inroads into the wider public domain. Without a distinctive break with the moribund cultural agenda of the past and a more appropriate and globalised perspective, it is not a progression that bodes well for the future of an Afrikaans community in post-apartheid South Africa.

It is then at the local level where diversity and a high degree of vibrancy among contemporary non-elite Afrikaans speakers are most apparent. The defence of Afrikaans language and culture might underwrite the most cohesive initiatives here as elsewhere, but the local logics of geographic location, generation and provincial politics carry substantial explanatory weight in accounting for the lack of any fundamental homogeneity. The language issue has provided a comfortable and stable core, but several initiatives have also rallied about more localised concerns including crime, material security, affirmative action and the nation-wide campaign to change place names. What is apparent is that the singular nationalist discourse of the past has all but disappeared as a new Other assumes shape. The traditional tendency for Afrikaans speakers to rally together as a community, ignoring their divisions against a common threat is more problematic because the nature of the threat is now far more complex. Solidarity remains imperfect even upon the local stage with diversity reinforced by all the global, national and local logics.

Even so, perceptions of marginalisation and alienation are coming to characterise an increasingly marked shift as many whites including Afrikaans speakers continue to withdraw from public life. This retreat takes many forms. Perhaps the most common comprises the 'stepping outside everyday rituals' or 'ethnic nesting' which is typified by the 'festivalisation of Afrikanerdom' and rise of consumerism.[16] Equally marked is the 'semi-gration' whereby whites give up their citizenship and withdraw to the gated communities now spread across the country.[17] But perhaps most stark is the loss of the white skills base and young professionals with rising emigration representing the key driving force behind the declining white population.[18] This 'huge cry of insecurity' is perhaps so profound because for many white Afrikaans speakers sovereignty is understood narrowly 'in terms of power and territory',[19] and the sense of loss – cultural and otherwise – remains acute. However, the manner in which different Afrikaans constituent parts have reacted to both the opportunities and challenges presented by neo-liberal globalisation has become the most significant catalyst in determining the process of identity adjustment among the grouping. For it is against the structural backdrop of the global economy and closely associated ideology of globalisation that the dynamics of identity politics and Afrikanerness can now be best understood.

On the basis of the conceptual analysis and empirical exploration within this book, it is not possible to suggest the presence of any broad-based communal dialogue or programmatic axis that would give impetus to an Afrikaans community as a whole. Certainly the beginnings of a new round of identity politics are apparent. But progress away from an exclusive identity towards even a heterogeneous but cohesive group identity has been gradual thus far. Whilst the formal minority grouping is protected to some extent within the ambit of the constitution, the complexity of the population suggests that it represents a far looser and overwhelmingly non-ethnic community. Indeed, there is a plurality of subjective meanings of Afrikanerness and 'being Afrikaans' no longer simply refers to a purely ethnic or even group-based identity. It has been shown that the acceptance of the global neo-liberal consensus in the domestic realm has overwhelmed and largely destroyed the ethnic slant of the social coalitions and sentiments that previously buoyed up Afrikaner solidarity. It comprises an echo of the class divisions which have afflicted the community since the 1960s. So whilst language might be the bottom line for many in this very heterodox community, even here initiatives have been circumscribed as much as sustained by their local origins.

It has become increasingly evident that the salience of ethnicity in the national political sphere has not been matched in ordinary life; that 'some forms of ethnic identity in fact represent, not the hardening but the *weakening* of ethnic boundaries'.[20] So whilst ethnicity is not disappearing – there are distinctive signs of what is termed a 'persisting subjective attachment to ethnicity'[21] – the concept of 'symbolic ethnicity represents 'a far better fit to the emerging nature of ethnic identity – essentially in the desire to retain a sense of being ethnic, but without any deep commitment to ethnic social ties or behaviours'.[22] Among Afrikaans speakers in South Africa today then, ethnicity is rather being pushed into the background by distinctions including most prominently class and race. This is the result of the changing structure of opportunities that must be set against the structural backdrop of globalisation and the character of the hegemonic project itself. Indeed, ethnic politics is unique in the manner in which it imparts a sense of belonging, loyalty, community and identity, whilst simultaneously being connected to the structure of power relations contained within the globalised economy.

There are certainly hints that a postmodern Afrikaans identity might yet emerge. That is, an identity that can forgo its hegemonic content, align its resources to appropriate subnational, national and supranational levels, and forge alliances in the common pursuit of economic, cultural and social interests.[23] Just how plausible this development might be is as yet a moot point. Some form of counter-hegemony would need to be assembled in order to overcome the 'sub-imperialist' consensus compiled by the ANC government, its hegemonic allies and connected global social forces. But contesting any hegemonic form of politics would require the participation of key Afrikaans speaking elites who presently form a critical part of this politics. Renewing the consensus need not mean a renewed process of ethnicisation. There can be no suggestion of any renegotiated pax Afrikaner, but the wideness of the spectrum suggested by that same label now encompasses the rudiments of more alternative if localised and perhaps even diasporic visions as well. What began life as a minority nationalist movement has come full circle, with political dominance exchanged for economic advantage and series of culturally-based and localised revivals in a new, globalised chapter of history. The challenge then surely is to build a degree of rapprochement not merely between these diverse Afrikaans constituencies, but also with the majority of South Africans.

NOTES

Chapter 1

1   In recent decades, the link between an Afrikaner nationalist identity, regime and state which characterised the years of apartheid government, and that sustained a balance of ethnic, racial and class forces commonly known as Afrikanerdom, has fractured. Whilst the group identity of Afrikaans speakers has fluctuated considerably over time, it was most coherent during the apartheid era when an organisational axis of the state and National Party offered privileged access to the state. In the post-apartheid era, the significant differences among Afrikaans speakers, especially in relation to class, have increased as the enrichment of Afrikaans business elites and the middle class has been paralleled by a marked rise in white poverty levels. Indeed, there is a diversity of meanings of 'being Afrikaans' or 'Afrikanerness' in contemporary South Africa.

2   D O'Meara 'Thinking Theoretically? Afrikaner nationalism and the comparative theory of the politics of identity' Paper delivered on 25 March 1999 at Dalhousie University (Halifax, Nova Scotia) as part of a lecture series entitled 'Africa in Focus': 7; and, C Marx 'The Afrikaners: Disposal of History or a New Beginning?' *Politikon* 2005; 32(1): 140.

3   'How Afrikaners are thriving in a black South Africa' *Financial Mail* 7 April 2000; 'If only the adults would behave like children' *The Economist* 21 April 2005.

4   Afrikaner control of the JSE has risen from 1 per cent in 1959, 25 per cent in 1991, 32 per cent in 1999 to 28 per cent during 2002. This progression has been most marked given the decline of English and Black capital, and the dramatic rise in foreign ownership of the JSE. This trend in Afrikaner control of market capitalisation is expected to continue: Personal communication to the author from Robin McGregor (Who Owns Whom) 29 September 2005.

5   'Courtship of convenience' *Business Day* 14 July 2005; 'Mbeki: Afrikaners tied to Africa' *Mail & Guardian* 16 April 2005; 'De Klerk invites Mbeki to speak at conference' *Mail & Guardian* 22 May 2007; 'Leading Afrikaners have say on farm BEE' *Business Day* 25 February 2007.

6   M Keating in: K Christie (ed) *Ethnic Conflict, Tribal Politics: A Global Perspective* London: Curzon, 1998: 41–2.
7   J Degenaar 'No Sizwe: The Myth of The Nation' *Indicator SA* 1993; 10(3): 15.
8   H Giliomee & C Simkins (eds) *The Awkward Embrace: One-Party Domination and Democracy* Cape Town: Tafelberg, 1999: 43.
9   'Fears of SA right-wing revival rise' *Mail & Guardian* 1 January 2002.
10 'Strangers in a new land' *Mail and Guardian* 8 July 2004. The Helen Suzman Foundation estimate that today 430 000 whites, of a total white population of 4.5 million, are 'too poor to live in traditional white areas' and 90 000 are in a 'survival struggle'. Of these, 305 000 are Afrikaans speaking whites and 215 000 are English speaking. Since 1998 these figures have increased year-on-year by 15 per cent. According to the South African Institute of Race Relations, white employment increased by 74.4 per cent using the expanded definition between 1998 and 2002, compared with the national average over the same period of 39.8 per cent. However, the growth of white unemployment is off a much lower population base than black unemployment and estimates of poverty headcount and poverty headcount ratio by race (1970–2000) demonstrate that whilst 1.4 per cent of whites were living in poverty (poverty line at R3000 per capita per annum) during 2000, this was comparable to estimates of 44.4 per cent–47.4 per cent of the black population: S van der Berg & M Louw 'Changing Patterns of South African Income Distribution: Towards Time Series Estimates of Distribution and Poverty' Stellenbosch Economic Working Papers: 2/2003. Stellenbosch: Bureau for Economic Research, Department of Economics, University of Stellenbosch, 2003. Research at the Universities of Leuven, Belgium and Free State has underlined the importance of looking more closely at the phenomenon of white poverty in contemporary South Africa: G Visser 'Unvoiced and invisible: on the transparency of white South Africans in post-apartheid geographical discourse' *Acta Academica* 2003; 1.
11 H Adam, F Van Zyl Slabbert & K Moodley *Comrades in Business: Post-Liberation Politics in South Africa* Cape Town: Tafelberg, 1997: 58.
12 H Giliomee and C Simpkins (eds) *The Awkward Embrace*: 117.
13 R Southall 'The ANC and Black Capitalism in South Africa' *Review of African Political Economy* 2004; 31(100): 326.
14 L Sklair and P Robbins 'Global capitalism and major corporations from the Third World' *Third World Quarterly*, 2002; 23 (1): 84–5.
15 The Big Business Working Group forms part of regular meetings between President Mbeki and key players in the economy including labour, the agricultural sector and black business. The Group consists of representatives for all the major corporations including Anglovaal, Sasol, Old Mutual, De Beers, Sanlam and Anglo American. It was established by the President at the request of the Business Trust with the purpose of providing business and government leaders with an opportunity for an exchange of opinions on a range of national issues.
16 'Big business "broadly satisfied" with government policies' *Mail & Guardian* 31 March 2003.

17 W M Gumede *Thabo Mbeki and the Battle for the Soul of the ANC* Cape Town: Zebra Press, 2005: 156. The author comments that: '[Mbeki] would like to be remembered as the person who brought economic, political and social benefits and equality to black South Africans and who led a change in the economic, political and social fortunes of the African continent.'
18 J Michie and V Padayachee (eds) *The Political Economy of South Africa's Transition: Policy Perspectives in the Late 1990s* Sydney: Harcourt Brace, 1997: 9.
19 P Williams and I Taylor 'Neoliberalism and the Political Economy of the "New" South Africa', *New Political Economy* 2000; 5(1): 21–40; S Terreblanche *A History of Inequality in South Africa 1652–2002* Pietermaritzburg: University of Natal Press, 2002; T Keolble 'Economic Policy in the Post-colony: South Africa between Keynesian Remedies and Neoliberal Pain', *New Political Economy* 2004: 9(1): 57–78; and, P Bond, *Against Global Apartheid: South Africa Meets the World Bank, IMF and International Finance* Cape Town: University of Cape Town Press, 2001.
20 H Marais *South Africa: Limits to Change: The Political Economy of Transition in South Africa* Cape Town: University of Cape Town Press, 2001; and, P Bond *Elite Transition: From Apartheid to Neoliberalism in South Africa* London: Pluto Press, 2005.
21 W Munro 'Revisiting Tradition, Reconstructing Identity? Afrikaner Nationalism and Political Transition in South Africa' *Politikon* 1995; 22(2): 26.
22 A Nash 'The New Politics of Afrikaans' *South African Journal of Philosophy* 2000; 19(4): 340.
23 'Ready to adapt' *Mail & Guardian* 28 June 2005.
24 During the ANC's General Council meeting during 2005, a number of discussion documents were released including one which considered the issue of a united South African nation with a common identity. In a controversial section, the document states: 'We must not regard the white group as monolithic. It is becoming clearer and clearer that white Afrikaners have a different emotional, psychological and material relationship to Africa and South Africa compared to other whites. There are many signs indicating that Afrikaners are embracing the new South Africa and an Africanism more readily than English-speaking whites.' For the full text see: African National Congress *Discussion Document: The National Question* (www.anc.org.za/ancdocs/ngcouncils/2005/nationalquestion.html).
25 B du Toit *The Boers in East Africa: Ethnicity and Identity* Westport: Bergin & Garvey, 1998; J van Rooyen *The New Great Trek: The Story of South Africa' White Exodus* Pretoria, Unisa Press, 2000.
26 This assorted faction includes organisations such as the Freedom Front Plus, *Afrikanerbond, Stigting vir Afrikaans, Afrikaanse Taal-en Kultuurvereninging*, Solidarity, *Pro-Afrikaanse Aksiegroep*, and the *Federasie Afrikaanse Kultuurvereniginge*, all wary of so-called 'Afrikaner alienation' under the ANC government to varying degrees.
27 I Taylor 'Globalisation Studies and the Developing World: making international political economy truly global' *Third World Quarterly* 2005; 26(7): 1028.

28 M Ebata & B Neufeld (eds) *Confronting the Political in International Relations* Basingstoke: Macmillan, 2000: 47–71.
29 R Tooze 'Understanding the Global Political Economy: Applying Gramsci' *Millennium* 1990; 19 (2): 278.
30 W Munro 'Revisiting Tradition, Reconstructing Identity? Afrikaner Nationalism and Political Transition in South Africa' *Politikon* 1995; 22(2): 7.
31 C Marx 'The Afrikaners: Disposal of History or a New Beginning' *Politikon* 2005; 32(1): 140.
32 A Butler *Democracy and Apartheid: Political Theory, Comparative Politics and the Modern South Africa State* London: Macmillan, 1998: 37.
33 A du Toit 'No Chosen People: The Myth of the Calvinist Origins of Afrikaner Nationalism and Racial Ideology' *American Historical Review* 1983; 88(4): 920–952; and, 'Puritans in Africa? Afrikaner "Calvinism" and Kuyperian Neo-Calvinism in Late Nineteenth-Century South Africa' *Comparative Studies in Society and History* 1985; 27(2): 209–240.
34 A Nash 'The New Politics of Afrikaans' *South African Journal of Philosophy* 2000; 19(4): 361.
35 H Adam & H Giliomee *The Rise and Crisis of Afrikaner Power* Cape Town: David Philip, 1979; and, D O'Meara *Volkskapitalismse: Class, capital and ideology in the development of Afrikaner nationalism, 1934–1948* Johannesburg: Ravan Press, 1983.
36 H Giliomee in: H Adam and H Giliomee *The Rise and Crisis of Afrikaner Power*: 107. For Giliomee's most recent thesis on the idea of Afrikaner distinctiveness, see: H Giliomee: *The Afrikaners: Biography of a People* Cape Town: Tafelberg, 2003: Chapter 17.
37 H Giliomee in: L Vail (ed) *The Creation of Tribalism in Southern Africa* Berkeley, CA: University of California Press, 1989: 49.
38 D O'Meara *Volkskapitalisme*: Chapter 11. Materialist analyses view the decline of the National Party as a 'process of class realignment' within its own ranks. For example, see: C Charney 'Class Conflict and the National Party Split' *Journal of Southern African Studies* 1984; 10(2): 269.
39 R Brubaker & F Cooper 'Beyond "identity"' *Theory and Society* 2000; 29(1): 27.
40 S Gill in: S Gill (ed) *Gramsci, Historical Materialism and International Relations* Cambridge: Cambridge University Press, 1993: 23.
41 S Cornelissen & S Horstmeier 'The social and political construction of identities in the new South Africa: an analysis of the Western Cape Province' *Journal of Modern African Studies* 2002; 40(1): 79.
42 J N Pieterse 'Deconstructing/reconstructing ethnicity' *Nations and Nationalism* 1997; 3(3): 366.
43 J Degenaar *The Roots of Nationalism* Cape Town: Academica, 1983: 40.
44 H Giliomee *The Afrikaners: Biography of a People* Cape Town: Tafelberg, 2003: xix.
45 W Munro 'Revisiting Tradition, Reconstructing Identity? Afrikaner Nationalism and Political Transition in South Africa' *Politikon* 1995; 22(2): 9.
46 D O'Meara *Forty Lost Years: The apartheid state and the politics of the National Party, 1948–1994* Randburg: Ravan Press, 1996: 148.
47 W Munro 'Revisiting Tradition, Reconstructing Identity? Afrikaner Nationalism and Political Transition in South Africa' *Politikon* 1995; 22(2): 12.

48 The author would like to thank Philip Nel for his comments on this issue.
49 P Cerny 'Paradoxes of the Competition State: The Dynamics of Political Globalisation' *Government and Opposition* 1997; 32(2): 256.
50 B Meyer & P Geschiere (eds) *Globalisation and Identity: Dialectics of Flow and Closure* Oxford: Blackwell, 1999: 7.
51 J Scholte 'The geography of collective identities in a globalising world' *Review of International Political Economy* 1996; 3(4): 578.
52 R Robertson in: M Featherstone, S Lash & R Robertson (eds) *Global Modernities* London: Sage, 1995: 35.
53 S Hall in: S Hall, D Held & A McGrew (eds) *Modernity and Its Futures* Cambridge: Polity Press, 1992: 310.
54 J Mittelman *The Globalisation Syndrome: Transformation and Resistance* Princeton: Princeton University Press, 2000: 227.
55 M Featherstone, S Lash & R Robertson (eds) *Global Modernities*: 2–3.
56 I Taylor & P Vale 'South Africa's Transition Revisited: Globalisation as Vision and Virtue' *Global Society* 2000; 14(3): 402.
57 W Munro 'Revisiting Tradition, Reconstructing Identity? Afrikaner Nationalism and Political Transition in South Africa' *Politikon* 1995; 22(2): 2.
58 During the 2004 elections, Pieter Mulder's Freedom Front rallied in the Platteland in a campaign which de-emphasised race and the hopeless project of a volkstaat for Afrikaners, and instead spoke the modern international language of minority rights and ethnic self-determination: 'And these little piggies had none' *Mail & Guardian* 16 April 2004.
59 A Morton 'Historicising Gramsci: situating ideas in and beyond their context' *Review of International Political Economy* 2003; 10(1): 136.
60 R Cox 'Gramsci, Hegemony and International Relations: An Essay in Method' *Millennium* 1983; 12(2): 164.
61 E Wilmsen & P McAllister (eds) *The Politics of Difference*: 83.
62 A Bielder & A Morton 'Introduction: International Relations as Political Theory' *Critical Review of International Social and Political Philosophy* 2005; 8(4): 383–4.
63 S Hall in: D Morley & K-H Chen (eds) *Stuart Hall: Critical Dialogues in Cultural Studies* London: Routledge, 1996: 429–30.
64 M Rupert in: S Gill (eds) *Gramsci, Historical Materialism and International Relations* Cambridge: Cambridge University Press, 1993; 81.
65 H Marais *South Africa: Limits to Change: The Political Economy of Transition in South Africa* Cape Town: University of Cape Town Press, 2001: 230–1.
66 J Netshitenzhe in: W Gumede *Thabo Mbeki and the Battle for the Soul of the ANC* Cape Town: Zebra Press, 2005: 116.
67 S Gill 'Globalisation, Market Civilisation and Disciplinary Neo-liberalism' *Millennium* 1995; 24(3): 402.
68 I Taylor & P Vale 'South Africa's Transition Revisited: Globalisation as Vision and Virtue' *Global Society* 2000; 14(3): 399.
69 R Cox 'Civil society at the turn of the millennium: prospects for an alternative world order' *Review of International Studies* 1999; 25: 12.
70 A number of policy discussion documents were distributed to ANC structures

as part of the preparations for the ANC National Policy Conference during June 2007, and the subsequent National Conference during December 2007. As part of the economic policy debate the nature of the post-apartheid state as a developmental state and the significance of state intervention were raised. For the full text see: African National Congress *Discussion Document: Economic Transformation for a National Democratic Society* (http://www.anc.org.za/ancdocs/policy/2007/discussion/econ_transformation.html).

71 'ANC succession dogfight taking on ideological edge' *Business Day* 12 September 2006; 'South Africa hit by strike as left challenges ANC leadership' *The Guardian* 13 June 2007.
72 H Marais *South Africa: Limits to Change*: 2.
73 W Munro 'Revisiting Tradition, Reconstructing Identity? Afrikaner Nationalism and Political Transition in South Africa' *Politikon* 1995; 22(2): 11.
74 I Taylor & P Vale 'South Africa's Transition Revisited: Globalisation as Vision and Virtue' *Global Society* 2000; 14(3): 406.
75 P Bond 'Pretoria's perspective on globalisation: a critique' *Politikon* 2001; 28(1): 85.
76 T Keolble 'Economic policy in the Post-colony: South Africa between Keynesian Remedies and Neoliberal Pain' *New Political Economy* 2004; 9(1): 59.
77 W Gumede *Thabo Mbeki and the Battle for the Soul of the ANC*: 91.
78 A Habib, D Pillay & A Desai 'South Africa and the Global Order: The Structural Conditioning of a Transition to Democracy' *Journal of Contemporary African Studies* 1998; 16(1): 105.
79 W Gumede *Thabo Mbeki and the Battle for the Soul of the ANC*: 64.
80 S Andreasson 'Economic Reforms and "Virtual Democracy" in South Africa and Zimbabwe: The Incompatibility of Liberalisation, Inclusion and Development' *Journal of Contemporary African Studies* 2003; 21(3): 391.
81 'ANC will win poll but lose credibility' *Business Day* 21 February 2006.
82 'ANC's year of shame' *Mail & Guardian* 21 November 2006.
83 'ANC papers over cracks in alliance' *Mail & Guardian* 26 February 2007.
84 P Bond 'The ANC's "Left Turn" and South African Sub-imperialism' *Review of African Political Economy* 2004; 102: 600–2.
85 'Foreign firms fret over BEE' *Mail & Guardian* 25 January 2006; 'SA losing out on billions in mining investment' *Business Day* 12 June 2007.
86 P Nel 'Conceptions of globalisation among the South African elite' *Global Dialogue* 1999; 4(1): 23.
87 'Afrikaans under threat, says FW de Klerk' *Mail & Guardian* 27 January 2007.
88 R Alba *Ethnic Identity: The Transformation of White America* New Haven, CT: Yale University Press, 1990: 3.

Chapter 2

1 J Degenaar *The Roots of Nationalism* Cape Town: Academica, 1983: 40. The author is careful to adjudicate Afrikaner nationalism in a strict sense as a

movement commencing in the 1930s, closely linked to the concept of volk and directly responsible for Afrikanerdom's rise to power in 1948.
2   A Butler *Democracy and Apartheid: Political Theory, Comparative Politics and the Modern South African State* London: Macmillan, 1998: 37.
3   A Grundlingh & H Sapire 'From Feverish Festival to Repetitive Ritual? The Changing Fortunes of Great Trek Mythology in an Industrialising South Africa, 1938–1988' *South African Historical Journal* 1989; 21: 25. Emphasis in the original.
4   H Giliomee in: H Adam & H Giliomee *The Rise and Crisis of Afrikaner Power* Cape Town: David Philip, 1979: 107.
5   Ibid: 156–7.
6   D O'Meara *Forty Lost Years: The apartheid state and the politics of the National Party, 1948–1994* Randburg: Ravan Press, 1996: 42.
7   D O'Meara *Volkskapitalisme: Class, Capital and Ideology in the Development of Afrikaner Nationalism* Cambridge: Cambridge University Press, 1983: 243.
8   Ibid: Chapter 11.
9   D Posel 'The Meaning of Apartheid Before 1948: Conflicting Interests and Forces within the Afrikaner Nationalist Alliance' *Journal of Southern African Studies* 1987; 14(1): 125.
10 H Giliomee 'Constructing Afrikaner Nationalism' *Journal of Asian and African Studies* 1983; 18(1–2): 91.
11 A Butler *Democracy and Apartheid: Political Theory, Comparative Politics and the Modern South African State* London: Macmillan, 1998: 46.
12 H Giliomee in: L Vail (ed) *The Creation of Tribalism in Southern Africa*: 22.
13 T Keegan *Colonial South Africa and The Origins of The Racial Order* London: Leicester University Press, 1996: 281.
14 S Marks & S Trapido in: S Marks & S Trapido (eds) *The politics of race, class and nationalism in twentieth-century South Africa* London: Longman, 1993: 3.
15 L Guelke in: R Elphick & H Giliomee (eds) *The Shaping of South Africa Society, 1652–1840* Cape Town: Longman, 1989: 93.
16 A Butler *Democracy and Apartheid*: 10.
17 A du Toit 'Captive to the Nationalist Paradigm: Professor F A van Jaarsveld and the historical evidence for the Afrikaner's ideas on his Calling and Mission' *South African Historical Journal* 1984; 16: 57.
18 A Butler *Democracy and Apartheid*: 12.
19 H Giliomee in: H Adam & H Giliomee *The Rise and Crisis of Afrikaner Power*: 103.
20 H Giliomee in: L Vail (ed) *The Creation of Tribalism in Southern Africa*: 32.
21 G Schutte in: E Tonkin, M McDonald & M Chapman (eds) *History and Ethnicity* London: Routledge, 1989: 222–23.
22 H Giliomee *Surrender Without Defeat: Afrikaners and The South African Miracle* Braamfontein: South African Institute of Race Relations, 1997: 10–11.
23 For a brief summary of this fundamental shift, see: S Dubow 'Afrikaner Nationalism, Apartheid and The Conceptualisation of "Race"' *Journal of African History* 1992; 33: 211.
24 D O'Meara *Forty Lost Years*: 27.
25 A Grundlingh & H Sapire 'From Feverish Festival to Repetitive Ritual? The

Changing Fortunes of Great Trek Mythology in an Industrialising South Africa, 1938–1988' *South African Historical Journal* 1989; 21: 23.
26 J Degenaar *The Roots of Nationalism*: 57.
27 For a more detailed investigation into the construction of ethnic identity using the Afrikaans language, see: I Hofmeyr in: S Marks & S Trapido (eds) *The politics of race, class and nationalism in twentieth-century South Africa*: Chapter Three.
28 D O'Meara *Forty Lost Years*: 40–41.
29 A Butler *Democracy and Apartheid*: 19.
30 Ibid: 19–20.
31 D Posel *The Making of Apartheid, 1948–61: Conflict and Compromise* Oxford: Clarendon Press, 1991: 60.
32 W Munro 'Revisiting Tradition, Reconstructing Identity? Afrikaner Nationalism and Political Transition in South Africa' *Politikon* 1995; 22(2): 8.
33 S Terreblanche in: U van Beek (ed) *South Africa and Poland in Transition: A Comparative Perspective* Pretoria: HSRC, 1995: 341–2.
34 For an exemplary examination of this mobilisation, see: D O'Meara *Volkskapitalisme*.
35 S Terreblanche in: U van Beek (ed) *South Africa and Poland in Transition*: 347.
36 D Posel 'The Making of Apartheid Before 1948: Conflicting Interests and Forces within the Afrikaner Nationalist Alliance' *Journal of Southern African Studies* 1987; 14(1): 125.
37 Ibid: 126. Emphasis in the original.
38 W Munro 'Revisiting Tradition, Reconstructing Identity? Afrikaner Nationalism and Political Transition in South Africa' *Politikon* 1995; 22(2): 9.
39 Ibid: 9.
40 D O'Meara *Forty Lost Years*: 43.
41 F van Zyl Slabbert in: L Thompson & J Butler (eds) *Change in Contemporary South Africa* Berkeley, CA: University of California Press, 1975: 9–10.
42 D O'Meara *Forty Lost Years*: 64–5.
43 D Posel *The Making of Apartheid*: 227. Posel offers four reasons for this shift, namely: concerns over the success of controlled urbanisation; the growing marginalisation of reformists within the alliance; the centralisation of the state apparatus; and, rising political confidence following the victorious 1958 election.
44 A Butler *Democracy and Apartheid*: 22.
45 R Price *The Apartheid State in Crisis: Political Transformation in South Africa, 1975–1990* Oxford: Oxford University Press, 1991: 14.
46 D O'Meara *Forty Lost Years*: 65. Emphasis added.
47 P Cillié 'Bestek Van Apartheid: Wat is apartheid?' *Die Suid-Afrikaan* Spring 1988: 18. Cited in: H Giliomee & L Schlemmer *From Apartheid to Nation-Building* Cape Town: Oxford University Press, 1989: 63.
48 A du Toit in: L Thompson & J Butler (eds) *Change in Contemporary South Africa*: 47.
49 H Marais *South Africa: Limits to Change*: 19.
50 M Morris in: S Gelb (ed) *South Africa's Economic Crisis*: 40.
51 D O'Meara *Forty Lost Years*: 148.
52 H Marais *South Africa Limits to Change: The Political Economy of Transition* Cape Town: University of Cape Town Press, 2001: 21.

53 J Saul *Recolonisation and Resistance: Southern Africa in the 1990s* Trenton, NJ: Africa World Press, 1993: 93–4.
54 For a full overview of the contradictions of the apartheid economy, see: S Gelb (ed) *South Africa's Economic Crisis*.
55 A Butler *Democracy and Apartheid*: 45–6.
56 S Gelb in: S Gelb (ed) *South Africa's Economic Crisis*: 20.
57 D O'Meara *Forty Lost Years*: 189.
58 M Morris in: S Gelb (ed) *South Africa's Economic Crisis*: 43.
59 *White Paper of Defence and Armaments Supply* Pretoria: Department of Defence, 1977: 5.
60 H Giliomee in: J Brewer (ed) *Can South Africa Survive?*: 126.
61 D O'Meara *Forty Lost Years*: 48.
62 Ibid: 166.
63 Ibid: 266–7.
64 H Marais *South Africa: Limits to Change*: 3.
65 W Munro 'Revisiting Tradition, Reconstructing Identity? Afrikaner Nationalism and Political Transition in South Africa' *Politikon* 1995; 22(2): 13.
66 Ibid: 12. My emphasis.
67 H Giliomee in: N Etherington (ed) *Peace, Politics and Violence in the New South Africa* Melbourne: Hans Zell, 1992: 177.
68 W Munro 'Revisiting Tradition, Reconstructing Identity? Afrikaner Nationalism and Political Transition in South Africa' *Politikon* 1995; 22(2): 12–3.
69 R Price *The Apartheid State in Crisis*: 145.
70 H Marais *South Africa: Limits to Change*: 56.
71 D O'Meara *Forty Lost Years*: 323.
72 H Giliomee *Surrender Without Defeat: Afrikaners and The South Africa Miracle* Braamfontein: South African Institute of Race Relations, 1997: 17.
73 H Giliomee in: N Etherington (ed) *Peace, Politics and Violence in the New South Africa*: 169.
74 D O'Meara *Volkskapitalisme*: 251.
75 Ibid: 144.
76 H Giliomee in: R Schrire (ed) *Malan to De Klerk: Leadership in the Apartheid State* London: Hurst and Company, 1994: 125.
77 W Munro 'Revisiting Tradition, Reconstructing Identity? Afrikaner Nationalism and Political Transition in South Africa' *Politikon* 1995; 22(2): 22.
78 D O'Meara *Forty Lost Years*: 313.
79 M McDonald & W James 'The Hand on the Tiller: the Politics of State and Class in South Africa' *Journal of Modern African Studies* 1993; 31(3): 365–6.
80 D O'Meara *Forty Lost Years*: 136–7.
81 H Giliomee in: H Adam & H Giliomee *The Rise and Crisis of Afrikaner Power*: 169.
82 D O'Meara *Forty Lost Years*: 141.
83 H Giliomee in: H Adam & H Giliomee *The Rise and Crisis of Afrikaner Power*: 118.
84 J Saul *Recolonisation and Resistance*: 94.

85 M Mann in: P Frankel, N Pines & M Swilling (eds) *State, Resistance and Change in South Africa* Johannesburg: Southern Books, 1988: 55.
86 D O'Meara *Forty Lost Years*: 177.
87 H Marais *South Africa:Limits to Change*: 65. My emphasis.
88 In this speech to the Natal Congress of the National Party on 15 August 1985, it was widely expected that Botha would announce fundamental reforms to the apartheid system; the so-called 'crossing of the rubicon'. Instead, he defiantly affirmed a commitment to change but at his own speed and on his terms. A debt standstill followed as foreign investment dried up and leading investors departed South Africa.
89 M Morris in: S Gelb *South Africa's Economic Crisis*: 41.
90 D O'Meara *Forty Lost Years*: 386.
91 A Wassenaar *Assault on private enterprise: the freeway to communism* Cape Town: Tafelburg, 1977.
92 R Davies, D O'Meara & S Dlamini *The Struggle for South Africa: A reference guide to movements, organisations and institutions* London: Zed Books, 1988: 122.
93 A Habib, D Pillay and A Desai 'South Africa and the Global Order: The Structural Conditioning of a Transition to Democracy *Journal of Contemporary African Studies* 1998; 16(1): 106.
94 R Schrire *Adapt or Die: The End of White Politics in South Africa* London: Hurst & Company, 1991: 134.
95 M Murray *Revolution Deferred: The Painful Birth of Post-Apartheid South Africa* London: Verso, 1994: 4.

Chapter 3

1 'Afrikaner Helping Hands' *Financial Mail* 19 May 2006.
2 J Seekings & N Nattrass *Class, Race, and Inequality in South Africa* Scottsville: University of KwaZulu-Natal Press, 2006: 305.
3 M MacDonald *Why Race Matters in South Africa* Scottsville: University of KwaZulu-Natal Press, 2006: 152.
4 T Koelble *The Global Economy and Democracy in South Africa* New Brunswick, NJ: Rutgers University Press, 1998: 23–4.
5 M Rupert & H Smith (eds) *Historical Materialism and Globalisation* London: Routledge, 2002: 291.
6 A Hurrell & N Woods 'Globalisation and Inequality' *Millennium* 1995; 24(3): 461.
7 P Bond *Elite Transition: From Apartheid to Neoliberalism in South Africa* London: Pluto Press, 2000: 54.
8 V Padayachee in: J Michie & V Padaychee (eds) *The Political Economy of South Africa's Transition: Policy Perspectives in the Late 1990s* Sydney: Harcourt Brace, 1997: 41.
9 H Marais *South Africa: Limits to Change*: 135.
10 T Jackson Lears 'The Concept of Cultural Hegemony: Problems and Possibilities' *American Historical Review* 1985; 90(3): 571.

11 T Lodge in: A Leftwich (ed) *Democracy and Development: Theory and Practice* Cambridge: Polity Press, 1996: 194–5.
12 H Marais *South Africa: Limits to Change*: 94.
13 Ibid: 94.
14 P Bond in: E Maganya & R Houghton (eds) *Transformation in South Africa? Policy Debates in the 1990s* Braamfontein: Institute for African Alternatives, 1996: 15.
15 W Gumede *Thabo Mbeki and the Battle for the Soul of the ANC* Cape Town: Zebra Press, 2005: 56.
16 Speech by Deputy President Thabo Mbeki at the opening of the debate in the National Assembly on 'Reconciliation and Nation-Building', Cape Town, 29 May 1998. For a full version of the speech see: http://www.anc.org.za/ancdocs/history/mbeki/1998/sp980529.html
17 T Lodge 'Policy processes within the African National Congress and the Tripartite Alliance' *Politikon* 1999; 26(1): 8.
18 A Marx *Lessons of Struggle: South African Internal Opposition, 1960–1990* Cape Town: Oxford University Press, 1992: 205.
19 'Labour, government reach a compromise' *Mail & Guardian* 16–22 February 2001.The relevant document indicates that labour has come into line with the government's vision of creating a competitive market: 'In order to make South Africa a destination of first choice for investment (domestic and foreign), the parties agree that it is necessary to have a competitive social and individual return on capital, measured over an appropriate time horizon (the individual return on capital refers to returns for investors and companies).'
20 'The new and improved Mbeki' *Mail & Guardian* 4 August 2006.
21 In response to another rise in interest rates by the Reserve Bank during August 2006, COSATU argued in a statement that: 'It seems the Reserve Bank is happy to choke off broader developmental strategies and long-term growth as long as it can keep inflation below 5 per cent – even though that is far stricter than the national policy.' 'Cosatu condemns interest rate hike' *Mail & Guardian* 4 August 2006.
22 I Taylor & P Vale 'South Africa's Transition Revisited: Globalisation as Vision and Virtue' *Global Society* 2000; 14(3): 412–4.
23 M Murray *Revolution Deferred: The Painful Birth of Post-Apartheid South Africa* London: Verso, 1994: 15–8.
24 R Fine & G Van Wyk 'South Africa: State, Labour, and the Politics of Reconstruction' *Capital and Class* 1996; 58: 29.
25 H Marais *South Africa: Limits to Change*: 85. Marais contends that until 1990 the ANC had no economic policy worthy of the description.
26 S Buhlungu 'The Building of the Democratic Tradition in South Africa's Trade Unions After 1973' *Democratization* 2004; 11(3): 133–58.
27 T Lodge 'Policy processes within the African National Congress and the Tripartite Alliance' *Politikon* 1999; 26(1): 30.
28 K Good 'Accountable to Themselves: Predominance in Southern Africa' *Journal of Modern African Studies* 1997; 35(4): 566.
29 H Marais *South Africa: Limits to Change*: 85.

30 J Michie & V Padayachee in: J Michie & V Padayachee (eds) *The Political Economy of South Africa's Transition*: 11.
31 J Hamill in: F Toase & E Yorke (eds) *The New South Africa: Prospects for Domestic and International Security* London: Macmillan, 1998: 67.
32 J Seekings & N Nattrass *Class, Race, and Inequality in South Africa*: 346–56.
33 S Robins in: S Robins (ed.) *Limits to Liberation: Citizenship and Governance After Apartheid* Cape Town: David Philip, 2006: 11.
34 H Marais *South Africa: Limits to Change* (First edition): 245.
35 J Saul 'Magical Market Realism' *Transformation* 1999; 38: 57.
36 Netshitenzhe in: W Gumede *Thabo Mbeki and the Battle for the Soul of the ANC*: 116.
37 H Marais *South Africa: Limits to Change*: 230–1.
38 Netshitenzhe in: W Gumede *Thabo Mbeki and the Battle for the Soul of the ANC*: 116.
39 P Bond *Elite Transition*: 347.
40 Speech by President Thabo Mbeki at the fourth Nelson Mandela annual lecture, University of Witwatersrand, Johannesburg, 29 July 2006.
41 E Maganya in: E Maganya & R Houghton (eds) *Transformation in South Africa?*: 5.
42 H Giliomee, quoted in: *Cape Times* 6 March 1997.
43 H Marais *South Africa: Limits to Change*: 241.
44 The Big Business Working Group forms part of regular meetings between President Mbeki and key players in the economy including labour, the agricultural sector and black business. The Group consists of representatives from all the major corporations including Anglovaal, Sasol, Old Mutual, De Beers, Sanlam and Anglo American. It was established by the President at the request of the Business Trust with the purpose of providing business and government leaders with an opportunity for an exchange of opinions on a range of national issues.
45 'Afrikaner helping hands' *Financial Mail* 19 May 2006. Willie Esterhuyse takes a group of all male and, until recently, all white Afrikaners to have tea with Thabo Mbeki once a month. The group includes leading businessmen such as Koos Bekker, GT Ferreira and Paul Cluver, as well as academics such as Anton van Niekerk and Bernard Lategan. Recently individuals including the recently appointed rector of Stellenbosch University, Russel Botman, have also been attending meetings: Personal communication to the author, 4 August 2006.
46 Whilst earlier National Executive Committee (NEC) meetings have endorsed the right of NEC leaders to be involved in business, at the NEC meeting in Ekurhuleni during July 2006 a team consisting of Minister of Finance Trevor Manuel, businessman and NEC member Saki Macozoma, ANC Deputy Secretary General Sankie Mthembi-Mahanyele, and Director General in the Presidency Frank Chikanke put forward a paper on the relationship between the ANC, government and business. It is intended as the first step towards the development of a code of conduct for presentation at the party's policy conference in June 2007, and will ultimately be written into the ANC's constitution: 'The new and improved Mbeki' *Mail & Guardian* 4 August 2006.
47 Most notable in recent years has been the intense debate which surrounded the

draft mining charter in 2002 which outlined the transformation of the mining sector in line with empowerment objectives. Prominent business leaders Nicky and Jonathan Oppenheimer of De Beers launched the Brenthurst Initiative during August 2003 in an effort to persuade government to manage empowerment without alienating foreign companies.

48 M Meyer 'Globalisation: An issue of contestation and struggle in South Africa' April 2000 http://www.arts.uwa.edu.au/MotsPluriels/MP1300mm.html: 4.
49 M Murray *Revolution Deferred*: 22.
50 J Hamill in: F Toase & E Yorke (eds) *The New South Africa*: 60. The other considerations included the accommodation of minority groups and the development of consensus.
51 Ibid: 69.
52 P Bond *Elite Transition*: 53.
53 T Koelble *The Global Economy and Democracy in South Africa*: 182.
54 H Marais *South Africa: Limits to Change*: 3–4.
55 Ibid: 4.
56 M Murray *Revolution Deferred*: 4.
57 For a fuller examination of this pivotal early policy document, see: H Marais *South Africa: Limits to Change*: 124–33.
58 D Lazar 'Competing economic ideologies in South Africa's economic debate' *British Journal of Sociology* 1996; 47(4): 614.
59 V Padayachee in: J Michie & V Padayachee (eds) *The Political Economy of South Africa's Transition*: 42.
60 H Marais *South Africa: Limits to Change*: 4.
61 D O'Meara *Forty Lost Years: The apartheid state and the politics of the National Party, 1948–1994* Randburg: Ravan Press, 1996: 82.
62 Central Economic Advisory Services *The Restructuring of the South African Economy, A Normative Model Approach* Pretoria: Government Printer, 1993.
63 M Morris in: S Gelb (ed) *South Africa's Economic Crisis* Cape Town: David Philip, 1991: 55.
64 A Butler *Democracy and Apartheid: Political Theory, Comparative Politics and the Modern South African State* London: Macmillan, 1998: 113.
65 I Taylor & P Vale 'South Africa's Transition Revisited: Globalisation as Vision and Virtue' *Global Society* 2000; 14(3): 405.
66 H Marais *South Africa: Limits to Change*: 89–90.
67 I Taylor & P Vale 'South Africa's Transition Revisited: Globalisation as Vision and Virtue' *Global Society* 2000; 14(3): 400.
68 For example, a number of policy discussion documents were distributed to ANC structures as part of the preparations for the ANC National Policy Conference during June 2007, and the subsequent National Conference during December 2007. As part of the economic policy debate the nature of the post-apartheid state as a developmental state and the significance of state intervention were raised. For the full text see: African National Congress *Discussion Document: Economic Transformation for a National Democratic Society* (http://www.anc.org.za/ancdocs/policy/2007/discussion/econ_transformation.html).

69 M Murray *Revolution Deferred*: 4.
70 M Rupert & H Smith (eds) *Historical Materialism and Globalisation*: 29.
71 Statement by Tito Mboweni to the Ninth Meeting of the International Monetary and Financial Committee of the IMF, 24 April 2004.
72 S Andreasson 'The ANC and its critics: "predatory liberalism", black empowerment and intra-alliance tensions in post-apartheid South Africa' *Democratization* 2006: 13(2): 303–22.
73 During 2004, FDI inflows to developing countries surged by 40 per cent to US$233bn which represents 36 per cent of the world total – the inflows are at their highest level since 1997. Nonetheless, Africa's FDI inflows have remained static at US$18bn despite substantial increases to Asia and South America: UNCTAD 'World Investment Report: Transnational Corporations and the Internationalisation of R&D' New York: United Nations, 2005.
74 H Marais *South Africa: Limits to Change*: 106.
75 In five of the last ten years, outward FDI has exceeded inward FDI. In addition, major foreign investments have been more or less restricted to the acquisition of stakes in state-owned utilities, and the re-entry of firms which had left the country during apartheid-era sanctions: N Chabane, A Goldstein & S Roberts 'The changing face and strategies of big business in South Africa: more than a decade of political democracy' *Industrial and Corporate Change* 2006; 15(3): 10–11.
76 H Marais *South Africa: Limits to Change*: 110.
77 S Gill 'Economic Globalisation and the Internationalisation of Authority: Limits and Contradictions' *Geoforum* 1992; 23(3): 269.
78 World Bank 'Accelerated Development in Sub-Saharan Africa: An Agenda for Action' Washington, DC: World Bank, 1981.
79 A Hurrell & N Woods 'Globalisation and Inequality' *Millennium* 1995; 24(3): 461.
80 S Andreasson 'The ANC and its critics: "predatory liberalism", black empowerment and intra-alliance tensions in post-apartheid South Africa' *Democratization* 2006: 13(2): 303–22.
81 The Washington Consensus refers to the 1980s–1990s ideology of the WB, IMF, US Treasury Department, Federal Reserve Board and assorted Washington think-tanks funded by large corporations and banks, as well as institutions outside Washington like the World Trade Organisation and sundry conservative university economics departments modelled on the Chicago school: P Bond *Elite Transition*: 156.
82 V Padayachee in: J Michie & V Padayachee (eds) *The Political Economy of South Africa's Transition*: 45.
83 D Hewson & M O'Donovan in: S Buhlungu, J Daniel, R Southall & J Lutchman (eds) *State of the Nation, South Africa 2005–2006* Cape Town: HSRC Press, 2006.
84 P Bond *Elite Transition*: 160.
85 H Marais *South Africa: Limits to Change*: 128. For a broader discussion, see: World Bank *Reducing Poverty in South Africa: Options for equitable and sustainable growth* Johannesburg: World Bank, 1994.
86 V Padayachee in: J Michie & V Padayachee (eds) *The Political Economy of South Africa's Transition*: 50.

NOTES

87 'Fischer sings SA's praises' *Business Day* 7 June 2001. During the World Economic Forum's Southern African Economic Summit in June 2001, the IMF's first deputy MD Stanley Fischer gave a ringing endorsement to South Africa's economic policies.

88 For example, in his capacity as Minister of Finance, Trevor Manuel serves as a Governor on the Board of the World Bank Group, the African Development Bank Group and the Development Bank of Southern Africa and has been touted as a future president of the World Bank itself. During April 2006, he was appointed to serve on the World Bank's new Commission on Growth and Development.

89 T Koelble *The Global Economy and Democracy in South Africa*: 10.

90 These six main groupings include Anglo American Corporation, Sanlam, Stanbic/Liberty Life, Rembrandt/Remgro, SA Mutual/Old Mutual and Anglovaal.

91 R Southall 'The New South Africa in the New World Order: beyond the double whammy' *Third World Quarterly* 1994; 15(1): 134.

92 D O'Meara *Forty Lost Years*: 385.

93 H Marais *South Africa: Limits to Change*: 84.

94 For example, the 'Mont Fleur' scenario exercise took place during 1991–2 and brought prominent South Africans from many backgrounds and across the ideological spectrum together to develop new ways forward on issues including economic policy, constitutional concerns and education among others using a scenario methodology. Those attending included: Saki Macozoma (Member of the National Executive Committee of the ANC), Tito Mboweni (Economist in the department of economic planning of the ANC), Trevor Manuel (Member of the National Executive Committee and the National Working of the ANC Committee), as well as a range of politicians, academics and businessmen.

95 E Webster & G Adler 'Toward a Class Compromise in South Africa's "Double Transition": Bargained Liberalisation and the Consolidation of Democracy' *Politics and Society* 1999; 27 (3): 370.

96 M Murray *Revolution Deferred*: 20.

97 See Chapter Two: P Bond *Elite Transition*.

98 H Marais *South Africa: Limits to Change*: 127.

99 A Butler *Democracy and Apartheid*: 152.

100 Ibid: 125.

101 P Bond *Elite Transition*: 56.

102 Ibid: 54.

103 T Lodge 'Policy processes within the African National Congress and the Tripartite Alliance' *Politikon* 1999; 26(1): 12.

104 T Koelble *The Global Economy and Democracy in South Africa*: 107.

105 'RIP the RDP committee' *Mail & Guardian* 20–26 August 1999.

106 P Bond *Elite Transition*: 118.

107 ANC *The Reconstruction and Development Programme: A Policy Framework* Johannesburg: ANC, 1994: 1.1.1.

108 Ibid: 6.5.17.

109 R Fine & G Van Wyk 'South Africa: State, Labour and the Politics of Reconstruction' *Capital and Class* 1996; 58: 20.

110 V Padayachee in: J Michie & V Padayachee (eds) *The Political Economy of South Africa's Transition*: 44.
111 P Bond *Elite Transition*: 89.
112 For a fuller discussion, see: D Hemson & M O'Donovan in: S Buhlungu, J Daniel, R Southall & J Lutchman (eds) *State of the Nation: South Africa 2005–2006*: 19–36.
113 H Marais *South Africa: Limits to Change*: 239. Emphasis in the original.
114 P Nel 'Conceptions of globalisation among the South African elite' *Global Dialogue* 1999; 4(1): 23.
115 GNU *Growth, Employment and Redistribution: A Macro-Economic Strategy* Cape Town: Government Printer, 1996: 1.1.
116 N Nattrass in: G Maharaj (ed) *Between Unity and Diversity: Essays on Nation-Building in Post-Apartheid South Africa* Cape Town: David Philip, 1999: 79–80.
117 D Hemson & M O'Donovan in: S Buhlungu, J Daniel, R Southall & J Lutchman (eds) *State of the Nation: South Africa 2005–2006*: 39.
118 Most telling in this stratagem have been the far-fetched predictions and lofty ideals relating to growth and jobs creation – an annual growth rate of 6 per cent and an average of 400 000 jobs annually by the year 2000 were the figures bandied about under the accelerated growth scenario. GNU *Growth, Employment and Redistribution: A Macro-Economic Strategy* Cape Town: Government Printer, 1996: 2.3.
119 D Hemson & M O'Donovan in: S Buhlungu, J Daniel, R Southall & J Lutchman (eds) *State of the Nation: South Africa 2005–2006* Cape Town: HSRC Press, 2006: 22.
120 R Southall 'The ANC and Black Capitalism in South Africa' *Review of African Political Economy* 2004; 31(100): 326.
121 C Marx 'Ubu and Ubuntu: on the dialectics of apartheid and nation building' *Politikon* 2002; 29(1): 50.
122 B von Lieres in: S Robins (eds) *Limits to Liberation after Apartheid*: 22.
123 H Marais *South Africa: Limits to Change*: 94.
124 S Hall in: D Morley & K-H Chen (eds) *Stuart Hall: Critical Dialogues in Cultural Studies* London: Routledge, 1996: 431.
125 H Marais *South Africa: Limits to Change*: 76.
126 M Murray *Revolution Deferred*: 12.
127 H Marais *South Africa: Limits to Change*: 89–90.
128 I Filatova 'The Rainbow Against the African Sky or African Hegemony in a Multi-Cultural Context?' *Transformation* 1997; 34: 50.
129 Speech made by Deputy President Thabo Mbeki to Parliament, 8 May 1996.
130 For a fuller discussion of the ANC's history of non-racialism, see: M MacDonald *Why Race Matters in South Africa*: 92–123.
131 H Marais 'Into the New South Africa' *South African Political and Economic Monthly* 1999; 12(3): 11.
132 H Marais *South Africa: Limits to Change*: 248.
133 T Bell *Unfinished Business: South Africa, Apartheid and Truth* London: Verso, 2003.
134 C Marx 'Ubu and Ubuntu: on the dialectics of apartheid and nation building' *Politikon* 2002; 29(1): 50.

135 J Gibson 'Overcoming Apartheid: Can Truth Reconcile a Divided Nation?' *Politikon* 2004; 31(2): 10.
136 J Hamill in: F Toase & E Yorke (eds) *The New South Africa: Prospects for Domestic and International Security*: 72.
137 The Director of the AHI is of the opinion that: 'Since 1994, the attitude of President Mandela towards the Afrikaner community has been very responsive. When the AHI delegation first met Deputy President Mbeki in 1995 an immediate friendship was struck. His daughter took up a position in one of our senior member's offices. His wife, Zanele Mbeki, in 1998 accepted to be the patron of the AHI Golfday, in aid of business development. Her involvement continues to this day. In 1999, President Mandela approached the AHI to erect a hostel in Qunu, at the Dalindyebo Senior Secondary School. We put together a consortium of members who completed the task in 2000. In 2002, [former] President Mandela accepted the highest honorary award from the AHI. To this day the refrain we hear in all our contacts with ministers and government officials is: "The Afrikaners are part of the solution, not part of the problem."' Interview with Jacob de Villiers, Director of the AHI: 21 August 2002.
138 H Marais *South Africa: Limits to Change*: 298–9.
139 For the full version, see: www.dfa.gov.za/docs/speeches/1998/mbek0529.htm.
140 C Halisi 'From Liberation to Citizenship: Identity and Innovation in Black South African Political Thought' *Comparative Studies in Society and History* 1997; 39(1): 61.
141 B von Lieres in: S Robins (eds) *Limits to Liberation after Apartheid*: 23.
142 'Nation-Formation and Nation Building: The National Question' ANC Discussion Document, July 1997: http://www.anc.org.za/ancdocs/discussion/nation.html
143 M MacDonald *Why Race Matters in South Africa*: 158.
144 I Filatova 'The Rainbow Against the African Sky or African Hegemony in a Multi-Cultural Context?' *Transformation* 1997; 34: 54.
145 G Olivier 'Is Thabo Mbeki Africa's saviour?' *International Affairs* 2003; 79(4): 815.
146 'Mandela slams "arrogant" black elite' *Sunday Times* 25 February 2001.
147 H Marais *South Africa: Limits to Change*: 74.
148 T Koelble *The Global Economy and Democracy in South Africa*: 185.
149 J Daniel, A Habib & R Southall (eds) *The State of the Nation, 2003–2004* Cape Town: HSRC Press, 2003: 20.
150 C Marx 'Ubu and Ubuntu: on the dialectics of apartheid and nation building' *Politikon* 2002; 29(1): 54.
151 I Taylor & P Nel 'New Africa, globalisation and the confines of elite reformism: 'Getting the rhetoric right, getting the strategy wrong' *Third World Quarterly* 2002; 23(1): 164.
152 H Marais *South Africa: Limits to Change*: 248.
153 P Vale & S Maseko 'South Africa and the African Renaissance' *International Affairs* 1998; 74(2): 277.
154 G Olivier 'Is Thabo Mbeki Africa's saviour?' *International Affairs* 2003; 79(4): 815.
155 H Marais *South Africa: Limits to Change*: 249.

156 T Mbeki 'Letter from the President: Bold steps to end the 'two nations' divide' *ANC Today* 22–28 August 2003; 33(3).

Chapter 4

1. Despite concern as to some aspects of the transformation process, the director of the AHI was adamant that: 'I do not believe there are major areas of unique discord, beyond the language issue, between Afrikaner capital and the ANC government.' At the same time, he stated that: 'I do not think that there is at this stage an appetite in the Afrikaner business community to itself initiate a broad based dialogue regarding the Afrikaner community.' Interview with Jacob de Villiers, Director of the AHI: 21 August 2002.
2. 'Is there an Afrikaner problem?' *Mail & Guardian* 19–25 March 1999.
3. Chairperson Pierre Theron continued: 'We are open to everyone who will subscribe to the principles of the Afrikanerbond. Whether they belong to what creed or colour . . .' 'Afrikanerbond seeks modern role' *Mail & Guardian* 3 August 2007.
4. E Bornman in: S Bekker and R Prinsloo (eds) *Identity? Theory, Politics, History* Pretoria: HSRC, 1999: 48.
5. H Giliomee *The Afrikaners: Biography of a People* Cape Town: Tafelberg, 2003: 661–6. The author offers a brief discussion of identifications among an Afrikaans 'community' in the new South Africa.
6. N Schuermans & G Visser 'On Poor Whites in Post-Apartheid Cities: The Case of Bloemfontein' *Urban Forum* 2005; 16(4): 259–94; and, G Visser 'Unvoiced and Invisible: on the transparency of white South Africans in post-apartheid geographical discourse' *Acta Academica* 2003: 1.
7. In Brink v Kitshoff NO 1996 (6) BCLR 752 at paragraph 42, the Constitution Court recognised that the right to equality in the Bill of Rights not only applies to the individual, but also to the group: 'Section 8 was adopted . . . in the recognition that discrimination against people who are members of disfavoured groups can lead to patterns of group disadvantage and harm.'
8. A Appadurai 'Disjuncture and Difference in the Global Cultural Economy' *Public Culture* 1990; 2(2): 1–24.
9. D Held, A McGrew, D Goldblatt and J Perraton *Global Transformations: Politics, Economics and Culture* Cambridge: Polity Press, 1999: 328. Emphasis in the original.
10. J Jenson 'Mapping, naming and remembering: globalisation at the end of the twentieth century' *Review of International Political Economy* 1995; 2(1): 105.
11. Sassen includes here new global corporate actors, and 'collectivities whose experience of membership has not been fully subsumed under nationhood in its modern conception, for example, minorities, immigrants, first-nation people, and many feminists.': S Sassen in: J Copjec & M Sorkin (eds) *Giving Ground: The Politics of Propinquity* London: Verso, 1999: 87.
12. S Hall in: S Hall, D Held and A McGrew (eds) *Modernity and Its Futures* Cambridge: Polity Press, 1992: 309.

13 M Keating in: K Christie (ed) *Ethnic Conflict, Tribal Politics: A Global Perspective* London: Curzon, 1998: 49–50. Using the examples of Quebec, Catalonia and Scotland, the author demonstrates that the 'move to support for free trade nonetheless represents a new form of nationalism, detaching it from economic protectionism. It also represents a shift in the historic nationalist mission in all three, but especially in Quebec and Catalonia and opens up a range of policy options and considerable scope for functional independence from the state.'
14 A Habib, D Pillay and A Desai 'South Africa and the Global Order: The Structural Conditioning of a Transition to Democracy' *Journal of Contemporary African Studies* 1998; 16(1): 103.
15 Ibid: 99.
16 P Nel 'Conceptions of globalisation among the South African elite' *Global Dialogue* 1999; 4(1): 23.
17 T Koelble *The Global Economy and Democracy in South Africa* New Brunswick, NJ: Rutgers University Press, 1998: 17.
18 Ibid: 2.
19 South African Government, Act No. 108 of 1996 *Constitution of the Republic of South Africa* Pretoria: Government Printers.
20 Swilling argues that the latter began to play with the numbers game: 'They've replaced group rights with majority rights. They've accepted 'the majority should rule,' and have gone for proportional representation as a mechanism for cosociational division. They began to realise that there's one advantage about democracy, and that is that it's a package deal that includes an electoral system, and electoral systems, as all good gerrymanderers will tell you, can be manipulated in all sorts of very different ways.' M Swilling in: A Callinicos *Between Apartheid and Capitalism: Conversations with South African Socialists* London: Bookmarks, 1992: 42–3.
21 S Bekker in: S Bekker and R Prinsloo (eds) *Identity? Theory, Politics, History*: 4.
22 C Halisi 'Citizenship and Populism in the New South Africa' *Africa Today* 1998; 43(3–4): 423.
23 K Nash *Contemporary Political Sociology: Globalisation, Politics and Power* Oxford: Blackwell, 2000: 157.
24 J Jenson 'Mapping, naming and remembering: globalisation at the end of the twentieth century' *Review of International Political Economy* 1995; 2(1): 103–4.
25 W Kymlicka *Multi-cultural Citizenship: a Liberal Theory of Minority Rights* Oxford: Clarendon Press, 1995: 19.
26 W Kymlicka *Politics in the Vernacular: Nationalism, Multiculturalism and Citizenship* Oxford: Oxford University Press, 2001: 6.
27 N Alexander in: G Maharaj (ed) *Between Unity and Diversity: Essays on Nation-Building in Post-Apartheid South Africa* Cape Town: David Philip, 1999: 18.
28 Minority rights are now too a matter of 'legitimate international concern'. Recent examples of this codification include: the Organisation on Security and Co-operation in Europe adopted principles regarding the rights of national minorities in 1991, and established a High Commissioner on National Minorities in 1993. The Council of Europe adopted a treaty on minority language rights in 1992 (the European Charter for Regional or Minority Languages) and a

Framework Convention for the Protection of National Minorities in 1995. On a wider scale, the United Nations has adopted a declaration on the Rights of Persons Belonging to National or Ethnic, Religious, and Linguistic Minorities (1993), and is currently debating a Draft Declaration on the Rights of Indigenous Peoples which both impact dramatically on the treatment of minorities worldwide: W Kymlicka *Politics in the Vernacular*: 6–7.

29 H Marais 'Into the New South Africa' *South African Political and Economic Monthly* 1999; 12(3): 11.
30 Interview by the author with Johann Rossouw, 7 August 2006.
31 Interview by the author with Danie Goosen, 31 July 2006.
32 For example, during 2006 the *Afrikanerbond* was 'transformed into a brand-new organisation with a new constitution, new structures and aim relevant to the times we live in'. One of the foremost aims of the organisation's new credo is to: 'Strive for the maintenance and development of all indigenous languages, with particular emphasis on Afrikaans': http://www.afrikanerbond.org.za
33 De Klerk commented that 'all communities should be regarded as valued bricks in the building of the overarching nation. To achieve this all communities must equally enjoy protection and bear responsibilities, regardless of their ethnic, religious or cultural origins: 'No leaders without their communities' *The Sunday Independent* 18 February 2001.
34 For example: A special report compiled for the F W de Klerk Foundation by Deon Geldenhuys & Johann Rossouw 'The International Protection of Minority Rights' Panorama: FW de Klerk Foundation, 2004: http://www.fwdklerk.org.za/download_docs/01_08_Minority_Rights_Protection_Publ.doc
35 P Strand 'Finalising the South African Constitution: the politics of the Constitutional Assembly' *Politikon* 2001; 28(1): 47.
36 South African Government, Act No. 108 of 1996 *Constitution of the Republic of South Africa*: Sections 185(1) (a) (b) and (2).
37 South African Government, Act No. 108 of 1996 *Constitution of the Republic of South Africa*: Section 181. The others include the Auditor General, Public Protector, and Human Rights, Gender Equality and Electoral Commissions.
38 Y Carrim in: G Maharaj (ed) *Between Unity and Diversity*: 263.
39 South African Government, Act No. 19 of 2002 *Commission for the Promotion and Protection of the Rights of Cultural, Religious and Linguistic Communities Act*.
40 South African Government, Act No. 108 of 1996 *Constitution of the Republic of South Africa*: Section 235 on self-determination: The right of the South African people as a whole to self-determination, as manifested in this Constitution, does not preclude, within the framework of this right, recognition of the notion of the right of self-determination of any community sharing a common cultural language and heritage, within a territorial entity in the Republic, or in any other way, determined by national legislation.
41 'A state of mind more likely than a piece of veld' *Financial Mail* 26 March 1999.
42 'Finger on the trigger of war' *The Sunday Independent* 25 March 2001.
43 Pieter Groenewald, Freedom Front spokesperson on safety and security and the party's provincial leader in the North West, said that the name change

disregards Afrikaner history and heritage. 'A petition opposing the proposed name change, containing more than 8 000 signatures, was submitted to the city council, but it is merely wiped off the table,' Groenewald said. 'It is nothing other than a total disregard of the cultural historical heritage of the Afrikaner, and the ANC is abusing its power to intimidate the Afrikaner.' He said Freedom Front leader Pieter Mulder will take up the name change with Minister of Arts and Culture Pallo Jordan, as such changes first have to be approved by the minister before becoming official. 'The Constitution of South Africa provides that the cultural historical heritage of all groups is acknowledged and the ANC of Potchefstroom is clearly ignoring this constitutional provision,' Groenewald said. 'It's Tlokwe, says Potchefstroom city council' *Mail & Guardian* 19 July 2006.

44 A Nash 'The New Politics of Afrikaans' *South African Journal of Philosophy* 2000; 19(4): 342.

45 'Report of the Government of the Republic of South Africa on the Question of the Afrikaners', presented by Deputy President Thabo Mbeki to the National Assembly on 24 March 1999.

46 African National Congress *Discussion Document: The National Question*. (*www.anc.org.za/ancdocs/ngcouncils/2005/nationalquestion.html*) 29 June – 3 July 2005.

47 For a fuller account of these discussions, see: P Waldmeir *Anatomy of a miracle: The end of apartheid and the birth of the new South Africa* London: Viking, 1997.

48 'Top Afrikaners support Mbeki' *The Sunday Independent* 20 February 2000. Willie Esterhuyse takes a group of male and, until recently, all white Afrikaans speakers to have tea with Mbeki once a month. The group includes leading businessmen such as Koos Bekker, GT Ferreira and Paul Cluver, as well as academics such as Anton van Niekerk and Bernard Lategan: Personal communication to the author, 4 August 2006.

49 Interview by the author with Marlene van Niekerk, 10 August 2006.

50 'Afrikaner debate about language and culture should involve all South Africans' *The Sunday Independent* 28 May 2000.

51 S May *Language and Minority Rights*: 148.

52 Interview by the author with Albert Grundlingh, 10 August 2006.

53 Interview by the author with Johann Rossouw, 7 August 2006.

54 A Nash 'The New Politics of Afrikaans' *South African Journal of Philosophy* 2000; 19(4): 352–3.

55 'Is there an Afrikaner problem?' *Mail & Guardian* 19–25 March 1999.

56 The then foremost organisation of prominent Afrikaans-speaking intellectuals was formed in May 2000. Intent on protecting Afrikaans and other minority languages in South Africa, this *taalstryd* has four principal motivations: firstly, to situate demands for group cultural rights for Afrikaans-speakers alongside similar rights for other minorities; secondly, to compel a 'democratisation of Afrikaans-speaking culture' in order to overcome racial and other distinctions; thirdly, to promote greater Afrikaans language and cultural rights as a cultural affair; and, finally, to view group rights as part of an international trend which views individual rights regimes as inadequate for the unique problems of

multicultural societies. Only shortly after its inception, a number of eminent figures withdrew their support, leaving spokesman Johann Rossouw to confirm that the Group of 63 was 'a loose group coming from various political strata, with a civil-society agenda in the Afrikaans community. We simply want to supplement and broaden what government is doing for the Afrikaans-speaking groups': 'Fighting for cultural space' *Mail & Guardian* 24–30 November 2000.
57　S Pillay in: S Robins (eds) *Limits to Liberation after Apartheid*: 58.
58　Interview by the author with Johann Rossouw, 7 August 2006.
59　For a wider discussion, see: I Hofmeyr in: S Marks and S Trapido (eds) *The politics of race, class and nationalism in twentieth-century South Africa* London: Longman, 1993: 95.
60　M Kriel 'Fools, Philologists and Philosophers: Afrikaans and the Politics of Cultural Nationalism' *Politikon* 2006; 33(1): 67.
61　Interview by the author with Hermann Giliomee, 18 August 2006.
62　Interview by the author with Johann Rossouw, 7 August 2006.
63　By mid-year 2006, figures show an increase in the coloured population (4 198 800 or 8.9 per cent of the total population). The 2001 Census demonstrated that Afrikaans is the predominant language among coloureds, with 79.5 per cent speaking Afrikaans as their first home language followed by 18.9 per cent speaking English. Among the declining white population (by mid-year 2006, 4 365 300 or 9.2 per cent of the total population), the 2001 Census demonstrated that 59.1 per cent speak Afrikaans as their first home language followed by 39.3 per cent speaking English. The proportion of those speaking Afrikaans declines gradually with decreasing age across both population groups: Statistics South Africa 'Mid-year population estimates, South Africa 2006' Statistical release P0302, August 2006; and, Statistics South Africa 'Achieving a better life for all: Progress between Census '96 and Census 2001' Pretoria: Statistics SA, 2005 (03–02–16 2001). Information from the All Media and Product Survey (AMPS) 2002A published by the South African Advertising Research Foundation (SAARF) puts the population share of Afrikaans speakers at 16.2 per cent. Personal communication to the author from Hedi Drunk, Statistical Information Office, Bureau of Market Research, Unisa, 28 March 2003.
64　Interview by the author with Danie Goosen, 31 July 2006.
65　S May *Language and Minority Rights: Ethnicity, Nationalism and the Politics of Language* Harlow: Longman, 2001: 135. Emphasis in the original.
66　The nation survey concerned with the reactions of language groups to major trends in language and cultural policy was conducted during 1997: L Schlemmer 'Factors in the Persistence or Decline of Ethnic Group Mobilisation: A conceptual review and case study of cultural group responses among Afrikaners in post-apartheid South Africa' Unpublished Ph.D. thesis, University of Cape Town, 1999: Chapter nine.
67　G de Klerk 'Mother-tongue education in South Africa: the weight of history' *International Journal of the Sociology of Language* 2002; 154: 41.
68　S May *Language and Minority Rights*: 150. May holds the latter process to be the more important of the two.

69 S May *Language and Minority Rights*: 148. Emphasis in the original.
70 The central role of the language in defining any Afrikaans community is widely acknowledged, but less frequently what has been termed a 'common content' including certain theology, politics and literature which has 'an engagement with Africa, the soil of Africa': Interview by the author with Willie Van Der Merwe, 1 August 2006.
71 For example, the Group of 63 was established in 2000 with the aim of protecting Afrikaans and other minority languages in South Africa initially included 10–15 coloured Afrikaans speakers. The low profile of these intellectuals therein and failure of Federasie van Afrikaanse Kultuurvereiniginge, established with similar aims, to gain little popular support from the wider coloured community is ascribed to the strong divisions and diffuseness of this community: Interview by the author with Johann Rossouw, 7 August 2006.
72 C S van der Waal 'Diverse approaches in a South African debate on language and diversity in higher education' *Anthropology Southern Africa* 2002; 25(3&4): 93.
73 W De Klerk *Afrikaners: Kroes, Kras, Kordaat* Cape Town: Human and Rousseau, 2000. The title literally translates as unhappy/worried; drastic/aggressive; self-assured/too big for one's boots.
74 His central proposal was that: 'To ensure existence . . . Afrikaners have to become an African nation, feel genuine guilt about the past, confess to apartheid, prove that they are a minority group, but not strive towards ethnic nationalism, and realise that they should be prepared to face serious criticism.' 'The Afrikaner today: listless, bewildered, morose and full of complaints' *The Sunday Independent* 4 June 2000.
75 C Louw *Boetman en die swanesang van die verligtes* Cape Town: Human & Rousseau, 2001.
76 Interview by the author with Herman Wasserman, 8 August 2006.
77 For example, a recent opinion piece published on Moneyweb (*www.moneyweb.co.za*) gained considerable attention: 'It's time for Afrikaans to go' 19 June 2006.
78 Kees van der Waal 'Essentialism in Language and Culture' Paper presented to Departmental Seminar 'Between Languages and Cultures,' Department of Sociology and Social Anthropology, Stellenbosch University, 26 May 2006.
79 Interview by the author with Johann Rossouw, 7 August 2006.
80 Higher Education Act 1997, Republic of South Africa; and, Education White Paper no. 3 1997, Department of Education, Republic of South Africa.
81 The revision of the university's language policy and the formulation of a language plan were to be carried out within the context of the university's approved Strategic Framework which states that the raison d'être of the University of Stellenbosch is the creation of an environment that promotes the production, sharing and application of knowledge, and also the pursuit of excellence: 'Nuwe taalbeleid en plan vir Universiteit' 25 July 2002. *http://www.sun.ac.za/news/NewsItem.asp?ItemID=2464&Zone=A05*
82 Ontwikkeling van 'n Taalplan 29 July 2002 *http://www.sun.ac.za/news/NewsItem.asp?ItemID=2479&Zone=A05*
83 C Brink *No lesser place: the taaldebat at Stellenbosch* Stellenbosch: Sunmedia, 2006.

84 The T-option describes dual medium tuition whilst the A-option denotes Afrikaans as a language of tuition. At its meeting of 15 December 2005, the Council of Stellenbosch University accepted the Senate's recommendation on language specifications for 2006 which included an extension of the T-option to the third year in the Faculty of Arts.
85 'FF leader describes new trend' *Business Day* 22 October 2002. Mulder was not so clear about the 'exact nature of the budding movement'.
86 'Without one university in the south and one in the north where the future of Afrikaans is secure, and without firm guidelines and rules for both these Afrikaans-orientated universities and for parallel medium instruction at two or three other universities, the turmoil in the Afrikaans community over language will continue. This cannot be in the interests of either government or the Afrikaans community.' Letter to Kader Asmal on 7 May 2001. *www.praag.org/Giliomee%20letter.htm*
87 For example: D Roodt *The Scourge of the ANC* Praag, 2005.
88 'Old split over Afrikaner identity fuels new terror' *Business Day* 28 November 2002. Roodt is the leader of the *Pro-Afrikaanse Aksiegroep* (Praag).
89 Interview by the author with Johann Rossouw, 7 August 2006.
90 Interview by the author with Herman Giliomee, 18 August 2006.
91 Interview by the author with Marlene van Niekerk, 10 August 2006.
92 At the height of the debate on diversity during 20 June to 16 July 2002, more than 70 letters on the language issue were published in the Afrikaans press including *Die Burger* and *Rapport*. All the letter writers were essentially in agreement that it was important to maintain Afrikaans as a medium of instruction at Stellenbosch University but differed on the approach needed to achieve this aim, as well as the position of English in higher education: C S van der Waal 'Diverse approaches in a South African debate on language and diversity in higher education' *Anthropology Southern Africa* 2002; 25(3&4): 91.
93 Interview by the author with Herman Wasserman, 8 August 2006.
94 Interview by the author with Marlene van Niekerk, 10 August 2006.
95 A Nash 'The New Politics of Afrikaans' *South African Journal of Philosophy* 2000; 19(4): 344.
96 Ibid: 359.
97 Ibid: 348.
98 Interview by the author with Johann Rossouw, 7 August 2006.
99 Interview by the author with Danie Goosen, 31 July 2006.
100 Interview by the author with Danie Goosen, 31 July 2006.
101 Interview by the author with Johann Rossouw, 7 August 2006.
102 Interview by the author with Danie Goosen, 31 July 2006.
103 Interview by the author with Andrew Nash, 16 August 2006.
104 Interview by the author with Sampie Terreblanche, 4 August 2006.
105 M Vestergaard 'Who's Got the Map? The Negotiation of Afrikaner Identities in Post-Apartheid South Africa' *Daedalus* 2001; 130(1): 24. Emphasis added.
106 Interview by the author with Johann Rossouw, 7 August 2006.
107 A Nash 'The New Politics of Afrikaans' *South African Journal of Philosophy* 2000; 19(4): 348.

108 H Marais *South Africa Limits to Change: The Political Economy of Transition* Cape Town: University of Cape Town Press, 2001: 300.
109 T Koelble *The Global Economy and Democracy in South Africa*: 187–8.
110 A nationwide survey conducted during July 2000 for the Institute for Justice and Reconciliation clearly demonstrates the attitudes of white and black South Africans on three crucial issues, namely: personal responsibility for the process of national reconciliation; material compensation for this same process (only 20 per cent of whites agreed in contrast to 70 per cent of blacks); and, the importance of the TRC in building a united South African nation (77 per cent of blacks approve of the work of the commission, against 29 per cent of whites). One of the report's authors comments that: 'The research clearly indicates that South Africa has a long road to travel in terms of reconciliation. Particularly among white South Africans, much work remains to be done in encouraging wider reconciliatory attitudes and some form of commitment towards restitution for having benefited from apartheid': *Truth – Yes, Reconciliation – Maybe* Cape Town: Institute for Justice and Reconciliation, 2000.
111 T Gouws 'Post Modern Identity: History, Language and Cultural Difference or The True Colours of the Rainbow Nation' *New Contree* 1996; 40: 18: 'the Afrikaner found himself in his predicament because he allowed ideology and politics to take his cultural identity hostage.'
112 www.homeforall.org.za/ENG/declarationENG.htm
113 'Sorry is still the hardest word in new South Africa' *The Sydney Morning Herald* 16–17 December 2000.
114 Interview by the author with Andrew Nash, 16 August 2006.
115 'Mbeki holds out olive branch' *Business Day* 26 June 2001.
116 During August 2006, the former South African cabinet minister Adriaan Vlok performed an act of contrition by washing the feet of the anti-apartheid activist, the Reverend Frank Chikane, who he alleged attempted to have murdered: 'SA debates atonement after Vlok apology' *Mail & Guardian* 4 September 2006.
117 Interview conducted by Paul Williams with Sampie Terreblanche, 7 July 1999.
118 Dan O'Meara *Volkskapitalisme: Class, capital and ideology in the development of Afrikaner nationalism, 1934–1948* Johannesburg: Ravan Press, 1983.
119 R Cox 'Civil society at the turn of the millennium: prospects for an alternative world order' *Review of International Studies* 1999; 25: 9.
120 Ibid: 12.
121 After two decades of Afrikaner upliftment under the auspices of the National Party government, the 'poor white problem' had been more or less solved. While the Afrikaners' per capita-income was less than 50 per cent of the income of English-speakers in 1948, it has risen to 75 per cent of the now higher income of English speakers: S Terreblanche 'The compatibility of inequality and democracy: The necessity and merit of nationalisation and redistribution' *The Investment Analysts Journal* 2003; 33(1).
122 S Terreblanche *A History of Inequality in South Africa 1652–2002* Pietermaritzburg: University of Natal Press, 2002: 391–2.
123 C Soudien 'Constituting the class: an analysis of the process of integration in

South African schools' in: J Daniel, A Habib & R Southall (eds) *State of the Nation: South Africa 2003–2004* Pretoria: HSRC Press, 2003: 111.

124 M Kahn & B Daya Reddy 'Science and Technology in South Africa: Regional Innovation Hub or Passive Consumer?' *Daedalus* 2001; 130(1): 214. During 2003, despite making up only 10 per cent of senior certificates, white pupils earned 65 per cent of A-aggregates; in mathematics they earned 53 per cent of all higher grades. In the tertiary sector, despite a massive increase in the number of black graduates and a small decrease in the number of white graduates, the latter remain more likely to graduate in areas such as engineering, commerce and management: South African Institute of Race Relations *2004/05 South Africa Survey* Braamfontein: SAIRR, 2006.

125 E Louw in: D Tanno & A Gonzalez (eds) *Communication and Identity Across Cultures* London: Sage, 1998: 153.

126 'A place in the sun' *Financial Mail*, 7 April 2000.

127 'Economic liberalisation falters on the JSE' *The Sunday Times*, 13 June 1999.

128 P Allanson, J Atkins & T Hinks 'No End to the Racial Wage Hierarchy in South Africa?' *Journal of Development Economics* 2002; 6(3) 442–59.

129 'A place in the sun' *Financial Mail* 7 April 2000. Indeed, white entrepreneurs, including many Afrikaans speakers, have swamped government efforts to incentivise small businesses, leaving Department of Trade and Industry officials scrambling to drum up interest from black entrepreneurs. Indian and then white South Africans constitute the most entrepreneurial groupings within the national population: 'Taking race out of job creation' *Business Day* 28 March 2006; 'BEE builds white business' *Mail & Guardian* 13 November 2006.

130 Thus Roussouw suggests that the 'economic logic [of globalisation] cuts into your identity', whilst Giliomee contends that 'consumerism does not satisfy the soul.' Interviews by the author with Johann Rossouw, 7 August 2006 and Herman Giliomee, 18 August 2006.

131 During 2004, British High Commissions issued 47 000 working holiday visas to Commonwealth citizens, with 47 per cent going to South African nationals, 43 per cent to Australians and 11 per cent to New Zealanders.

132 The data on emigration is patchy and unreliable but it is clear that between 1994–2000 there was a net outflow of skilled migrants. Nonetheless, the migration of professionals in the post-apartheid era has fluctuated considerably. Whilst a variety of factors prompt the decision to emigrate, the change of government in South Africa coincided with the onset of neo-liberal globalisation and relaxation of exchange controls: M Brown, D Kaplan & J-B Meyer 'The Brain Drain: An Outline of Skilled Emigration from South Africa' in: D McDonald & J Crush (eds) *Destinations Unknown: Perspectives on the Brain Drain in Southern Africa* Pretoria: Africa Institute of South Africa, 2002.

133 The total of white unemployed had risen from 3 per cent in 1995 to 4.9 per cent in 2004, increasing from 38 000 to 104 000 or 174 per cent: South African Institute of Race Relations *2004/05 South Africa Survey* Braamfontein: SAIRR, 2006.

134 Whilst overall levels of inequality have changed little, the income shares of different racial groups have shifted. A range of different data suggests that the

white population's share of total income declined from a high point in 1970 to current levels of between 36–46 per cent of total income during 2000, depending on the data. The racial composition of the higher income deciles suggests that between 1995–2000 there were large shifts as the white proportion dropped by either 12 or 18 percentage points: J Seekings & N Nattrass *Class, Race, and Inequality in South Africa* Scottsville: University of KwaZulu-Natal Press, 2006: Chapter nine. Overall, white household incomes increased by 67 per cent between 1995–2004 whilst the number of households increased by only 5 per cent. African household income was only 24 per cent of whites in 2004, a mere 1 per cent higher than 23 per cent in 1995: South African Institute of Race Relations *2004/05 South Africa Survey* Braamfontein: SAIRR, 2006.

135 'Behind the myth that affirmative action is hurting white prospects' *Business Day* 7 April 2006.
136 J Seekings & N Nattrass *Class, Race, and Inequality in South Africa*: 345.
137 P Nel 'Conceptualisations of globalisation among the South African elite' *Global Dialogue* 1999; 4(1): 23.
138 D Randall 'Prospects for the Development of a Black Business Class in South Africa' *Journal of Modern African Studies* 1996; 34(4): 675.
139 Total investment overseas amounted to R652, 53bn at the end of December 2002 according to the South African Reserve Bank, almost double the figure of R333, 17bn at the end of 1998. At the end of 2002, South Africa held most of its foreign assets in Britain, amounting to R223, 99bn or 34.3 per cent of the total, followed by assets in the rest of Europe at R203, 84bn or 31.2 per cent. The US was next in line with R124, 56nn or 19.1 per cent of the total. About 4.6 per cent or R30, 01bn was invested in Africa, comprising a 300 per cent increase during 1997–2001.
140 A Nash 'The New Politics of Afrikaans' *South African Journal of Philosophy* 2000; 19(4): 342.
141 Interview by the author with Jacob de Villiers, 21 August 2002.
142 N Chabane, A Goldstein & S Roberts 'The changing face and strategies of big business in South Africa: more than a decade of political democracy' *Industrial and Corporate Change* 2006; 15(3): 10.
143 Interview by the author with Sampie Terreblanche, 4 August 2006.
144 N Chabane, A Goldstein & S Roberts 'The changing face and strategies of big business in South Africa: more than a decade of political democracy' *Industrial and Corporate Change* 2006; 15(3): 23.
145 'Naspers seeks R5bn war chest for growth' *Business Day* 28 February 2007.
146 H Wasserman 'Private culture, public sphere: media, race and economics in the Afrikaans media after apartheid' Paper presented as part of a panel: 'Forms of media, change and resistance in postcolonial Africa' at the Conference of the Association of Cultural Studies, Istanbul, July 2006.
147 'Business fails to deliver on promise to make amends' *The Sunday Independent*, 19 September 2004.
148 A Hirsch *Season of Hope: Economic Reform Under Mandela and Mbeki* Pietermaritzburg: University of KwaZulu-Natal Press, 2005: 213.

149 H Marais *South Africa Limits to Change: The Political Economy of Transition*: 173.
150 R Southall 'The ANC and Black Capitalism in South Africa' *Review of African Political Economy* 2004; 31(100): 323.
151 'Charters light a fire under BEE deals' *Business Day*, 1 April 2005.
152 R Southall 'The ANC and Black Capitalism in South Africa' *Review of African Political Economy* 2004; 31(100): 319–20.
153 Ibid: 318.
154 BusinessMap Foundation *Empowerment 2004 – Black Ownership: Risk or Opportunity?* Johannesburg: BusinessMap Foundation, 2004: 56.
155 R Southall 'The ANC and Black Capitalism in South Africa' *Review of African Political Economy* 2004; 31(100): 318.
156 BusinessMap Foundation *Empowerment 2004 – Black Ownership: Risk or Opportunity?*: iii.
157 'A place in the sun' *Financial Mail*, 4 August 2000.
158 'Minerals bill deal satisfies mine players' *Business Day*, 11 June 2001.
159 'De Beers signs £333m deal on black economic empowerment' *The Guardian*, 9 November 2005.
160 African Labour Research Network *Mining Africa: South African MNCs labour and social performance* Helsinki: Trade Union Solidarity Centre of Finland, 2005.
161 Disinvestment exceeded the levels of inward investment: 'Disinvestment blow to mining' *Business Day* 14 March 2007.
162 R Southall 'The ANC and Black Capitalism in South Africa' *Review of African Political Economy* 2004; 31(100): 327.
163 'ANC urges business to speed up BEE' *Business Day*, 15 September 2005.
164 'ANC bigwigs buy Sun stake in BEE deal' *Business Day*, 8 November 2005.
165 I Taylor 'Globalisation Studies and the Developing World: making international political economy truly global' *Third World Quarterly* 2005; 26(7): 1026.

Chapter 5

1 Munro argues that ethno-nationalist and class-based approaches (that tend to use bounded groupness as a self-evident given) do not 'offer a satisfactory account of the cultural politics of ethnic solidarity and the internecine struggles over the character of that solidarity in the 1980s'. W Munro 'Revisiting Tradition, Reconstructing Identity? Afrikaner Nationalism and Political Transition In South Africa' *Politikon* 1995; 22(2): 7.
2 A Butler *Democracy and Apartheid: Political Theory, Comparative Politics and the Modern South African State* London: Macmillan, 1998: 12.
3 D O'Meara *Forty Lost Years: The apartheid state and the politics of the National Party, 1948–1994* Randburg, Ravan Press, 1996: 53.
4 For a wider examination of these regional rifts, see: D O'Meara *Forty Lost Years*: Chapter Four.
5 D O'Meara *Volkskapitalisme: Class, Capital and Ideology in the Development of Afrikaner Nationalism* Cambridge: Cambridge University Press, 1983: Chapter 11.

6 D O'Meara *Forty Lost Years*: 54.
7 Ibid: 55.
8 Ibid: 55. Indeed, the common insult used by the Transvaal establishment for this Cape establishment referred to the *geldmag* (financial power) of the Cape.
9 Ibid: 87.
10 Where leadership battles led, the regional press groups (Cape-based Nasionale Pers and its Transvaal competitors) were never far behind. O'Meara is convinced that, aside from the obvious political reasons, the so-called 'great Afrikaner press war' was linked to very lucrative government printing contracts for the house publisher of the victorious province. See: D O'Meara *Forty Lost Years*: 129–131.
11 For a discussion of the ideological struggles for control of the verkrampte-dominated Broederbond, see: D O'Meara *Forty Lost Years*: 159–164.
12 Ibid: 296.
13 For a comprehensive discussion of the far right in South Africa, see: J van Rooyen *Hard Right: The New White Power in South Africa* London: I.B.Tauris, 1994.
14 D O'Meara 'Thinking Theoretically? Afrikaner nationalism and the comparative theory of the politics of identity' Paper delivered on 25 March 1999 at Dalhousie University, Halifax, Canada: 7. He comments that: 'Only fairly late in the game, and under very specific conditions and circumstances, did [key groups of Afrikaners] come to assimilate the subjectivity embodied in the nationalist discourse. Moreover, the hold of this generalised Afrikaner nationalist identity lasted for a relatively short period – from the early 1950s to the end of the 1970s.'
15 H Giliomee in: R Schrire (ed) *Malan to De Klerk: Leadership in the Apartheid State* London: Hurst and Company, 1994: 125.
16 W Munro 'Revisiting Tradition, Reconstructing Identity? Afrikaner Nationalism and Political Transition in South Africa' *Politikon* 1995; 22(2): 15.
17 Ibid: 14.
18 Interview by the author with Sampie Terreblanche, 4 August 2006.
19 C Charney 'Class conflict and the National Party split' *Journal of Southern African Studies* 1984; 10(2): 273–4. Following the 1982 NP split, approximately a quarter of Transvaal district and branch committee members deserted the NP for the ranks of the CP. By-election swings to the CP were most marked in working class and farming constituencies, ranging from between 10 per cent to 27 per cent.
20 W Munro 'Revisiting Tradition, Reconstructing Identity? Afrikaner Nationalism and Political Transition in South Africa' *Politikon* 1995; 22(2): 16.
21 D O'Meara *Forty Lost Years*: 310.
22 Ibid: 311–2.
23 W Munro 'Revisiting Tradition, Reconstructing Identity? Afrikaner Nationalism and Political Transition in South Africa' *Politikon* 1995; 22(2): 20.
24 J Grobbelaar, S Bekker and R Evans *Vir Volk en Vaderland: A Guide to the White Right* Durban: Indicator Project South Africa, 1989.
25 D O'Meara *Forty Lost Years*: 125. Emphasis in the original.

26 O Figes *Natasha's Dance: A Cultural History of Russia* London: Allen Lane, 2002: xxviii.
27 N Alexander in: G Maharaj (ed) *Between Unity and Diversity: Essays on Nation-Building in Post-Apartheid South Africa* Cape Town: David Philip, 1999: 18.
28 A Nash 'The New Politics of Afrikaans' *South African Journal of Philosophy* 2000; 19(4): 352.
29 'Bitter with a twist' *Mail & Guardian* 8 December 2006. According to the founders, Conrad Botes and Anton Kannemeyer: 'As long as you remain harshly self-critical, anybody and anything is fair game.'
30 D O'Meara 'Thinking Theoretically? Afrikaner nationalism and the comparative theory of the politics of identity' Paper delivered on 25 March 1999 at Dalhousie University, Halifax, Canada: 7.
31 D O'Meara *Forty Lost Years*: 370. '*Eie*' literally translates as [one's] own – i.e., essential characteristics, essence.
32 Giliomee argues that: 'Many of the younger generation were delighted to be rid of the stifling cultural conformity of Afrikaner society and the security anxieties of the final decades of apartheid. They were proud to live in a democracy and loved the country's inclusive national symbols. Unlike their parents, they could travel all over the world. National sports teams were welcome in international competitions.': H Giliomee *The Afrikaners: Biography of a People*: 664.
33 O Figes 'Birth of a nation' *The Guardian* (London) 14 September 2002.
34 D O'Meara *Forty Lost Years*: 126–7. The incidence revolved around the award of the 1964 Hertzog Prize for prose by the *Akademie vir Wetenskap en Kuns* to Etienne Leroux's controversial novel, *Sewe Dae by die Silbersteins*. Despite the beginnings of an all-out cultural war, the award stood.
35 Ibid: 127.
36 Ibid: 371.
37 O'Meara argues that: 'Outside the relatively small fundamentalist circles, most urban Afrikaner nationalists were intensely proud of what the Sestigers wrought for Afrikaans literature and language.' Ibid: 370–1.
38 For a more detailed investigation into the invention of ethnic identity using the Afrikaans language, see: I Hofmeyr in: S Marks & S Trapido (eds) *The politics of race, class and nationalism in twentieth-century South Africa* London: Longman, 1993: Chapter three.
39 A Nash 'The New Politics of Afrikaans' *South African Journal of Philosophy* 2000; 19(4): 346.
40 Ibid: 348.
41 Ibid: 357.
42 'Old split over Afrikaner identity fuels new terror' *Business Day* 28 November 2002. Dan Roodt is the leader of the *Pro-Afrikaanse Aksiegroep* (Praag).
43 D Roodt *The Scourge of the ANC* Praag, 2005.
44 'Is there an Afrikaner problem?' *Mail & Guardian* 19–25 March 1999.
45 For example, Giliomee argues that many of the younger generation reject the idea of waging a struggle on behalf of Afrikaans as a public language as part of their revolt with patriarchy. He quotes a participant in a television programme

(*Rapport* 24 November 2002 on the KykNet program *Jonk en Afrikaans*): 'The older people have a tendency to turn everything into an issue. The language issue. The university issue. Everything is issues. The young people must survive, that's our issue.' H Giliomee *The Afrikaners: Biography of a People*: 664.

46 A Nash 'The New Politics of Afrikaans' *South African Journal of Philosophy* 2000; 19(4): 349.
47 Degenaar has identified this with 'a commitment to pluralism "which leaves room for the individual to come of age as an Afrikaner in a way which does not necessarily presuppose a nationalist identity"'. Quoted in: Ibid: 350.
48 Ibid: 352.
49 Ibid: 340 and 352. Emphasis added.
50 Interview by the author with Johann Rossouw, 7 August 2006.
51 Interview by the author with Danie Goosen, 31 July 2006.
52 Quoted in: A Nash 'The New Politics of Afrikaans' *South African Journal of Philosophy* 2000; 19(4): 353.
53 See: www.solidaritysa.co.za
54 'White workers flock to unions' *Mail & Guardian* 9–15 March 2001.
55 'Eskom race dispute: Union is wrong' *Mail & Guardian* 21 March 2006. The union has consistently claimed that affirmative action policies contravene the guidelines of the International Labour Organisation.
56 'End rugby quotas, say white authors' *Mail & Guardian* 1 January 2002. The authors of a book concerned with promoting an end for quotas in rugby – 'it is now time for normal sport' – included Kallie Kriel, the director of the research institute at Solidarity.
57 The tour drew heavy criticism from other trade unions including COSATU and the National Union of Mineworkers where the general secretary, Gwede Mantashe, commented: 'They have recycled themselves to exactly where they were decades ago': 'Solidarity returns to its white-right roots' *Business Report* 17 February 2006.
58 For example: B Lohnert, S Oldfield & S Parnell 'Post-apartheid social polarisations: the creation of sub-urban identities in Cape Town' *South African Geographical Journal* 1998; 80(2): 86–92; C Rogerson 'The Economic and Social Geography of South Africa: Progress Beyond Apartheid' *Tijdschrift voor Economische en Sociale Geografie* 2000; 19(4); and, M Ramutsindela 'Down the post-colonial road: reconstructing the post-apartheid state in South Africa' *Political Geography* 2001; 20(1): 57–84.
59 S Jackson 'Coloureds don't Toyi-Toyi: Gesture, Constraint and Identity in Cape Town' in: S Robins (eds) *Limits to Liberation after Apartheid: Citizenship, Governance and Culture* Cape Town: David Philip, 2006: 211.
60 S Cornelissen & S Horstmeier 'The social and political construction of identities in the new South Africa: an analysis of the Western Cape Province' *Journal of Modern African Studies* 2002; 40(1): 57. Emphasis added.
61 Statistics South Africa *Primary tables Western cape: Census '96 and 2001 compared* (Report no.: 03-02-13 (2001)) Pretoria: Statistics SA, 2005. It is likely that numbers among the African/black population group will rise due to an influx

of migrants from other provinces. Aside from the Northern Cape, the Western Cape is the only province with a coloured majority population.

62 In a survey conducted by the Human Sciences Research Council (HSRC) during March 1999, it was suggested that: 'Exclusive subgroup identities with an absent overarching shared national identity was characteristic of how South Africans defined themselves under apartheid rule. This has now changed. While a range of subgroup identities is very much in place, these identities are shared with a strong overarching national identity. In present day South Africa subgroup identities have become important elements in support of the national identity. Furthermore, these inter-linked identities are important for building societal cohesion.' HSRC 'Am I a South African?' Media Release, 2 December 1999 http://www.hsrc.ac.za/media/1999/12/19991202.html

63 Personal correspondence to the author from Scarlett Cornelissen 12 February 2003.

64 Electoral briefing 'Party support in South Africa's third democratic election' Cape Town: IDASA, March 2004.

65 S Cornelissen & S Horstmeier 'The social and political construction of identities in the new South Africa: an analysis of the Western Cape Province' *Journal of Modern African Studies* 2002; 40(1): 58.

66 'ANC undisputed – if blemished – poll victor' *Business Day* 4 March 2006.

67 Sheval Ardense in: 'Coloured in the drinking water' *Mail & Guardian* 9 June 2006.

68 S Cornelissen & S Horstmeier 'The social and political construction of identities in the new South Africa: an analysis of the Western Cape Province' *Journal of Modern African Studies* 2002; 40(1): 59. Emphasis in the original.

69 Ibid: 69 and 67. In addition, seven of these 15 opinion-makers believed that Afrikaans is the predominant and unifying language in the Western Cape, and saw this as 'signifying a common culture in the province'.

70 Six variables including geographic location, ethnicity, language, religion, socio-economic standing and age were used to select the communities.

71 S Cornelissen & S Horstmeier 'The social and political construction of identities in the new South Africa: an analysis of the Western Cape Province' *Journal of Modern African Studies* 2002; 40(1): 72–3.

72 Ibid: 77.

73 S Jacobs & R Krabill 'Mediating Manenberg in the post-Apartheid Public Sphere: Media, Democracy and Citizenship in South Africa' in: S Robins (eds) *Limits to Liberation after Apartheid*: 163.

74 M Vestergaard 'Who's Got the Map? The Negotiation of Afrikaner Identities in Post-Apartheid South Africa' *Daedalus* 2001; 130(1): 35. Emphasis added.

75 D O'Meara *Forty Lost Years*: 368.

76 Ralph Rabie (aka Johannes Kerkorrel) in P de Vos 'Nuwe lied van jong Suid-Afrika' *Die Suid Afrikaan* 21 June/July 1989. Quoted in: D O'Meara *Forty Lost Years*: 368.

77 Ibid: 369–70.

78 'Wake up and smell the moerkoffie' *Mail & Guardian* 22–28 June 2001.

79 A Nash 'The New Politics of Afrikaans' *South African Journal of Philosophy* 2000; 19(4): 352.

80   M Vestergaard 'Who's Got the Map? The Negotiation of Afrikaner Identities in Post-Apartheid South Africa' *Daedalus* 2001; 130(1): 35.
81   'Is there an Afrikaner problem?' *Mail & Guardian* 19–25 March 1999.
82   'Rocking the laager' *The Sunday Times* 13 October 2002. Emphasis added. The bands include Koos Kombuis, Valiant Swart, Beeskraal, Kobus!, the Brixton Moord en Roof Orkes, battery9, Diff-olie, Brasse vannie Kaap, Not My Dog, Akkedis, Spinnekop, Plank, The Buckfever Underground, Tynhys, Riku Latti, Karen Zoid and Pieter Smit amongst many other recorded artists.
83   Haddad Viljoen, head of marketing for DStv's Afrikaans music channel MK89, quoted in: 'Afrikaans music gets interesting' *Mail & Guardian* 4 May 2007.
84   'Afrikaans music gets interesting' *Mail & Guardian* 4 May 2007.
85   Ryk Benade of kidofdoom, quoted in 'Afrikaans music gets interesting' *Mail & Guardian* 4 May 2007.
86   Roof Bezuidenhout of Brixton Moord en Roof, quoted in 'Rocking the laager' *The Sunday Times* 13 October 2002.
87   Bok van Blerk, quoted in: 'Boer roar' *The Financial Times* 21–22 July 2007.
88   'Afrikaans music gets interesting' *Mail & Guardian* 4 May 2007.
89   'Straight to hell' *Mail & Guardian* 7–13 May 2004.
90   'Leader of the pack' *Mail & Guardian* 3 October 2006.
91   'Rocking the laager' *The Sunday Times* 13 October 2002.
92   'Fewer bitterbekke, more art at Aardklop' *The Sunday Independent* 14 October 2001.
93   Interview by the author with Albert Grundlingh, 10 August 2006. It was suggested that rugby is perhaps the only other cultural area or space where a similar 'ethnic nesting' occurs.
94   'More than mother tongue' *Mail & Guardian* 8 April 2005.
95   Interview by the author with Marlene van Niekerk, 10 August 2006.
96   Interview by the author with Albert Grundlingh, 10 August 2006.
97   Interview by the author with Herman Wasserman, 8 August 2006.
98   S Hall in: A King (ed) *Culture, Globalisation and The World System*: 34–5.
99   'A hundred years of attitude' *Mail & Guardian* 8–14 October 1999.
100 A Krog *Country of My Skull* London: Vintage, 1999: 238.
101 F Fanon *Black Skin, White Masks* New York: Grove Weidenfeld, 1991: 17–8.
102 'Climbing Mount Improbable' *The Guardian* (London) 15 June 2002.
103 Interview by the author with Tom Dreyer, 5 November 2001.
104 'Climbing Mount Improbable' *The Guardian* (London) 15 June 2002.
105 'Is English the new Afrikaans?' *Mail & Guardian* 1 June 2006.
106 'What the Boer wore' *Mail & Guardian* 1 April 2005.
107 'Where have all the book readers gone?' *Business Day* 12 November 2001.
108 Interview by the author with Johann Rossouw, 7 August 2006.
109 It is contended that group solidarity and resilience are premised upon fears concerning security and cultural identity being at least on a par with material interests. For example, see: J van Rooyen *Hard Right: The New White Power in South Africa* London: IB Tauris, 1994; and, K Manzo & P McGowan 'Afrikaner Fears and the Politics of Despair: Understanding Change in South Africa' *International Studies Quarterly* 1992; 36(1).

110 W Munro 'Revisiting Tradition, Reconstructing Identity? Afrikaner Nationalism and Political Transition In South Africa' *Politikon* 1995; 22(2): 22. Emphasis added.
111 Ibid: 7.
112 'FF+ 'a home for former NNP supporters" *Mail & Guardian* 27 February 2006.
113 http://www.vryheidsfront.co.za/index.asp
114 'The Role of the Afrikaner in a Multicultural South Africa' Speech given on 21 October 2002 by Dr Pieter Mulder as part of the Africa Dialogue Lecture Series at the University of Pretoria. http://www.vryheidsfront.co.za/index.asp
115 W Munro 'Revisiting Tradition, Reconstructing Identity? Afrikaner Nationalism and Political Transition In South Africa' *Politikon* 1995; 22(2): 25. It is suggested that Viljoen's ascendancy 'also indicates that the character of Afrikaner nationalism had by no means solidified. While pressing for negotiations, Viljoen also pressed for a postponement of the election date (agreed in June 1993), admitting that the Afrikaners needed more time to work out a clearer concept of self-determination, one which would be both politically workable and ultimately negotiable'.
116 Aside from the Free State (2.07 per cent), in these key provinces the FF+ won less than 2 per cent of the vote, achieving only 1.49 per cent of the vote in Northern Cape, 1.24 per cent in the Western Cape and 1.2 per cent in Gauteng: http://www.elections.org.za/Elections2004_Static.asp
117 'Freedom Front could be the unexpected beneficiary' *Business Day* 20 November 2001. Mulder told the party's federal congress that: 'Opposition will only be sensible if there is a definite possibility that your party can defeat the government in the next election after which you can implement your policies. For the next 10 to 15 years that simply is not possible. Shouting at the ANC from the opposite benches for the next 50 years can never be the answer to the problems and frustrations of the Afrikaner.'
118 He continued: 'For example, in the Western Cape, during their three-year rule of Cape Town, the ANC used national rather than provincial demographic figures in employment-equity appointments, blatantly discriminating against 60 per cent of the [coloured] population.' 'DA bemoans "silent war"' *Mail & Guardian* 20 August 2006.
119 'FF satisfied with growth as indicated by election' http://www.vryheidsfront.co.za/index.asp?l=e
120 'What ideals in the beer and boerewors belt will protect Afrikaners now?' *The Sunday Independent* 22 October 2000.
121 'Solidarity seeks Cosatu aid against farm killings' *Business Day* 21 July 2006. According to the farmers organisation AgriSA, two farmers a week are murdered whilst Solidarity estimates that since 1987, 2017 murders have occurred on farms of which 70 per cent were directed against farmers. There is considerable debate about whether the high toll is due to outside criminal elements and/or exploitation and abuse in the sector. Whilst the figures have not risen, an average of 180 farmers are murdered every year which has raised questions as to whether there will be a wide-scale abandonment of the criminal justice system. Rumours of a conspiracy against white farmers are rife.

122 South African Human Rights Commission (SAHRC) *Final Report on the Inquiry into Human Rights Violations in Farming Communities* Johannesburg: SAHRC, 2003. After a series of public hearings during 2002 and 2003, the wide-ranging SAHRC report which looked at labour conditions, economic and social rights, as well as safety and security for farm workers and farmers themselves, was completed during August 2003.
123 'ANC urges land reform to meet poverty-relief, growth targets' *Business Day* 23 January 2007. The government's Land Redistribution for Agricultural Development programme underlines the massive contribution land reform will make to economic development. It expects that land claims will be finalised by 2008 and by 2014 over 14 per cent of farmland will have been transferred to black farmers.
124 'Fresh spate of farm murders reignites feud' *Business Day* 13 June 2001. In places like the Potchefstroom district in North West Province, membership of the local commando dropped from more than a thousand in 1989, to approximately 150 in 1999.
125 'Farmers threaten armed struggle' *Mail & Guardian* 7 September 2005.
126 'Nervous farmers turn to the ANC' *Mail & Guardian* 20–26 October 2002. Other FF members joined the defections, with Dannie Wanneberg on the party's candidate list for Pretoria, and Monica Muller on its list for the North Eastern District in Gauteng.
127 Executive director of AgriSA Hans van der Merwe explained that whilst there are concerns about the reduction in commercial farmers that restitution and land reform will effect: 'We never asked to be paid more than a reasonable commercial price for our properties.' 'Good response to land reform initiative' *Mail & Guardian* 16 August 2006.
128 'Building bridges in the Free State' *Mail & Guardian* 22 October 2002.
129 'Afrikaner helping hands' *Financial Mail* 19 May 2006. Naspers chairman, Ton Vosloo, believes Afrikaners have a long history of co-operation, especially among farmers communities: 'We call it *helpmekaar* – the idea that you can't help yourself if you don't help your neighbour in times of need. Only then can you live in peace. Now we are extending *helpmekaar* across the colour line.'
130 'Farmers rising to market challenges' *Business Day* 17 July 2001.
131 The Centre for Development and Enterprise (CDE) *Land Reform in South Africa: A 21st century perspective* Johannesburg: CDE Research Report no. 14, 2005. Commercial agriculture has been in long-term decline (during 2002 it represented only 3.4 per cent of GDP) and today comprises a fragile, relatively small knowledge- and not labour-intensive sector.
132 'What ideals in the beer and boerewors belt will protect Afrikaners now?' *The Sunday Independent* 22 October 2000.
133 'Whites protest against African name changes' *Mail & Guardian* 28 July 2006.
134 For example, the Freedom Front Plus' euphemistically entitled manifesto for the 2004 national elections 'A Programme of Hope:' http://www.vryheidsfront.co.za/english/Manifesto2004.htm
135 'Moving beyond the yawn on Afrikaans' *The Sunday Independent* 22 April 2001.

136 During a debate in the National Assembly on 24 March 1999, the then leader of the NNP Marthinus van Schalkwyk argued that: 'We in the New NP say there are no colour or political requirements to be an Afrikaner. It is an inclusive concept based on only one criterion: language.'

137 For example, Flip Buys is General Secretary of Solidarity and was a founding member of the Group of 63.

Chapter 6

1 The white population comprises 9.2 per cent (4 365 300) of the total population and is expected to decline to under 8 per cent by 2021: Statistics South Africa *Mid-year population estimates, South Africa: 2006* (Statistical release: P0302) Pretoria: StatsSA, August 2006.

2 'Whites to drive economic growth, says survey' *Mail & Guardian* 4 April 2006. According to the annual *South Africa Survey* of the South African Institute for Race Relations (SAIRR), whites continue to dominate certain vital academic fields. A co-author of the report commented: 'As long as the school system does not produce suitable university candidates, the private sector will find it difficult to meet employment and management equity targets, as qualified candidates will remain in short supply. No amount of empowerment legislation can serve as a substitute for a quality education system.'

3 I Taylor 'Globalisation Studies and the Developing World: making international political economy truly global' *Third World Quarterly* 2005; 26(7): 1026.

4 S Hall in: D Morley & H-K Chen (eds) *Stuart Hall: Critical Dialogues in Cultural Studies* London: Routledge, 1996: 447.

5 P Spencer & H Wollman in: K Brehony & N Rassoll (eds) *Nationalisms Old and New* London: Macmillan, 1999: 105.

6 A Appadurai *Modernity at Large: Cultural Dimensions of Globalisation* Minneapolis, MN: University of Minneapolis Press, 1997: 581.

7 H Marais *South Africa: Limits to Change: The Political Economy of Transition* Cape Town: University of Cape Town Press, 2001: 231.

8 Ibid: 234–5.

9 S Hall *The Hard Road to Renewal: Thatcherism and the Crisis of the Left* London: Verso, 1988: 8.

10 'Friends of Mbeki tee off together' *Business Day* 18 August 2006.

11 A Nash 'The New Politics of Afrikaans' *South African Journal of Philosophy* 2000; 19(4): 340.

12 Interview with Jacob de Villiers, Director of the AHI: 21 August 2002. Where there are areas of difference, Afrikaner capital elites 'are not inclined to fight the government in public. [Indeed], the AHI is constructive in our approach to help make the economy work.' De Villiers is adamant that, at this stage, there is no 'appetite in the Afrikaner business community to itself initiate a broad-based dialogue regarding the Afrikaner community.'

13 'Transformation: Agencies get into GEAR' *Financial Mail* 4 August 2000.

14 The sixth annual report of the Commission for Employment Equity released in September 2006 demonstrated that whites still dominate top and senior management positions within the economy. In top management, 72.6 per cent of positions were filled by whites which represents a decrease of 2.1 per cent from 2001 to 2005. The figure is roughly comparable in senior management: 'Mdladlana names 'too-white' firms' *Business Day* 12 September 2006.

15 The *taaldebat* runs the entire spectrum of sentiments from *verloopte* Afrikaans speakers to the *taalstryders*. The debate is largely concentrated within the white Afrikaans grouping so that coloured and black Afrikaans speakers represent a 'whole world lost from sight': Interview by the author with Herman Wasserman, 8 August 2006. The views represented here are equally diverse, as demonstrated by the social exclusion concerns of the academic, Neville Alexander, to the belief that protection is not necessary because the language is, according to Conrad Sidego, Chair of the *Stigting vir die Bemagtiging deur Afrikaans* (Foundation for Empowerment through Afrikaans), 'now warts and all part of our African heritage.' 'Stop Agonising About Afrikaans' *Mail & Guardian* 1 June 2006.

16 Interview by the author with Albert Grundlingh, 10 August 2006.

17 Richard Ballard of the University of KwaZulu-Natal in: 'Fear and loathing in gated communities' *Mail & Guardian* 1 March 2005.

18 'More of SA's executives leaving the country' *Mail & Guardian* 10 August 2006. A national survey conducted by consultancy firm Deloitte found that the number of executives leaving the country rose between 2005–2006 in spite of higher pay packages. The main reason given for the exodus was better jobs abroad.

19 Interview by the author with Marlene van Niekerk, 10 August 2006.

20 J N Pieterse 'Deconstructing/reconstructing ethnicity' *Nations & Nationalism* 1997; 3(3): 381. Emphasis in the original.

21 R Alba *Ethnic Identity: The Transformation of White America* New Haven, CT: Yale University Press, 1990: xiii.

22 Ibid: 306.

23 C McCall *Identity in Northern Ireland: Communities, Politics and Change* London: Macmillan, 1999: 204.

BIBLIOGRAPHY

Books, chapters in books and unpublished theses

Heribert Adam, Frederik Van Zyl Slabbert and Kogila Moodley *Comrades in Business: Post-Liberation Politics in South Africa* Cape Town: Tafelberg, 1997.

——and Hermann Giliomee *The Rise and Crisis of Afrikaner Power* Cape Town: David Philip, 1979.

Walter Adamson *Hegemony and Revolution: A Study of Antonio Gramsci's Political and Cultural Theory* Berkeley, CA: University of California Press, 1980.

Richard Alba *Ethnic Identity: The Transformation of White America* New Haven, CT: Yale University Press, 1990.

Benedict Anderson *Imagined Communities: Reflections on the Origins and Spread of Nationalism* London: Verso, 1983.

Arjun Appadurai *Modernity At Large: Cultural Dimensions of Globalisation* Minneapolis, MN: University of Minneapolis Press, 1997.

Simon Bekker and Rachel Prinsloo (eds) *Identity? Theory, Politics, History* Pretoria: HSRC, 1999.

Terry Bell *Unfinished Business: South Africa, Apartheid and Truth* London: Verso, 2003.

Patrick Bond *Against Global Apartheid: South Africa meets the World Bank, IMF and International Finance* Cape Town: UCT Press, 2001.

——*Elite Transition: From Apartheid to Neoliberalism in South Africa* London: Pluto Press, 2000 (first edition).

Kevin Brehony and Naz Rassool (eds) *Nationalisms Old and New* London: Macmillan, 1999.

John Brewer (ed) *Can South Africa Survive? Five Minutes to Midnight* London: Macmillan Press, 1989.

Chris Brink *No lesser place: the taaldebat at Stellenbosch* Stellenbosch: Sunmedia, 2006.
Sakhela Buhlungu, John Daniel, Roger Southall & Jessica Lutchman (eds) *State of the Nation, South Africa 2005–2006* Cape Town: HSRC Press, 2006.
Anthony Butler *Democracy and Apartheid: Political Theory, Comparative Politics and the Modern South African State* London: Macmillan, 1998.
Alex Callinicos (ed) *Between Apartheid and Capitalism: Conversations with South African Socialists* London: Bookmarks, 1992.
Kenneth Christie (ed) *Ethnic Conflict, Tribal Politics: A Global Perspective* Richmond: Curzon Press, 1998.
Joan Copjec and Michael Sorkin *Giving Ground: The Politics of Propinquity* London: Verso, 1999.
Robert Cox *Production, Power and World Order: Social Forces in the Making of History* New York: Columbia University Press, 1987.
John Daniel, Adam Habib & Roger Southall (eds) *The State of the Nation, 2003–2004* Cape Town: HSRC Press, 2003.
Rob Davies, Dan O'Meara and Sipho Dlamini *The Struggle for South Africa: A reference guide to movements, organisations and institutions* London: Zed Books, 1988.
Johan Degenaar *Nations and Nationalism: The Myth of a South African Nation* Cape Town: IDASA, 1991.
——*The Roots of Nationalism* Cape Town: Academica, 1983.
Frederik Willem de Klerk *The Last Trek – A New Beginning* London: Macmillan, 1998.
Brian du Toit *The Boers in East Africa: Ethnicity and Identity* Westport: Bergin & Garvey, 1998.
Micha Ebata & Beverly Neufeld (eds) *Confronting the Political in International Relations* Basingstoke: Macmillan: 2000.
Richard Elphick and Hermann Giliomee (eds) *The Shaping of South African Society, 1652–1840* Cape Town: Maskew Miller Longman, 1989.
Norman Etherington *The Great Treks: The Transformation of Southern Africa, 1815–1854* London: Longman, 2001.
——(ed) *Peace, Politics and Violence in the New South Africa* Melbourne: Hans Zell, 1992.
Frantz Fanon *Black Skin, White Masks* New York: Grove Weidenfeld, 1991.
Mike Featherstone, Scott Lash and Roland Robertson (eds) *Global Modernities* London: Sage, 1995.
——(ed) *Global Culture: Nationalism, globalisation and modernity* London: Sage, 1990.

Orlando Figes *Natasha's Dance: A Cultural History of Russia* London: Allen Lane, 2002.
David Forgacs (ed) *A Gramsci Reader: Selected Writings 1919–1935* London: Lawrence and Wishart, 1999.
Philip Frankel, Noam Pines, and Mark Swilling (eds) *State, Resistance and Change in South Africa* Johannesburg: Southern Books, 1988.
Stephen Gelb (ed) *South Africa's Economic Crisis* Cape Town: David Philip, 1991.
Ernest Gellner *Encounters with Nationalism* Oxford: Blackwell, 1994.
——*Plough, Sword and Book: The Structure of Human History* Chicago, IL: Chicago University Press, 1988.
——*Nations and Nationalism* Oxford: Basil Blackwell, 1983.
Dante Germino *Antonio Gramsci: Architect of a New Politics* Baton Rouge, LO: Louisiana State University Press, 1990.
Anthony Giddens *The Nation-State and Violence* Berkeley, CA: University of California Press, 1985.
Hermann Giliomee *The Afrikaners: Biography of a People* Cape Town: Tafelberg, 2003.
——and C Simkins (eds) *The Awkward Embrace: One-Party Domination and Democracy* Cape Town: Tafelberg, 1999.
——*Surrender Without Defeat: Afrikaners and the South African Miracle* Braamfontein: South African Institute of Race Relations, 1997.
——and Jannie Gagiano (eds) *The Elusive Search for Peace: South Africa, Israel and Northern Ireland* Cape Town: Oxford University Press, 1990.
——and Lawrence Schlemmer *From Apartheid to Nation-Building* Cape Town: Oxford University Press, 1989.
Stephen Gill (ed) *Gramsci, Historical Materialism and International Relations* Cambridge: Cambridge University Press, 1993.
Barry Gills (ed) *Globalisation and the Politics of Resistance* London: Macmillan, 2000.
Henri Goverde, Philip Cerny, Mark Haugaard and Howard Lentner (eds) *Power in Contemporary Politics: Theories, Practices, Globalisations* London: Sage, 2000.
Antonio Gramsci *Selections from the Prison Notebooks* London: Lawrence and Wishart, 1971.
Janis Grobbelaar, Simon Bekker and Robert Evans *Vir Volk en Vaderland: A Guide to the White Right* Durban: Indicator Project South Africa, 1989.
William Gumede *Thabo Mbeki and the Battle for the Soul of the ANC* Cape Town: Zebra Press, 2005.
Stuart Hall, David Held and Anthony McGrew (eds) *Modernity and Its Futures* Cambridge: Polity Press, 1992.

―――*The Hard Road to Renewal: Thatcherism and the Crisis of the Left* London: Verso, 1988.

David Held, Anthony McGrew, David Goldblatt and Jonathan Perraton *Global Transformations: Politics, Economics and Culture* Cambridge: Polity Press, 1999.

Alan Hirsch *Season of Hope: Economic Reform Under Mandela and Mbeki* Pietermaritzburg: University of KwaZulu-Natal Press, 2005.

Eric Hobsbawm *Nations and nationalism since 1780: Programme, myth, reality* Cambridge: Cambridge University Press, 1990.

―――and J Ranger (eds) *The Invention of Tradition* Cambridge: Cambridge University Press, 1983.

Ankie Hoogvelt *Globalisation and the Postcolonial World: The New Political Economy of Development* Basingstoke: Palgrave, 2001.

Tim Keegan *Colonial South Africa and The Origins of The Racial Order* London: Leicester University Press, 1996.

Anthony King (ed) *Culture, Globalisation and The World-System: Contemporary Conditions For The Representation of Identity* London: Macmillan, 1991.

Thomas Koelble *The Global Economy and Democracy in South Africa* New Brunswick, NJ: Rutgers University Press, 1998.

Antjie Krog *Country of My Skull* Johannesburg: Random House, 1998.

Will Kymlicka *Politics in the Vernacular: Nationalism, Multiculturalism, and Citizenship* Oxford: Oxford University Press, 2001.

―――*Multi-cultural Citizenship: a Liberal Theory of Minority Rights* Oxford: Clarendon Press, 1995.

Adrian Leftwich (ed) *Democracy and Development: Theory and Practice* Oxford: Polity Press, 1996.

Michael Macdonald *Why Race Matters in South Africa* Scottsville: University of KwaZulu-Natal Press, 2006.

Ernest Maganya and Rachel Houghton (eds) *Transformation in South Africa? Policy Debates in the 1990s* Braamfontein: Institute for African Alternatives, 1996.

Gitanjali Maharaj (ed) *Between Unity and Diversity: Essays on Nation-Building in Post-Apartheid South Africa* Cape Town: David Philip, 1999.

Hein Marais *South Africa Limits to Change: The Political Economy of Transition* Cape Town: University of Cape Town Press, 2001 (second edition).

Shula Marks and Stanley Trapido (eds) *The politics of race, class and nationalism in twentieth-century South Africa* London: Longman, 1993.

Anthony Marx *Lessons of Struggle: South African Internal Opposition, 1960–1990* Cape Town: Oxford University Press, 1992.

Stephen May *Language and Minority Rights: Ethnicity, Nationalism and the Politics of Language* Harlow: Longman, 2001.

Cathal McCall *Identity in Northern Ireland: Communities, Politics and Change* London: Macmillan, 1999.
David McDonald and Jonathan Crush (eds) *Destinations Unknown: Perspectives on the Brain Drain in Southern Africa* Pretoria: Africa Institute of South Africa, 2002.
Birgit Meyer and Peter Geschiere (eds) *Globalisation and Identity: Dialectics of Flow and Closure* Oxford: Blackwell, 1999.
Jonathan Michie and Vishnu Padayachee (eds) *The Political Economy of South Africa's Transition: Policy Perspectives in the Late 1990s* Sydney: Harcourt Brace, 1997.
James Mittelman and Norani Othman *Capturing Globalisation* London: Routledge, 2001.
——*The Globalisation Syndrome: Transformation and Resistance* Princeton, NJ: Princeton University Press, 2000.
David Morley and Kuan-Hsing Chen (eds) *Stuart Hall: Critical Dialogues in Cultural Studies* London: Routledge, 1996.
Chantal Mouffe (ed) *Gramsci and Marxist Theory* London: Routledge and Kegan Paul, 1979.
Martin Murray *Revolution Deferred: The Painful Birth of Post-Apartheid South Africa* London: Verso, 1994.
Tom Nairn *The Breakup of Britain* London: Verso, 1981.
Kate Nash *Contemporary Political Sociology: Globalisation, Politics, and Power* Oxford: Blackwell, 2000.
Dan O'Meara *Forty Lost Years: The apartheid state and the politics of the National Party, 1948–1994* Randburg: Ravan Press, 1996.
——*Volkskapitalisme: Class, Capital and Ideology in the Development of Afrikaner Nationalism, 1934–1948* Cambridge: Cambridge University Press, 1983.
Deborah Posel *The Making of Apartheid, 1948–61: Conflict and Compromise* Oxford: Clarendon Press, 1991.
Robert Price *The Apartheid State in Crisis: Political Transformation in South Africa, 1975–1990* Oxford: Oxford University Press, 1991.
Steven Robins (ed) *Limits to Liberation: Citizenship and Governance After Apartheid* Cape Town: David Philip, 2006.
Dan Roodt *The Scourge of the ANC* Praag, 2005.
Mark Rupert and Hazel Smith (eds) *Historical Materialism and Globalisation* London: Routledge, 2002.
John Saul *Recolonisation and Resistance: Southern Africa in the 1990s* Trenton, NJ: Africa World Press, 1993.
Lawrence Schlemmer 'Factors in the Persistence or Decline of Ethnic Group

Mobilisation: A Conceptual Review and Case Study of Cultural Group Responses Among Afrikaners in Post-Apartheid South Africa' Ph.D. thesis – Department of Political Studies, University of Cape Town, August 1999.

Robert Schrire (ed) *Malan to De Klerk: Leadership in the Apartheid State* London: Hurst and Company, 1994.

——*Adapt or Die: The End of White Politics in South Africa* London: Hurst and Company, 1991.

Jeremy Seekings and Nicoli Nattrass *Class, Race, and Inequality in South Africa* Scottsville: University of KwaZulu-Natal Press, 2006.

Anne Showstack Sasson (ed) *Approaches to Gramsci* London: Writers and Readers, 1982.

Roger Simon *Gramsci's Political Thought: An Introduction* London: Lawrence and Wishart, 1991.

Mark Suzman *Ethnic Nationalism and State Power: The Rise of Irish Nationalism, Afrikaner Nationalism and Zionism* London: Macmillan, 1999.

Dolores Tanno and Alberto Gonzalez (eds) *Communication and Identity Across Cultures* London: Sage, 1998.

Ian Taylor 'Hegemony, "Common Sense" and Compromise: A Neo-Gramscian Analysis of Multilateralism in South Africa's Post-Apartheid Foreign Policy' D. Phil. Thesis – Department of Political Science, University of Stellenbosch, March 2000.

Sampie Terreblanche *A History of Inequality in South Africa 1652–2002* Pietermaritzburg: University of Kwa-Zulu-Natal Press, 2002.

Leonard Thompson and Jeffrey Butler (eds) *Change in Contemporary South Africa* Berkeley, CA: University of California Press, 1975.

Francis Toase and Edmund Yorke (eds) *The New South Africa: Prospects for Domestic and International Security* London: Macmillan, 1998.

Elizabeth Tonkin, Mayron McDonald and Malcolm Chapman (eds) *History and Ethnicity* London: Routledge, 1989.

Leroy Vail (ed) *The Creation of Tribalism in Southern Africa* Berkeley, CA: University of California Press, 1989.

Ursula van Beek (ed) *South Africa and Poland in Transition: A Comparative Perspective* Pretoria: HSRC, 1995.

Johann van Rooyen *The New Great Trek: The story of South Africa's white exodus* Pretoria: Unisa Press, 2000.

——*Hard Right: The New White Power in South Africa* London: I B Tauris, 1994.

Frederik Van Zyl Slabbert *Tough Choices: Reflections of an Afrikaner African* Cape Town: Tafelberg, 2000.

Patti Waldmeir *Anatomy of a miracle: The end of apartheid and the birth of the new South Africa* London: Viking, 1997.

Andreas Wassenaar *Assault on private enterprise: the freeway to communism* Cape Town: Tafelberg, 1977.

Richard Werbner and Terence Ranger (eds) *Postcolonial Identities in Africa* London: Zed, 1996.

Edwin Wilmsen and Patrick McAllister (eds) *The Politics of Difference: Ethnic Premises in a World of Power* Chicago, IL: University of Chicago Press, 1996.

David Yudelman *The emergence of modern South Africa: State, Capital, and the Incorporation of Organised Labour on the South African Goldfields, 1902–1939* Cape Town: David Philip, 1984.

Journal articles

Iraj Abedian and Barry Standish 'Poor Whites and The Role of The State: The Evidence' *South African Journal of Economics* 1985; 53(2): 141–65.

Walter Adamson 'Gramsci and The Politics of Civil Society' *Praxis International* 1987/8; 7(3/4): 320–39.

John Agnew 'Mapping Political Power Beyond State Boundaries: Territory, Identity, and Movement in World Politics' *Millennium* 1999; 28(3): 499–521.

Neville Alexander 'Afrikaner Identity Today: A Response to Giliomee' *New Contree* 1996; 40: 83–5.

Paul Allanson, Jonathan Atkins and Timothy Hinks 'No End to the Racial Wage Hierarchy in South Africa?' *Journal of Development Economics* 2002; 6(3) 442–59.

Stefan Andreasson 'The ANC and its critics: "predatory liberalism", black economic empowerment and intra-alliance tensions in post-apartheid South Africa' *Democratization* 2006; 13(2): 303–22.

——'Economic Reforms and "Virtual Democracy" in South Africa and Zimbabwe: The Incompatibility of Liberalism, Inclusion and Development *Journal of Contemporary African Studies* 2003; 21(3).

Vicki Birchfield 'Contesting the hegemony of market ideology: Gramsci's "good sense" and Polanyi's "double movement".' *Review of International Political Economy* 1999; 6(1): 27–54.

Andreas Bielder and Adam Morton 'Introduction: International Relations as Political Theory' *Critical Review of International Social and Political Philosophy* 2005; 8(4).

Patrick Bond 'The ANC's "Left Turn" and South African Sub-imperialism' *Review of African Political Economy* 2004; 102.

———'Pretoria's perspective on globalisation: a critique' *Politikon* 2001; 28(1): 81–94.
Rogers Brubaker and Frederick Cooper 'Beyond "identity"' *Theory and Society* 2000; 29(1): 1–47.
Sakhela Buhlungu 'The Building of the Democratic Transition in South Africa's Trade Unions After 1973' *Democratization* 2004; 11(3): 133–58.
Philip Cerny 'Paradoxes of the Competition State: The Dynamics of Political Globalisation' *Government and Opposition* 1997; 32(2): 251–74.
Neo Chabane, Andrea Goldstein and Simon Roberts 'The changing face and strategies of big business in South Africa: more than a decade of political democracy' *Industrial and Corporate Change* 2006; 15(3).
Craig Charney 'Class conflict and the National Party split' *Journal of Southern African Studies* 1984; 10(2)
Elsie Cloete 'Afrikaner Identity: Culture, Transition, Gender' *Agenda* 1992; 13: 42–56.
Carli Coetzee 'Individual and Collective Notions of the "Promised Land": The "Private" Writings of the Boer Emigrants' *South African Historical Journal* 1995; 32: 48–65.
John Comaroff 'Of totemism and ethnicity: Consciousness, practice, and the signs of inequality' *Ethnos* 1987; 52: 301–23.
Scarlett Cornelissen and Steffen Horstmeier 'The social and political construction of identities in the new South Africa: an analysis of the Western Cape Province' *Journal of Modern African Studies* 2002; 40(1): 55–82.
Robert Cox 'Civil society at the turn of the millennium: prospects for an alternative world order' *Review of International Studies* 1999; 25.
———'Gramsci, Hegemony, and International Relations Theory: An Essay in Method' *Millennium* 1983; 2: 162–75.
———'Social Forces, States and World Order: Beyond International Relations' *Millennium* 1981; 10(2): 126–55.
Gerda de Klerk 'Mother-tongue education in South Africa: the weight of history' *International Journal of the Sociology of Language* 2002; 154.
Johan Degenaar 'No Sizwe: The Myth of the Nation' *Indicator SA* 1993; 10(3): 11–6.
Loet Douwes Dekker 'Business Interest Groups' *Industrial Democracy Review* 1996; 5(2): 6–12.
Martin Doornbos 'Linking the Future to the Past: Ethnicity and Pluralism' *Review of African Political Economy* 1991; 52: 53–65.
Saul Dubow 'Ethnic Euphemisms and Racial Echoes' *Journal of Southern African Studies* 1994;20(3): 355–70.

―― 'Afrikaner Nationalism, Apartheid and The Conceptualisation of "Race"' *Journal of African History* 1992; 33: 209–37.

Andre du Toit 'Puritans in Africa? Afrikaner 'Calvinism' and Kuyperian Neo-Calvinism in Late Nineteenth-Century South Africa' *Comparative Studies in Society and History* 1985; 27(2): 209–40.

―― 'Captive to the Nationalist Paradigm: Professor F A van Jaarsveld and the historical evidence for the Afrikaner's ideas on his Calling and Mission' *South African Historical Review* 1984; 16: 49–80.

―― 'No Chosen People: The Myth of the Calvinist Origins of Afrikaner Nationalism and Racial Ideology' *American Historical Review* 1983; 88(4): 920–52.

Louise du Toit 'Cultural identity as narrative and performance' *South African Journal of Philosophy* 1997; 16(3): 85–93.

Robert Fine and Graham van Wyk 'South Africa: State, Labour, and the Politics of Reconstruction' *Capital and Class* 1996; 58: 19–31.

Irina Filatova 'The Rainbow Against the African Sky or African Hegemony in a Multi-Cultural Context?' *Transformation* 1997; 34: 47–56.

David Forgacs 'Gramsci and Marxism in Britain' *New Left Review* 1989; 176: 70–88.

Fred Gale 'Cave Cave! Hic dragones: a neo-Gramscian deconstruction and reconstruction of international regime theory' *Review of International Political Economy* 1998; 5(2): 252–83.

Herbert Gans 'Symbolic ethnicity: the future of ethnic groups and cultures in America' *Ethnic and Racial Studies* 1979; 2(1): 1–20.

Randall Germain and Michael Kenny 'Engaging Gramsci: international relations theory and the new Gramscians' *Review of International Studies* 1998; 24: 3–21.

James Gibson 'Overcoming Apartheid: Can Truth Reconcile a Divided Nation?' *Politikon* 2004; 31(2).

Hermann Giliomee, James Myburgh and Lawrence Schlemmer 'Dominant Party Rule, Opposition Parties and Minorities in South Africa' *Democratization* 2001; 8(1): 161–82.

―― 'Being Afrikaans in The New (Multilingual) South Africa' *New Contree* 1996; 40: 59–74.

―― 'Being Afrikaans As A Presumed Identity: A Response to Adam' *New Contree* 1996; 40: 79–82.

―― 'Democratisation in South Africa' *Political Science Quarterly* 1995; 110(1): 83–104.

―― 'Survival in Justice: An Afrikaner Debate Over Apartheid' *Comparative Studies in Society and History* 1994; 36(3): 527–48.

——'Constructing Afrikaner Nationalism' *Journal of Asian and African Studies* 1983; 18(1–2): 83–98.

Stephen Gill 'Globalisation, Market Civilisation and Disciplinary Neoliberalism' *Millennium* 1995; 24(3).

——'The Global Panopticon? The Neoliberal State, Economic Life, and Democratic Surveillance' *Alternatives* 1995; 20(1): 1–49.

——'Economic Globalisation and the Internationalisation of Authority: Limits and Contradictions' *Geoforum* 1992; 23(3): 269–83.

Barry Gills 'Re-orienting the New (International) Political Economy' *New Political Economy* 2001; 6(2): 233–45.

Kenneth Good 'Accountable to Themselves: Predominance in Southern Africa' *Journal of Modern African Studies* 1997; 35(4): 547–73.

Tom Gouws 'Post Modern Identity: History, Language and Cultural Difference or: The True Colours of The Rainbow Nation' *New Contree* 1996; 40: 13–25.

Janis Grobbelar 'Afrikaner Nationalism: the End of a Dream?' *Social Identities* 1998; 4(3): 385–98.

Albert Grundlingh and Hilary Sapire 'From Feverish Festival to Repetitive Ritual? The Changing Fortunes of Great Trek Mythology in an Industrialising South Africa, 1938–1988' *South African Historical Journal* 1989; 21: 19–57.

Adam Habib, Devan Pillay and Ashwin Desai 'South Africa and the Global Order: The Structural Conditioning of a Transition to Democracy' *Journal of Contemporary African Studies* 1998; 16(1): 95–115.

C R D Halisi 'Citizenship and Populism in the New South Africa' *Africa Today* 1998; 43(3/4): 423–38.

——'From Liberation to Citizenship: Identity and Innovation in Black South Africa Political Thought' *Comparative Studies in Society and History* 1997; 39(1): 61–85.

Andrew Hurrell and Ngaire Woods 'Globalisation and Inequality' *Millennium* 1995; 24(3): 447–70.

Jonathan Hyslop 'Problems of Explanation in the Study of Afrikaner Nationalism: A Case Study of the West Rand' *Journal of Southern African Studies* 1996; 22(3): 373–85.

T J Jackson Lears 'The Concept of Cultural Hegemony: Problems and Possibilities' *American Historical Review* 1985; 90(3): 567–93.

Jane Jenson 'Mapping, naming and remembering: globalisation at the end of the twentieth century' *Review of International Political Economy* 1995; 2(1): 96–116.

Chris Jooste 'A Volkstaat for Afrikaners?' *Indicator SA* 1998; 15(3): 21–7.

Courtney Jung 'After Apartheid: Shaping a New Afrikaner Volk' *Indicator SA* 1996; 13(4): 12–6.

Michael Kahn and B Daya Reddy 'Science and Technology in South Africa: Regional Innovation Hub or Passive Consumer?' *Daedalus* 2001; 130(1): 205–34.

Thomas Keolble 'Economic Policy in the Post-colony: South Africa between Keynesian Remedies and Neoliberal Pain' *New Political Economy* 2004; 9(1): 57–78.

Johan Kinghorn 'Social Cosmology, Religion and Afrikaner Ethnicity' *Journal of Southern African Studies* 1994; 20(3): 393–404.

Hennie Kotze and Pierre du Toit 'Reconciliation, Reconstruction and Identity Politics in South Africa: A 1994 Survey of Elite Attitudes After Apartheid' *Nationalism and Ethnic Politics* 1996; 2(1): 1–17.

Mariana Kriel 'Fools, Philologists and Philosophers: Afrikaans and the Politics of Cultural Nationalism' *Politikon* 2006; 33(1).

David Lazar 'Competing economic ideologies in South Africa's economic debate' *British Journal of Sociology* 1996; 47(4): 599–626.

Oupa Lehulere 'The Political Significance of GEAR' *Debate* 1997; 3: 73–88.

Tom Lodge 'Policy processes within the African National Congress and the Tripartite Alliance' *Politikon* 1999; 26(1): 5–32.

Beate Lohnert, Sophie Olfield and Susan Parnell 'Post-apartheid social polarisations: the creation of sub-urban identities in Cape Town' *South African Geographical Journal* 1998; 80(2): 86–92.

Michael Macdonald 'Power Politics in the New South Africa' *Journal of Southern African Studies* 1996; 22(2): 221–33.

——and Wilmot James 'The Hand on the Tiller: the Politics of State and Class in South Africa' *The Journal of Modern African Studies* 1993; 31(3): 387–405.

Kate Manzo and Patrick McGowan 'Afrikaner Fears and the Politics of Despair: Understanding Change in South Africa' *International Studies Quarterly* 1992; 36: 1–24.

Hein Marais 'Into the New South Africa' *South African Political and Economic Monthly* 1999; 12(3): 10–15.

Peter Marden 'Geographies of dissent: globalisation, identity and the nation' *Political Geography* 1997; 16(1); 37–64.

Christoph Marx 'The Afrikaners: Disposal of History or a New Beginning' *Politikon* 2005; 32(1).

——'Ubu and Ubuntu: on the dialectics of apartheid and nation building' *Politikon* 2002; 29(1).

James Mittelman 'Coxian Historicism as an Alternative Perspective in International Studies' *Alternatives* 1998; 23(1): 63–92.

Adam Morton 'Historicising Gramsci: situating ideas in and beyond their context' *Review of International Political Economy* 2003; 10(1).

——'On Gramsci' *Politics* 1999; 19(1): 1–8.

William Munro 'Revisiting Tradition, Reconstructing Identity? Afrikaner Nationalism and Political Transition in South Africa' *Politikon* 1995;22(2): 5–33.

Andrew Nash 'The New Politics of Afrikaans' *South African Journal of Philosophy* 2000; 19(4): 340–64.

Nicoli Nattrass and Jeremy Seekings 'Two Nations? Race and Economic Inequality in South Africa Today' *Daedalus* 2001; 130(1): 45–70.

Philip Nel 'Conceptions of globalisation among the South African elite' *Global Dialogue* 1999; 4(1): 22–35.

Gerrit Olivier 'Is Thabo Mbeki Africa's saviour?' *International Affairs* 2003; 79(4).

Jan Nederveen Pieterse 'Deconstructing/reconstructing ethnicity' *Nations and Nationalism* 1997; 3(3): 365–95.

Deborah Posel 'The Meaning of Apartheid Before 1948: Conflicting Interests and Forces within the Afrikaner Nationalist Alliance' *Journal of Southern Africa Studies* 1987; 14(1): 123–39.

Maano Ramutsindela 'Down the post-colonial road: reconstructing the post-apartheid state in South Africa' *Political Geography* 2001; 20(1): 57–84.

Duncan Randall 'Prospects for the Development of a Black Business Class in South Africa' *Journal of Modern African Studies* 1996; 34(4).

Christian Rogerson 'The Economic and Social Geography of South Africa: Progress Beyond Apartheid' *Tijdschrift voor Economische en Sociale Geografie* 2000; 19(4).

John Saul 'Magic Market Realism' *Transformation* 1999; 38: 49–67.

Jan Aart Scholte 'The geography of collective identities in a globalising world' *Review of International Political Economy* 1996; 3(4): 565–607.

Nick Schuermans & Gustav Visser 'On Poor Whites in Post-Apartheid Cities: The Case of Bloemfontein' *Urban Forum* 2005; 16(4): 259–94.

Tim Shaw 'Ethnicity as the Resilient Paradigm for Africa: From the 1960s to the 1980s' *Development and Change* 1986; 17(4): 587–605.

Leslie Sklair and Peter Robbins 'Global capitalism and major corporations from the Third World' *Third World Quarterly* 2002; 23(1).

Roger Southall 'The ANC and Black Capitalism in South Africa' *Review of African Political Economy* 2004; 31 (100).

———'The New South Africa in the New World Order: beyond the double whammy' *Third World Quarterly* 1994; 15(1): 121–37.

Tjaart Steenekamp 'The income distribution of Afrikaners: implications for a new South Africa' *Acta Academica* 1992; 24(4): 1–17.

Per Strand 'Finalising the South Africa Constitution: the politics of the Constitutional Assembly' *Politikon* 2000; 28(1): 47–63.

Stanley Tambiah 'Ethnic Conflict in The World Today' *American Ethnologist* 1989; 16(2): 335–49.

Ian Taylor 'Globalisation Studies and the Developing World: making international political economy truly global' *Third World Quarterly* 2005; 26(7).

———and Philip Nel 'New Africa, globalisation and the confines of elite reformism: "Getting the rhetoric right," getting the strategy wrong' *Third World Quarterly* 2002; 23(1).

———and Peter Vale 'South Africa's Transition Revisited: Globalisation as Vision and Virtue' *Global Society* 2000; 14(3): 399–414.

Sampie Terreblanche 'The compatibility of inequality and democracy: The necessity and merit of nationalisation and redistribution' *The Investment Analysts Journal* 2003; 33(1).

Roger Tooze 'Understanding the Global Political Economy: Applying Gramsci' *Millennium* 1990; 19(2): 273–80.

Peter Vale and Sipho Maseko 'South Africa and the African Renaissance' *International Affairs* 1998; 74(2): 271–89.

C S Kees van der Waal 'Diverse approaches in a South African debate on language and diversity in higher education' *Anthropology Southern Africa* 2002; 25(3&4).

Mads Vestergaard 'Who's Got the Map? The Negotiation of Afrikaner Identities in Post-Apartheid South Africa' *Daedalus* 2001; 130(1): 19–44.

Gustav Visser 'Unvoiced and invisible: on the transparency of white South Africans in post-apartheid geographical discourse' *Acta Academica* 2003; 1.

Eddie Webster and Glenn Adler 'Toward a Class Compromise in South Africa's 'Double Transition': Bargained Liberalisation and the Consolidation of Democracy' *Politics and Society* 1999; 27(3): 347–85.

Paul Williams and Ian Taylor 'Neoliberalism and the Political Economy of the "New" South Africa' *New Political Economy* 2000; 5(1): 21–40.

Zoe Wicomb 'Five Afrikaner Texts and the Rehabilitation of Whiteness' *Social Identities* 1998; 4(3): 363–84.

Organisation and government documents, speeches, official papers and conference proceedings

African Labour Research Network *Mining Africa: South African MNCs labour and social performance* Helsinki: Trade Union Solidarity Centre of Finland, 2005.

African National Congress 'The Reconstruction and Development Programme: A Policy Framework' Johannesburg: ANC, 1994.

BusinessMap Foundation *Empowerment 2004 – Black Ownership: Risk or Opportunity?* Johannesburg: BusinessMap Foundation, 2004.

Central Economic Advisory Services *The Restructuring of the South African Economy, A Normative Approach* Pretoria: Government Printer, 1993.

The Centre for Development and Enterprise (CDE) *Land Reform in South Africa: A 21st century perspective* Johannesburg: CDE Research Report no. 14, 2005.

Government of National Unity 'Growth, Employment and Redistribution: A Macro-Economic Strategy' Cape Town: Government Printer, 1996.

Dan O'Meara 'Thinking Theoretically? Afrikaner nationalism and the comparative theory of the politics of identity' Paper delivered on 25 March 1999 at Dalhousie University, Halifax, Canada.

South African Government, Act No. 108 of 1996 *Constitution of the Republic of South Africa* Pretoria: Government Printers.

South African Human Rights Commission (SAHRC) *Final Report on the Inquiry into Human Rights Violations in Farming Communities* Johannesburg: SAHRC, 2003.

Servaas Van Der Berg and Megan Louw 'Changing Patterns of South African Income Distribution: Towards Time Series Estimates of Distribution and Poverty' Stellenbosch Economic Working Papers: 2/2003. Stellenbosch: Bureau for Economic Research, Department of Economics, University of Stellenbosch, 2003.

UNCTAD 'World Investment Report: Transnational Corporations and the Internationalisation of R&D' New York: United Nations, 2005.

C S Kees van der Waal 'Essentialism in Language and Culture' Paper presented to Departmental Seminar 'Between Languages and Cultures,' Department of Sociology and Social Anthropology, Stellenbosch University, 26 May 2006.

Volkstaatraad 'First Interim Report of the Volkstaat Council' May 1995.

Herman Wasserman 'Private culture, public sphere: media, race and economics in the Afrikaans media after apartheid' Paper presented at the Conference of the Association of Cultural Studies, Istanbul, Turkey, July 2006.

World Bank 'Reducing Poverty in South Africa: Options for equitable and sustainable growth' Johannesburg: World Bank, 1994.

——'Accelerated Development in Sub-Saharan Africa: An Agenda for Action' Washington DC: World Bank, 1981.

Interviews

Tom Dreyer – 5 November 2001.
Jannie Gagiano – 28 July 2006.
Hermann Giliomee, 18 August 2006.
Danie Goosen – 31 July 2006.
Albert Grundlingh, 10 August 2006.
Willie van der Merwe, 1 August 2006.
Andrew Nash, 16 August 2006.
Marlene van Niekerk, 10 August 2006.
Johann Rossouw, 7 August 2006.
Sampie Terreblanche, 4 August 2006.
Jacob de Villiers – 21 August 2002.
Herman Wasserman – 8 August 2006.

Newspapers

Business Day (Johannesburg)
Cape Argus (Cape Town)
Cape Times (Cape Town)
The Economist (London)
Financial Mail (Johannesburg)
Financial Times (London)
The Guardian (London)
Mail and Guardian (Johannesburg)
The Sunday Independent (Johannesburg)
The Sunday Times (Johannesburg)
Sydney Morning Herald (Sydney)

INDEX

Absa 97
Accelerated and Shared Growth Initiative for South Africa (Asgi-SA) 63, 93
accumulation
　crisis 8, 31, 32, 33, 34, 57
　strategy 36, 39–43, 54, 55
African labour movement 34
African National Congress *see* ANC
African Peer Review Mechanism 79
African Renaissance 63–70, 133
Afrikaanse Handelsinstituut (AHI) 42, 94–5, 134
Die Afrikaanse Oorlegplatform group 86
Afrikaanse Protestante Kerk 104
Afrikaanse Taal-en Kultuurvereniging (Afrikaans language and culture society) 82
Afrikaanses, use of term 4
Afrikaner capital 1, 72, 94
　maturation of 39–43
　see also capital/business elite
Afrikaner Economic Movement 20
Afrikaner Eenheidsbeweging (AEB) 127
Afrikaner identity
　alternative 105–16
　and apartheid legacy 90–1, 107–8, 109–10, 111, 112, 117, 118, 122, 134
　arts festivals 81, 120–1, 135
　capital/business elite *see* capital/business elite

captains of industry 93
consensus renewal in post-apartheid era 130–7
contemporary manifestations of 71–98
and cultural boundaries 72–4, 104, 106, 108
and cultural projects 81–91, 106
cultural self-determination 79–80, 105, 107, 108–21, 123–5, 127, 134–5
cultural visions, new 117–23
definitions 8, 18, 100
development of 19–25
and dissident activism 109–10, 111
early tensions and splits 20
economic and cultural importance of 1, 2, 3–4, 5, 6, 9–10, 16, 24, 25, 52
and English speakers, closing gap between 40, 41, 84
fundamental homogeneity, lack of 106–7
and globalisation 8, 71–98, 112, 117, 118, 121, 128, 131–5
language and cultural survival 22–3, 82–8
and language, official 25
language, promotion of 22–3, 105–6, 108–10, 112, 116, 118–19, 121–2, 124, 128, 133–5
and literature 108–9, 117, 121–3

'logic of the local' in contemporary 99–129
and minority rights 4, 64–5, 74, 76–81, 82–3, 91, 111, 125, 128, 135
and music 104, 108, 119–20, 121
non-white 3, 7, 52–3, 83, 84
post-apartheid 4–9, 10
and postmodernism 111–12
provincial level politics 123–9, 135
provincial power sharing in Western Cape 113–16, 123, 124–5
regional differentiation 100, 121
right-wing local politics 123–5, 127
social transformation 38, 39–40
taaldebat (language debate) 85, 86, 87–8
trade union membership 93, 112–13, 116
transformation politics 74–5
working class 34, 38, 40
and younger generation 107–8, 111, 112, 117–18, 119–20, 121–2, 125

Afrikaner nationalist project
alliances 27–9, 30, 31
alliances, problems with 31–6, 37–8, 43
apartheid as ideological axis 29, 30, 31, 36, 37, 40–1, 43
consensus building 25–31, 43
division and conflict 25–6, 37–9
and economic development 30, 31, 34–5
and entrepreneurship 20
group consciousness 19, 22
identity development 18, 19–25, 102, 103
legitimacy crises 33, 34, 36
and National Party *see* National Party
post-apartheid 20
racial protectionism 20
reform agenda 34–6, 37
unravelling of 37–9
volksbeweging (national movement) 28, 34, 39
volkseenheid (unity of the volk) 26, 38

white racial domination 27, 28, 30, 34, 35, 36, 37–8
Afrikanerbond 77
Afrikaners: Kroes, Kras, Kordaat (De Klerk) 85
Afrikaners, first use of term 7
Agaat (van Niekerk) 122
Agri SA 126
agriculture *see* farmers
Alba, R. 17
Alexander, Neville 85
ANC government
Accord on Afrikaner Self-Determination 79
accumulation strategy 54
and African Renaissance 63–70, 133
alliance partners 2, 3, 4, 15, 47–51, 62, 89, 103, 115, 132
black middle class, pursuit of 59–60
business support 53, 54, 57–8, 59–60, 66, 94–5, 96, 98, 133
and Charterist traditions 64, 65
compromise position 45, 48–9, 53–4, 59–63, 68
Constitution 4, 50, 64, 65, 68–9, 74–5, 76–80, 82, 86
corruption allegations 14
credibility crisis 14–15
criticism of 49, 51
and cultural nationalism 63–4, 67–8, 69
delivery failures 51, 56, 63
democratic organisational culture 49–50, 74–5
Discussion Document on Economic Policy (1990) 54
dominance consolidation 45–51
dual citizenship philosophy 75
and economic restructuring 46–63, 93–8
electoral promises 61, 62
executive monitoring 74
farmers' support for 126–7
Freedom Charter 47, 48, 61, 65, 68
GEAR (Growth, Employment and Redistribution) strategy 12, 14, 38, 47, 48, 50, 51, 53, 54, 60, 61, 62–3, 97

and global economics 45, 52–6, 58–9, 60, 62, 69, 74, 94, 98, 132
Higher Education Act (1997) 85
inclusion policies 45, 64, 75
leadership succession 13, 50
nation-building project 63–70, 75, 80–1, 90
'Nation-Formation and Nation Building' 67
National General Council (2005) 80–1
National Plan for Higher Education (2001) 85, 86
neo-liberal hegemonic consensus 10, 12–16, 44–70, 72, 74–5, 93, 103, 133, 137
and non-racialism 65, 66–7, 68, 69
parliamentary debate on Afrikaners (1999) 80
party rebuilding, recent 56
popular support 24, 52, 60, 69, 75
and post-apartheid growth path 45, 49, 51, 55, 57–8, 64, 67, 93
proportional representation 74
Reconstruction and Development Programme (RDP) 14, 50, 58, 61–2, 63
Record of Understanding 55
and social transformation 12, 47–8, 50, 52–3, 56, 60–5, 68–9, 75, 78, 94
Structural Adjustment Programme (SAP) 53
succession crisis 48–9
Truth and Reconciliation Commission (TRC) 65–6, 90–1
'two nations' thesis 66–7, 69
and white privileged minority, relationship with 48, 49
see also Mbeki, Thabo
Anglo American 32, 96, 98
apartheid
Afrikaner nationalist project *see* Afrikaner nationalist project
dissident critics of 109
and educational disparities 92, 94
forced removals, mass 30
government election victory (1948) 20, 24, 25, 26
government subsidies 20, 243
high (grand plan) 29
as ideological axis 29, 30, 31, 36, 37, 40–1, 43
ideology 5, 16
interpretations, divergent 27, 30, 31
job reservation 20, 23, 29
legislation 29
low (1948–60) 29, 31
modernisation process 33, 35–6
and retribalisation 30
Sauer Report 26
in sport 38
Total Strategy 33, 34, 35, 36
welfare protection 20
Ardense, S. 115*n*
arts festivals 81, 120–1, 135
Asmal, Kader 85, 86, 87, 110

banking sector 53
bankruptcies 103
battery9 119
Benade, Ryk 119
Bitterkomix (magazine) 107
black
economic empowerment 97, 98
farmers 126, 127
inundation of (*oorstroming*) cities 29
middle class 3, 42, 51, 59, 63, 67, 96
power-sharing 34
Black Economic Empowerment (BEE) 15, 63, 93, 95, 96–7, 98, 127
Blom, Francois 120
Boer War 22, 23–4, 121
Boeremag, bombing campaign 2
Boetman 85
Boetman is die Bliksem in! (Fourie) 117
Bond, P. 13
Botha, P.W. 31–2, 34, 36, 39, 41
Rubicon speech (1985) 42
Botman, Russell 86
Breytenbach, Breyten 108, 109, 110, 117
Brink, Andre 108, 109
Brink, Chris 85–6

Broad-Based Black Empowerment Act (2003) 97
Broederbond 24–5, 26, 39, 101, 102, 106
Die Burger (newspaper) 4, 85, 110
Businees Trust 66
Buthelezi, Mangosuthu 80
Butler, A. 21, 22, 60(*n*)
Buts, Flip 112–13

Cape
  Afrikaans language in 104, 114
  coloured community, claims of marginalisation 115
  economic development 100, 101
  Great Trek 22, 24
  provincial power sharing in Western 101, 102, 113–16, 123, 124–5
  territorial homeland demands 4
  voting patterns 114
  wheat farmers 20
capital/business elite
  and Afrikaner nationalisation 25, 39–43
  and Black Economic Empowerment (BEE) legislation 15
  and globalisation 13, 92, 94–6, 134
  Mandela factor 66
  and neo-liberal orthodoxy 59–60
  success of 1, 3, 19, 34, 46, 48, 52–3, 67–8
  see also entrepreneurship; petty bourgeoisie
capitalism 13, 20, 22, 24, 25, 31–3, 40, 45, 61, 102, 134
Carnegie Commission 24
Cerny, P. 8
Charterist traditions 64, 65
Christian nationalism 20, 25, 26, 101, 107, 124
Cillié, Piet 30
cities, black inundation of (*oorstroming*) 29
citizenship 67, 76
Cold War, end of 47
colonialism 21
colour bar, lowering 38
Come Home Campaign 113
Commission for the Promotion and Protection of the Rights of Cultural, Religious and Linguistic Communities 78–9
communal group rights 75
competitiveness 45
Congress of South African Trade Unions (COSATU) 15, 48, 49, 50, 54
Conservative Party (CP) 38–9, 104, 105, 127
consumerism 93, 135
corporate restructuring 95
crime 110, 113, 125
Cronin, Jeremy 89
Curriculum vitae (Letoit) 117

De Beers 97
De Klerk, F.W. 34, 43, 55, 75, 77, 85
de la Rey, Koos 119–20
de Villiers, Jacob 94–5
Degenaar, Johan 24–5(*n*), 109–10
Democratic Alliance (DA) 113, 114, 115, 125
Depression 24
deregulation of labour markets 45, 48, 125–6, 127
Dreyer, Tom 122
Du Toit, A. 5, 22
Dutch language 21
Dutch Reformed Churches 39, 104

economic crisis 8, 31–2, 33, 34, 57
economic liberalisation 34–5, 41, 46, 103–4, 125–7
Economic Volkskongres 20
education, disparities in 92, 94
education projects 42, 65, 77, 104
  and language 85–8, 112
emigration 4, 89, 93, 136
employment, job reservation 20, 23, 29
entrepreneurship 40, 93, 103
  see also capital/business elite; petty bourgeoisie
Equatoria (Dreyer) 122
exchange controls 95

farmers
  black 126, 127

and economic liberalisation 20, 34, 103–4, 125–7
human rights abuses 125–6
murders 110, 125
nationalist alliance 27, 40, 101, 103
protectionist demands 32
and social transformation 38
support for ANC government 126–7
trekboer communities 21–2
FDI 54, 57, 58
Federasie Afrikaanse Kultuurvereiniginge (FAK) 77, 116
Federasie van Afrikaanse Kultuurvereiniginge 82, 89
Fellowship of True Afrikaners (*Genootskap van Regte Afrikaners*) 22–3
Figes, O. 108*n*
finance power (*geldmag*) 40
Fischer, Bram 85
FK de Klerk Foundation 77
Fokofpolisiekar (song) 120
Fordism 32, 39
foreign exchange constraints 32
Fourie, Peter 117
Fragmente (journal) 81, 89, 112
Freedom Front Plus 80, 86, 124–5, 126, 127
Fusion Pact 24

gated communities 135
GDP growth 62–3
GEAR (Growth, Employment and Redistribution) strategy 12, 14, 38, 47, 48, 50, 51, 53, 54, 60, 61, 62–3, 97
Gereformeerde Blues Band 104
Gerwel, Jakes 84
Giliomee, H. 5, 6, 19, 20, 21, 37, 38, 86
Gill, S. 6(*n*)
globalisation
and Afrikaner identity 8, 71–98, 112, 117, 118, 121, 128, 131–5
and ANC liberalisation project 45
cultural 73–4
division of labour and power (GDLP) 92
ideology of 4–5, 8–9, 12–13
international banking community 45
of liberalism 76
Goosen, Anton 119
Goosen, D. 89
Government of National Unity (GNU) 46
Gramsci, Antonio 6, 10–12, 16, 44, 52, 107, 131–2, 134
grensliteratuur (border literature) 108
Group of 63 82
Guelke, L. 21–2
Gurnede, W. 14(*n*)

Hall, S. 9, 11, 73–4, 121, 132
health provision 51, 62
Hemson, D. and M.O'Donovan 62(*n*)
Herstigte (Reconstituted) National Party (HNP) 38, 105
Hertzog, Albert 20, 24, 38
Home for All initiative 91
housing projects 42, 51, 62
human rights 64, 75, 77, 125–6
Hurrell, A. and N. Woods 58(*n*)

IMF 58–9, 74
import-substitution policy 32
income inequalities 51, 93–4
individualistic materialism 93
industrial policy 13, 32, 94, 97
industrial revolution, second 24
inflation 46, 57
influx control 29, 35
interest rates 57
international banking community 45
international relations 33, 35
IT sector 62, 92–3

Jameson Raid 22
Johannesburg Stock Exchange (JSE) 1, 32, 93, 97
Johnson, Stephen 122–3
Jonker, Ingrid 108

Kerkorrel, Johannes 104, 116*n*, 117*n* 119
Klein Karoo Nasionale Kunstefees arts festival 120, 121
Koelbe, T. 46(*n*), 90(*n*)
Kombuis, Koos 119

Krog, Antjie 91, 121–2
Kymlicka, W. 76

labour legislation 29, 32, 35, 41, 49–50, 93
labour market access 93–4
land reform 7, 126
language
　Afrikans as official 25
　Dutch 21
　freedoms 65, 78, 84
　promotion of 22–3, 105–6, 108–10, 112, 116, 118–19, 121–2, 124, 128, 133–5
　Stellenbosch University policy 85–6, 87, 88
　taaldebat (language debate) 85, 86, 87–8
Leon, Tony 125
Letoit, Andre 117
literature 108–9, 117, 121–3
Litnet (website) 81

Malan, D F 20, 102
Mandela, Nelson 1, 54, 66, 68, 81
manufacturing industry 62
Marais, H. 13, 31(*n*), 41(*n*), 52, 53–4, 64(*n*), 66(*n*), 70(*n*)
markets
　liberalisation 40, 45, 47–8, 53, 57–8
　political importance of 35, 94–5
　poor domestic 32
Marks, S. and S. Trapido 21(*n*)
Mbeki, Thabo
　and Afrikaners 111
　and agriculture 126–7
　Big Business Working Group 3, 53
　and black economic empowerment 97, 98
　'I Am An African' speech 65, 66
　material wealth, warning against 52
　policy-making style 14, 48, 56, 68–9, 70, 79, 80, 81, 91, 94
　and poverty 89
　State of the Nation address (2006) 63
　see also ANC
Mboweni, Tito 57

Meyer, Roelf 79
Michie, J. and V. Padayachee 50
middle class
　black 3, 35, 42, 51, 59–60, 63, 67, 96
　globalised 1, 9–10, 72, 73, 90, 92, 93, 128, 134
　and historic bloc 12
　urbanised 103
militancy, right-wing 2
Milnerism 23, 87
Mineral Development Bill 97
mining industry 22, 24, 32, 42
　disinvestment 97–8
Minority Front 125
minority rights 4, 14, 64–5, 74, 76–81, 82–3, 91, 111, 125, 128, 135
MK89 music channel 120
Mont Fleur 60
Morris, M. 42(*n*), 55(*n*)
Mulder, Pieter 86, 124, 125
Munro, W. 26(*n*), 27(*n*), 35(*n*), 103–4(*n*), 123
music 104, 108, 119–20, 121

Nash, A. 3–4, 89*n*, 110*n*, 111*n*, 118, 134*n*
Naspers 88, 95–6, 101, 121
National Party
　Accord on Afrikaner Self-Determination 79
　and Afrikaner ideology 26, 27, 107, 134
　and Afrikaner nationalism 7–8
　alliances 25, 28, 55, 103
　apartheid, policies at odds with 55
　broedertwis divisions 37, 39, 101, 102
　and business support 55
　constituency changes and capital maturation 39–43
　Constitution (1984) 35
　economic policy 31, 42, 43, 47, 50–1, 52, 55
　Herstigte (Reconstituted) National Party (HNP) 38, 105
　internal discord 37, 38
　liberal nationalism 13, 16, 101–2

national democracy 74
Normative Economic Model (NEM) 55
pluralist power centres 34
and provincialism 100–1, 102–3, 113
reform agenda 34–6, 37
right wing groups 105, 123
split (1982) 38–9
structure of 33–4, 35
Tricameral Parliament 35
National Security Council 35
nationalism, *volk* consciousness 7, 19, 26, 31, 35, 37–8, 101, 102, 103
Native Policy 24
Nedcor 60
Netherlands, colonialism 21
Netshitenzhe 12(*n*)
New National Party 4, 114
'New' South Africa, consensus in 44–70
Ngonyama, Smuts 98, 133
Niehaus, Carl 91

oil crisis 2
Old Mutual 60, 97, 98
O'Meara, D. 6, 20, 28(*n*), 31(*n*), 33, 34(*n*), 36, 37, 37–8(*n*), 107, 108(*n*)
Orange Free State (OFS) 20, 100, 101, 102, 104, 105
Orania 127
Ossewa Brandwag 101

Padaychee, V. 58(*n*), 61–2
Pahad, Essop 80
pass law system 29
petty bourgeoisie 20, 27, 38, 40, 52, 59, 102, 105
see also capital/business elite; entrepreneurship
Phosa, Matthews 80
Pillay, S. 82*n*
Posel, D. 20, 26(*n*), 30(*n*)
Potchefstroom name change 80
Potchefstroom University 85, 86
poverty 51, 52, 62, 69, 89
white 23, 24, 93
Price, R. 30

private sector investment 62–3
privatisation 45, 49, 95
productivity costs 32
professional employment 40
property rights 64, 74
provincial level, and National Party 100–1, 102–3, 113
provincial level politics 123–9, 135
power sharing in Western Cape 113–16, 123, 124–5
public sector 63, 93

Rabie, Jan 108
racial hierarchies 21
racial segregation 22, 29, 30
Reconstruction and Development Programme (RDP) 14, 50, 58, 61–2, 63
Reddingsdaad (Rescue Action) 20, 39
religious freedom 78
Rembrandt 95, 101
Riekert, Paul 119
right-wing
groups, National Party 105, 123
local politics 123–5, 127
militancy 2
Robbertze, Hendrik 79
Robertson, R. 8–9
rock music 119–20
Roodt, Dan 86–7, 88, 90
Roussouw, Arrie 4, 89, 90
Rugby World Cup (1995) 66
Rumney, Reg 98
Rupert, Anton 42

SANLAM 42, 96, 101
'Platform for Investment' 60
Sauer Report 26
Schutte, G. 23
security 34, 35, 36, 104
Sestiger writers 108–9
Sewe Dae by die Silbersteins (Leroux) 108
Sisulu, Max 61
skills shortage 32, 35, 93, 113, 125, 136
slave trade prohibition 21
Smit, Bartho 108
Smit, Pieter 120

Smuts, J.C. 24, 101
Solidarity 93, 112–13, 116
South Africa Foundation 42
   'Growth for All' 60
South Africa Party 24
South African Chamber of Business (SACOB), 'Economic Options for South Africa' 60
South African Communist Party (SACP) 15, 48–9, 89, 127
Southall, R. 3(*n*), 59
sport
   and apartheid 38
   rugby 66, 113
   Rugby World Cup (1995) 66
Springbok Nude Girls 120
State Security Council 27
Stellenbosch University, language policy 85–6, 87, 88
Stigting vir Afrikaans (Foundation for Afrikaans) 82
Stinkafrikaners (Dreyer) 122
strike action 49
Strydom, J G 102
Die Suid Afrikaan 104

tariff controls 45, 95
taxation 46, 53, 66
Taylor, I. 5(*n*), 9
technology 62, 92–3
Terreblanche, Sampie 26(*n*), 27(*n*), 90, 95
Die Toneelstuk (Breytenbach) 117
Tooze, R. 5
trade unions 15, 48, 49, 50, 54, 93, 112–13, 116
Transvaal 20, 100, 101, 102, 104, 105
Treurnicht, Andries 38–9, 102
Triomf (van Niekerk) 122
Tutu, Archbishop Desmond 97

Ubuntu 69
UK
   and Boer War 22, 23

   colonialism 21, 23
UN conventions 4
unemployment 51, 62, 93, 103, 125
United Party 24
universal suffrage 65, 74
Urban Foundation 42
urbanisation policies 22, 24, 35, 41

van Blerk, Bok 119–20
van Niekerk, Marlene 88, 122
Van Rooyen, Johan 126
Van Zyl Slabbert, F. 109
Verwoerd, Wilhelm 91
Verwoerd, Hendrik 31, 34, 35, 38, 66, 100, 101, 102
Viljoen, Constand 79, 124
Voëlvry music 108, 119
volk consciousness 7, 19, 26, 31, 35, 37–8, 101, 102, 103
Volkstaat Council Report 79
Vorster, John 34, 35, 38, 41
Die Vrye Afrikaan (newspaper) 81, 89, 104, 112

wage levels 93, 103
wage restraint 45
Washington Consensus 58
Wassenaar, Andreas 42
Wasserman, H. 96*n*
welfare programmes 20, 29, 61
Willemse, Hein 84
working class 12, 20, 34, 38, 40, 52, 93, 103
working holiday visas 93
World Bank 58–9, 74
   Berg Report 58
World War Two 24

younger generation 107–8, 111, 112, 117–18, 119–20, 121–2, 125

Zille, Helen 113
Zoid, Karen 120